Elsie Dunn (Evelyn Scott) at age seven

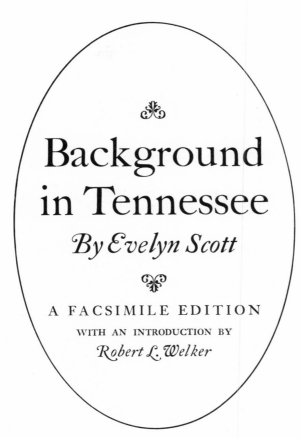

Background
in Tennessee

By Evelyn Scott

A FACSIMILE EDITION

WITH AN INTRODUCTION BY

Robert L. Welker

THE UNIVERSITY OF TENNESSEE PRESS
KNOXVILLE

TENNESSEANA   EDITIONS

Library of Congress Cataloging in Publication Data

Scott, Evelyn, 1893–
  Background in Tennessee.
  (Tennesseana editions)
  Photoreprint of the 1st ed (1937) published by
R. M. McBride, New York.
  Includes bibliographical references.
    1. Scott, Evelyn, 1893–   —Biography—Youth.
2. Tennessee—Social life and customs.
3. Novelists, American—20th century—Biography.
I. Title. II. Series.
PS3537.C89Z463   1980   813′.52 [B]   80–15703
ISBN 0-87049-297-7

Introduction

TO THE NEW EDITION

THE dust jacket of the 1937 issue of *Background in Tennessee* states: *This book is rich in content, possessing all those characteristics which have made Evelyn Scott so very important a personality in American writing. In this new work Miss Scott has set herself against her native background, Tennessee. Despite the author's intimate revelations about her immediate ancestors and collateral relations the book is singularly free from bitterness and stricture. A good natured wisdom permeates the scenes of childhood and early adolescence.* The blurb continues:

Miss Scott's main purpose . . . has been to throw light on the character of the Tennessee pioneer and emphasize the social influence which were factors in her own development and a background for Tennessee's cultural evolution. She has selected a most informal method so that her material suggests personal experience rather than formal history.

In her view of southern tradition, she is completely unorthodox. At the same time her sympathy with things southern persists; she cannot escape her identity with the region described.

Except for the statement that her view of southern tradition is completely unorthodox, the dust jacket commentary is an accurate description that holds after the passage of forty-three years. Like each of Evelyn Scott's works, the book is unique, rich in thought and exquisite prose. It is intensely personal and at the same time passionately objective, evocative rather than explicit, and for its time highly innovative in form and technique.

As to the orthodoxy of her view of southern tradition, Evelyn Scott wrote: "I had rebelled; courted disapproval: Tennessee, I considered, had disowned me; I, in return, with self-respecting arrogance, would disown it."[1] The mutual disowning, she was to recognize, was far from valid. Her rebellion was not so complete as she might have supposed. Her view of southern tradition proved not so much completely unorthodox as prophetically typical.

Her view seemed unorthodox at a time when the usual printed fare was either local-color celebrations of moonlight and magnolias or sociological tirades against the benighted South, but in reality she had much more in common with the view of her "orthodox" peers among the Southern Renaissance writers. The Fugitives, for example, were rebels too, fleeing both the false sentiments and overblown myths of the South and the pseudo-scientific myths of America. Like fellow southerners considered orthodox, she recognized the importance of place and knew that "expatriatism was a myth." She wrote from the belief that the "individual experience, set forth honestly, is bound to reveal aspects that are typical and have a catholic significance. . . ." She held to the concreteness of life and the necessity to test abstractions and grand designs by the reality of experience. She knew well the fragility of civilizations and the perilous

---

[1] *Background in Tennessee*, p. 2.

balance between the natural and supranatural. Above all, deeply involved with history, she had the southern obsession with the need to unify history into vital meaning by relating personal and family past into a living context of larger movements. (One of the more recent efforts similar to *Background in Tennessee* is from another Tennessean, Andrew Lytle in his *A Wake for the Living*.)

Still another facet of Evelyn Scott's orthodoxy is reflected in her statement: *It can be said with accuracy that, both literally and metaphorically, "I have traveled far" from the South of my childhood. But I owe it to the general aristocratic pretensions of the South, that I still prize most in myself and in others a man's control of his own spirit and mind—man's self-direction in the development of an inner life. And I owe it to the South that I never did and do not now see virtue in any proposal to make other people "good" by force. The frail Puritan in me has died, and I hope will never be reborn.*[2]

Evelyn Scott's public rebellion was against those cultural, aesthetic, political, and economic forces which wastefully violated individual integrity and constricted intellectual and spiritual life. In her private life, rebellion took the form of rejecting the feminine role prescribed by her society and of refusing to accept her era's conventional view of marriage.

It is clear that from her birth in 1893 she had all the trappings that could have equipped her for the role of Southern Belle. Born Elsie Dunn into a prominent family with aristocratic pretensions and a majestic antebellum Greek revival mansion, she possessed physical beauty and was educated in all the social graces, including the training to be blind to prescribed injustices, contradictions,

[2] Quoted by Kunitz and Haycraft, eds., *Twentieth-Century Authors*, 1942, p. 1252.

conventional immorality, and male chauvinism. She was too intelligent to accept unquestioningly the cultural myth's pretensions and false sentiments urged upon her, and she was too honest to pretend acceptance. She rejected the proffered role and became a voluntary exile, a fugitive.

Essential good manners—respect for ideals and beliefs of others—combined with negative capability and Arnoldian "disinterestedness" kept her from blatant protest and flamboyant public shockings. With the quiet deliberativeness commensurate with personal integrity, she went, shortly before her twenty-first birthday, into chosen exile with Frederick Creighton Wellman, director of the division of tropical medicine at Tulane University. At the time Dr. Wellman was married to his second wife and in his second career, having previously been a medical missionary to Africa.[3]

Taking nothing with them but minimal travel funds, a few clothes, a volume of Keats' poetry, and Tolstoy's *War and Peace*, Elsie Dunn and Frederick Creighton Wellman left for England on the first leg of a journey to Brazil. Evelyn Scott wrote that, until aboard ship at sea, she "was a virgin with contempt for a view of chastity as psychological rather than of the spirit. We went away knowing we could draw reprehension on ourselves. No one guessed we had gone until we were well away, and the expected *and* unexpected happened."[4]

What happened was that Frederick Wellman and Elsie

[3] Dr. Wellman, as Cyril Kay Scott, was to have three more careers: a mining engineer in Brazil, a novelist after his return to the United States, and, finally, a water colorist and art teacher. Cyril and Evelyn Scott's common-law marriage was dissolved by legal divorce in 1928. The circumstance of the last years of their marriage is fictionalized in Evelyn Scott's novel *Eva Gay*.

[4] Marginalia in her personal copy of my *Evelyn Scott: A Literary Biography*, Ph.D. diss., Vanderbilt Univ., 1958.

viii

Dunn became Cyril Kay and Evelyn Scott, generally condemned by the conventional society they had formerly known and threatened with the Mann Act should they return to the United States. For six years, from 1913 to 1919, they endured horrendous hardships in Brazil. Destitute, often near starvation, homesteading in the wilds of pioneer Baia, they assumed the additional burden of Evelyn Scott's helpless mother who had come to visit but, never sent funds by her husband to return to the United States, was divorced on grounds of desertion. Further trammeled in misery, Evelyn Scott suffered from chronic weakness and severe pain resulting from botched surgery following the birth of her son.

In the agony of her exile and isolation, Evelyn Scott became poet and novelist, anticipating and paralleling many of the innovations usually associated with Virginia Woolf, D.H. Lawrence, James Joyce, and the imagist poets, and almost immediately upon her return to the United States and the publication of her first novel in 1921 she became a literary sensation.

By the time she wrote *Background in Tennessee*, she probably considered that she was leaving for posterity a partial record of the personal and cultural matrix which developed an important American author. To have so thought of herself was no unfounded vanity. Cooly objective and marvelously clear-eyed, she was neither vain nor unreasonably egotistical, although she did place value on the individual above all things collective. She thought the artist (capable of passionately involved objectivity and exceptionally aware sensitivity) could deliver an ideal, a vision, a myth of far greater worth than the collective psycho-socio-economic realities against which the vision is tested and from which it is gleaned.

She had just reason to suppose her importance to

American literature. She was at the height of her career and behind her were thirteen novels, two volumes of poetry, a volume of novellas, a biography, a play produced by the Provincetown Players, and numerous contributions of poems, short stories, and criticisms to anthologies and journals. With the publication of her first novel, *The Narrow House* (1921), she was hailed by prominent critics as an innovator of the first order; even the powerful H.L. Mencken, apparently not knowing she was a southerner, praised her work with the same breath that condemned the "Sahara of the Bozart." Two books and two years later, her lyrical transformation of hard surface reality and unrelenting psychological insight into spiritual vision in *Escapade* (the account of her Brazilian ordeal) further solidified her reputation, fairly summarized by Ludwig Lewisohn: *By her cold acuteness of psychological observation, by her peering exactness of physical vision, she succeeds in giving "The Narrow House" and "Narcissus" and above all "Escapade" a hardness of surface that seems to protect these books from decay. They have an intellectual lucidity and a powerful and bitter moral vision that keeps them fresh and memorable.*[5]

With *Migrations* in 1927, the first of a giant four-volume trilogy, the minute psychological observations and poetic symbolism combined with an epic sweep. It was as if the negative capability and sensory evocations of Keats had combined with the grand scope of Tolstoy. Evelyn Scott was now a novelist in the grand tradition, bursting through the bounds of conventional forms to create innovations suitable to her epic vision. She needed, like Faulkner, a vast canvas and a long view that could encompass an empire and a century, yet, since each in-

---

[5] Ludwig Lewisohn, *Expression in America* (1932), pp. 408–409.

dividual is center of his universe, she also needed a micro-
scopic inspection of each soul in its struggle to find or
maintain identity. Her trilogy, *Migrations, The Wave*
(1929), and a *Calendar of Sin* (1931), combined the
minutiae of the psychological and symbolic novel of inner reality with the broad, mythical sweep of the epic.
She opposed one myth against another—one Northern,
one Southern; one scientific, one Biblical; one radical,
one traditional; one individual, one communal. Both individual and collective destiny in their separateness and
oneness were vividly manifest. Thus was delivered, simultaneously, the godlike, objective view and the emotional
intensity of personal involvement. Joyce's artist was par-
ing his fingernails, but he had cut them to the quick.
Critical voices were almost unanimous in calling Evelyn
Scott great. She was named honorary vice-president of
the Author's League of America, and it was said that the
publication of *The Sound and the Fury* should place its
up-and-coming author in company with Evelyn Scott
among the outstanding literary figures of the time.[6]

Three other novels of undiminished power (*Eva Gay*,
1933; *Breathe Upon These Slain*, 1934; *Bread and a
Sword*, 1937), mainly concerned with the relation of the
artist and society, were to follow. After *Background in*

[6] With access to the manuscript before publication, Evelyn Scott
wrote her publisher an unsolicited letter which, with little revision,
was issued as a pamphlet along with Faulkner's novel. The pamphlet
provided remarkable insight into Faulkner's art and doubtlessly had
a considerable effect in calling attention to the value of Faulkner's
work. The publisher's foreword reads as follows: "This essay by
Evelyn Scott, whose recent novel *The Wave* placed her among the
outstanding literary figures of our time, has been distributed to those
who are interested in Miss Scott's work and the writing of Faulkner.
The Sound and the Fury should place Faulkner in company with
Evelyn Scott. The publishers believe in the issuance of this little book
that a valuable and brilliant reflection of the philosophies of two important American authors is presented to those who care for such
things."

Tennessee, however, private circumstances became so dire that she was able to publish only one more novel, *The Shadow of the Hawk*, 1941.

Publishing nineteen books within a span of seventeen years from 1920 to 1937, Evelyn Scott had worked at an exhausting pace. Also her unsettled life doubtlessly took its toll: in 1930 she had married British novelist John Metcalfe and the demands of their individual careers frequently necessitated their separation and moving between the United States, England, and France where their meager income could be furthest stretched. By 1939 World War II was raging and John Metcalfe was called to active duty as an officer in the Royal Air Force, first in Canada and later in England. During this separation which lasted four years, Evelyn Scott led a hand-to-mouth existence shuttling between the United States and Canada, trying to make ends meet by accepting journalistic assignments and lecturing at Swarthmore, all the while awaiting, on a nerve-wracking, stand-by basis, transportation to England. She endured ill health, great emotional stress, personal harassment, loss or theft of manuscripts, and finally in 1944 when she at last rejoined her husband, the horrors of London bombings.

At some time during this decade she suffered some sort of breakdown, probably a stroke, which left her with her voices—a multitude of separate mumblings and whisperings in her head. Fighting this almost constant distraction, along with a heart condition which developed after her sickness in Brazil, she published a few occasional pieces and continued to work on two long novels which were never published. Under these conditions she all but disappeared from the American literary scene. Her finances were such that she could not leave war-ravaged England until 1954, when continuing her valiant struggle to recoup her publishing career she returned to the United States.

During the last decade of her life, conditions did not improve. Another stroke left her with expressive aphasia —seemingly the final blow to end a writer's career! Nevertheless, her spirit fought back and after a period of agonizing effort she regained her full power and continued to work on her novels. Extreme but proud poverty confined her with her husband to one room and communal kitchen privileges in a cheap New York hotel. With clothes scarcely decent to appear on the street, she never lost her intense drive and striking physical beauty.

Fine boned, lithe, and thin with a quick grace of movement, she wore a coronet of bright honey and gray hair braided about her head. Her chiseled features were such as a sculptor would cherish. Flushed cheeks and a clear complexion with the tight, scrubbed look of youth belied her advanced years and disciplined days. A generous, humorous mouth, ready to laugh or smile, ready with a quick wit, was equally ready with a terrible tongue if a matter of integrity were involved. Her eyes were astounding: immense, steady, clear, gray as dawn, and as haunted as a summer eve's afterglow. Rasputin would have envied them but that they belonged to Melpomene.

That last harsh decade ended in 1963. Hospitalized for treatment of cancer for several weeks, she was temporarily dismissed and returned to her one-room home. With a great reckoning in a little room, during the first night of her return, she died quietly in her sleep by her husband's side. At last she had reached that peace that ends *Background in Tennessee*, that *peace for which life strives so unavailingly we come at last to bless the failures which conclude our efforts—raptures of ending, bland, desireless, passing thought! Triumphs of negation and ac-*

ceptance quite beyond the scope of our imaginings as children! . . . Where Snow White, with her seven dwarfs, Jesus and Hercules, Brunhild, Siegfried and Phaëthon, and Meg and Jo and Beth, lay down together, like the lions and the lambs! And vultures quit their heckling of Prometheus and three poor lynched Negroes simultaneously!

Thus were the endings. The beginnings were in Tennessee.

The account of these beginnings provides a multitude of riches for both the casual and the scholarly reader. For literary and cultural historians there is an evocation of the living facts of a mythology that shaped the views of an aristocratic society at the turn of the century, a society still suffering the stings of reconstruction while embroiled in the agrarian-commercial conflicts that, among other troubles, caused the Black Patch Tobacco Wars in Kentucky and Tennessee, the subject of Robert Penn Warren's *Night Riders*. One may speculate that Clarksville, Tennessee, at the time of Evelyn Scott's beginnings, was a border-town pocket of culture caught in a rich current of ideas which forced it to consider what it was in relation to what it was being urged to become. Something extraordinary was afoot. From this one small area of scarcely 10,000 population, within a ten-year period, were to emerge three prominent artists, Evelyn Scott, Caroline Gordon, and Robert Penn Warren, besides a considerable number of lesser writers, artists, and journalists. *Background in Tennessee* provides a perceptive look into one of the pockets from which came the Southern Renaissance.

For the more casual reader there is a lively account of the "way it was" for a sensitive and intelligent young girl seeking her self and personal liberation into the social and spiritual freedom proper for womanhood.

With the reissue of *Background in Tennessee*, perhaps the evidence is more clear that the pact of mutual disinheritance is indeed not valid: Tennessee reclaims with pride one of its own.

ROBERT L. WELKER
The University of Alabama
in Huntsville

BOOKS BY EVELYN SCOTT

Precipitations (1920). *Love: A Drama in Three Acts* (1921). *The Narrow House* (1921). *Narcissus* (1922). *Escapade* (1923). *In the Endless Sands: A Christmas Book for Boys and Girls*, with Cyril Kay Scott (1925). *The Golden Door* (1925). *Ideals: A Book of Farce and Comedy* (1927). *Migrations: An Arabesque in Histories* (1927). *The Wave* (1929). *Witch Perkins: A Story of the Kentucky Hills* (1929). *On William Faulkner's "The Sound and the Fury"* (1929). *Blue Rum* (1930). *The Winter Alone* (1930). *A Calendar of Sin, American Melodramas* (1931). *Eva Gay: A Romantic Novel* (1933). *Breathe Upon These Slain* (1934). *Billy the Maverick* (1934). *Bread and a Sword* (1937). *Background in Tennessee* (1937). *The Shadow of the Hawk* (1941). Works unpublished: "Before Cock Crow: A Novel" (1930–62). "Escape Into Living: A Novel" (1952–62). "The Gravestones Wept," poetry (1950–60). "The Youngest Smiles," poetry (1955–60).

Background in Tennessee

. . . these are counsellors
That feelingly persuade me what I am.—SHAKESPEARE

To Lenore Marshall

NOTE: The stimulus for writing this book has come in large measure from the letters and conversation of a friend of my childhood, Harper Leech, of the Chicago *Daily News*, who is equipped as I am not to be a real state historian. I owe as much to his provocative disagreement with most of my theories, as to his fine fund of information, of which I have failed to take advantage when I might . . .

1

WHEN it was first suggested to me that I "write something about Tennessee," I wondered what I, who had not delved deeply into the history of the region, could offer that had been anticipated by scores of historians. In a life already consumed by a variety of antecedent preoccupations, it was not plausible to suppose the dedication of a few months to "research" would allow me to unearth unsuspected documents or discover facts to reillumine well-thumbed archives. I felt I was prepared neither to be originally informing about the past of the Tennessee people nor to qualify with distinction as a traveller in my native state. Though from 1893, when I was born, until 1909, when I was sixteen, I was never absent from Tennesssee for more than a few months together, the impressions of the locality I carried with me into a voluntary exile which lasted twenty years were derived from such exclusively personal associations I doubted they could supply anything generally informing. All I possessed which might be regarded as Tennessee documenta to be presented to a public, seemed to be myself. . . .

And yet, I decided, on second thought, surely the doubt engendered by these reflections was inconsistent and contradictory, since it has always been a part of my philosophy to assume that the individual experience, set forth honestly, is bound to reveal aspects that are typical and have a catholic significance of some sort or other. When I was first in England, in 1914, Britishers accustomed to the Yankee accent sometimes asked me from what colony I came; and when I told them I was not a colonial, I always disclaimed more than a technical identification with the land of my origin. I had rebelled; courted disapproval: Tennessee, I considered, had disowned me; I, in return, with self-respecting arrogance, would disown it. But the pact of disinheritance has turned out not very valid. No more valid, on my side, than any other rejection by youth of the real world behind the imagined—perpetually such a disappointment to those envisaging perfection for the first time!

Some have said of my writings that they constitute an act of treachery toward the "real" South; but I think there may be different critics who recognize the attack should be directed against the faulty but sincere exponent of the "natural," who could exist anywhere. I do know this: expatriotism is a myth. During twenty-three years, I have not spent a quarter of the time in America, and my sojourns in Tennessee have been limited to a few days or a few weeks together; yet, though I possessed the genius for disguises attributed to the late Lon Chaney, I could not successfully camouflage my Americanism to the foreigner, who, just because he is detached from the scene, recognizes the embodiment of the indigenous character. And I remain, also, more specifically, a Tennesseean; let those from my own state disparage as much as they please a vocabulary in which the Southernisms have all got a little the worse for wear! And though, at this moment, if I were to walk down Franklin Street, in Clarksville, and ask, consecutively, of each person I met, an opinion on the weather, I should probably find not one who would not prophesy clear skies where I anticipated rain, still I should be speaking the language of my background, to which could be traced influences responsible for my present disparate opinions. In theory, I may be far removed from most of those among whom I was reared; yet I have not, on that account, ceased to be a Tennesseean, any more than the Oriental student at Columbia—collegiate sport clothes and John Bull pipe of tobacco notwithstanding!—has ceased to be Chinese. To observe how much of all a man, on coming of mental age, casts aside, he yet carries with him to the ends of the earth, should be a lesson to reformers—who will, of course, refuse this modest instruction. . . . And so I dare recall a Tennessee which is neither represented in textbooks, nor wholly indicated in old records; and not actually visible to the most alert eye of a traveller sojourning for a while among southerners on his way to somewhere else. This, though the artificiality of mathematically arbitrary time measurement is never more apparent than when one hesitates midway toward the nonexistingness of the self after death and contemplates the new chapter assumed to have begun with one's birth!

When the individual life span is viewed objectively, one thing is seen to follow another as inevitably as the hooves of the horse and the breath of the rider follow, by yards and inches, the circle around the racecourse from the starting point to the goal; but this, though many fictionists content themselves with such a description, is no full account of experiencing. Two-dimensional histories may satisfy moralists; not persons for whom moralizing is only the little aftermath of an ineffable knowledge,

common to, and yet different for, all men. I defy anybody beginning honestly to set down his own past, not to
feel, as he attempts to fit this and that impression into the
orthodox time pattern, so reliably concerned with precipitated events, that he is lying! Laws of perspective are
really based upon predigested concepts of externals.
They represent experiences already passed upon by mankind at large. Anything still in the realm of purely personal vision escapes these laws and refutes their control.
In the view of a man attempting to project for others
happenings in which, though they are over and done
with, he is yet immersed, as in a stream, what ought to
be seen as remote may appear terribly near; presumed
cause may, on examination, turn out to be a consequence
of its own supposed effect; there is no yesterday to juxta-
pose to today, because, in memories vividly invoked,
everything is *now*. . . . Nothing for it then but to
plunge—since writing is not so much an exposition of
crystallized understanding as a voyage of discovery for
the writer himself. I want to know what people are recognizing when, after an introduction, they say to me:
"You are from the South!" challengingly, with the air of
cunningly proclaiming something I have been trying to
hide. . . .

I wonder, for instance, which, if any, of the signs they
are reading can be attributed to my rather startling first
recollection of a human figure—that of a dark-skinned
man, entirely naked except for the white cloth nicely
snaring his middle!'An Indian, in fact—a spectacle so
bizarre, intruding as it did on the "ramshackle Victoria"
(I think I am quoting Miss Marianne Moore) represented
by a small southern town, it might easily be mistaken for
a vision of prenatal origin. Isn't it possible this red man

was never actually seen by me, but is one encountered somewhere by my maternal great-grandfather, Captain Joseph Thomas, a lawyer of Winchester, Virginia, who, after equipping at his own expense a company of militia he (naturally) commanded during Jackson's campaign against the British, became so enamoured of adventure that he and his French-Irish wife, not content with the rewards of a national victory, set out on a tour of pioneering? By 1822, they had advanced as far west as Elkton, Kentucky; and though they did not remove to Tennessee until 1829, after the Indian warfare of that region had been officially concluded, there were still Indians aplenty in the neighbourhood.

Or granting, for art's sake, a yet further elaboration of the premise expanded by Eugene O'Neill when he wrote *Emperor Jones*, mightn't the buck I conjured before me for so many years have descended to me, as imaginative inheritance, through an even earlier impression—one made on the retina of great-*great*-grandfather—an attorney, too—while he was winning modest honours in the struggle for Independence, from which he retired a major? In his day, Tennessee, existing, nameless, as a hinterland of North Carolina, was known only as a lost range of mountains which were wild citadels for the Cherokees; while even at home, in Virginia, the presence of a friendly band of them was no rarity. The new territories, neglected by their remote governors nearer the coast, protected themselves as they could, through stressful periods, by organizing an impromptu defence; but it was not always effectual. The Chickamaugas, most remorseless of all Cherokees, often guilefully insinuated themselves into newly erected cabins, and left behind them the silence of death.

5

Tradition says De Soto once traversed an eastern section of this territory which, later, became Tennessee, and that he encamped near Chicsa, on the site of the present city of Memphis. Queen Elizabeth gave Raleigh, by royal patent, the right to discover and possess, in her name, if it were possible, the bald quiet of these hills and valleys, where only birds, of creatures that were different, entered with licence. And Charles II, in 1663, granted to Clarendon, General Monk, Lord Ashley and other serviceable creditors of the Crown, all of the New World between the thirty-first and thirty-sixth parallels of latitude; Locke and Spinoza, it is said, having been invited to frame a form of government suitable for the proposed colony, which was to cover most of a continent. But in 1719 the government passed from the control of the proprietors directly into the hands of the King again, and South and North Carolina grew as independent colonies. And still, while the hardier English, joined by a positively pestilential number of Scotch-Irish and Welsh, persisted with the attempt to force from nature a welcome for the paleface; and the Spaniards planted, in blood, in the sand of Florida, a culture they hoped was deep-rooted; and the French, brave yet with an indomitable hunger for gain and glory, treasured the Mississippi as if it were a very stream of life; the Indian knew what he knew, and remained where he was, though the grip he kept on his own country had to be furtive, stealthy, defended by perpetual hostile skirmishing. Oh, my great-great-grandfather, my great-grandfather—even my grandmother!—saw Indians!

In 1769, one William Bean constructed a log house at the junction of the Watauga River and Boone's Creek, in a section now east Tennessee, then west North Caro-

6

lina; and though La Salle had already, long before, built Fort Prud'homme, on the Chickasaw Bluffs, he and Marquette had carried the sword and Cross only along the western border; so that the erection, by the French, of blockhouses on the Kentucky, Ohio, Wabash and Cumberland, and their exploits, religious and military, do not detract from Bean's distinction as a bona fide first settler— the first to enter this district and thus boldly display an intention to remain. When Bean's axe was ringing on boles of virgin trees, there were listeners—not friendly. In 1748 an expedition of Virginians, directed by Dr. Thomas Walker, had penetrated into this secret verdure, scaled crags through dense timber, looked down from heights toward the false smiling of beautiful valleys; and gone back. Either Walker, or Governor Spotswood, who preceded him across the Appalachian range, or the Wood or Wallen parties of explorers, had commemorated discouragement by giving the region the name "Cumberland," to honour a royal duke. But they had not lingered.

Daniel Boone and Sam Calloway had likewise passed, with their rifles, where a footprint left unwisely was as good as a warrant to be shot with an arrow. European powers refused to admit the sovereignty of the Indians. The Iroquois, who composed the Five Nations, had claimed part of Tennessee; the claim had been ignored, as the ghost of many a Frenchman could have testified. The Cherokees, the Creeks, the Miamis and the Choctaws together protested their right to consider land confined by the Cumberland, the Tennessee and the Holston a common hunting ground; and in 1768 the English compromised their arrogance by descending to an arrangement for a purchase of this property; and began the "century of dishonour," in which agreements evasively couched were made and broken, pacts entered into and discarded, over and over—their perfidy toward the Indian so monotonously patterned, it took on a paradoxical quality of dependableness.

And when, in 1779, Evan Shelby and his son Isaac, having wangled from the governor the command of two thousand men who were—*this* time!—determined to wipe out the Chickamaugas so that they would never be heard from any more, did destroy their great stronghold on the banks of the Tennessee River; even this victory prepared only for longer, more lingering hatreds which would be paid for by white men right up to the time of my great-grandfather Captain Joseph.

In the double parlours of the house in Clarksville where I was born, in rooms once perfect as a museum—with their pier glasses, console tables and antique bric-a-brac—there were some paintings by early Americans which my grandfather had collected. There was never a scene, of those depicted, in which, by some great river like a bluer Mississippi, on some palisade more grandly towering than any above the real Hudson, there did not appear a solitary redskin, tiny in the foreground of the picture, but indomitably erect with the dignity he invoked to withstand encroachments from the magnificent austerity of the wilderness surrounding him. These Indians were always on the watch, as if, in their view of the world, the threat of death were never absent; they were ready to face it and defy it in the same instant; yet, the very next moment, could have resumed with unalloyed pleasure an indolence we surrendered with the invention of clocks and sundials.

Paul Wellman has written a story he himself disparages as "a yarn of adventure": *Broncho Apache*. The

8

style is not all equal to the moving narrative simplicity of the first chapters, and there are interludes which are shallowly melodramatic; yet the author is almost unique in recognizing, through genuine self-identification with red men, what the resources of primitives are. He has taken a figure, which might easily have been descended from those embalmed by James Fenimore Cooper, straight out of legend, into a life of the senses—a genuine animal life! He has defined, by implication, what constitutes pure animal courage, with its limited wisdom. I think he shows us what savages are when not tricked into false, strutting behaviour for literature and the theatre.

Savages like Mr. Wellman's were present, animate with the cunning of fear and increasing despair, when the Watauga settlements were being added to by men who had other desperations to fire their bravado. After the War of Independence, there were many who had been named "Tories," who were obliged to trek west hastily, toward a constantly retreating horizon. There were criminals—in that era any small lapse, any trivial error of judgement, might make a criminal overnight! There were obstinate heretics who had militantly despised the orthodox church of Ireland. There were those adversity-goaded who dreamed of revenging themselves on fate where no shrewd competitor could interfere. There were men who were artists at heart and had to live out their fantasies.

One of my great-grandmothers had a French father, Mareen Duval, who settled in Maryland, at a time when French people, for all sorts of reasons—political, religious and purely personal—thought of the New World, and could feel, in advance, their wounds healing as if some magical unguent were being applied. He married a Miss Curran, a young Irish girl. America was already the melting pot. I have a grandmother from an opposite line, so Irish (though her father was from Ulster) I, who inherited, with the snobbery engendered by the milieu in which I was reared, a contemptuous view of a race that, even in the nineties, had already surfeited America with cheap labor, and was making a bad reputation for itself through its disastrous fondness for strong drink, used to be ashamed of her name. It was McGinty—and "down went McGinty to the bottom of the sea," as everybody knows. There seems to have been a large connection, all dissatisfied with the state of things in the old country. . . . Where I was brought up—at any rate, for the generation to which I belong—anti-Irishism was almost as prevalent as anti-Semitism today! Almost as bitter as anti-Semitism in Germany! "That *Mick*!" "Shanty Irish!" Such expressions registered the utmost in contempt and disapproval. There was a shade of preference for the north of Ireland, a hairsplitting degree of greater tolerance for the Irishman who was not a Roman Catholic—I think this gain the result of deliberate propaganda; for, among the numbers pouring tidally into the territories at the beginning of the last century, Ulstermen and Scots were predominant. There has been a similiar drive to convince Americans that the flower of French aristocracy is, was, and always will be, of the Huguenot persuasion. My mother stoutly maintained the Huguenot tradition in our own family, the last surviving near relations, a pair of wealthy and decorous spinsters in Ellicott City, Maryland, devout Papists, notwithstanding. *How,* I used to wonder, was she going to answer *that*?

But she did answer it, and tried to persuade me the

McGintys—*our* McGintys!—were of the stuff of kings.
However, I did not believe her. Already at six, maybe
seven, years of age I had sufficient experience of the Irish
to be sure the Shannahans, who kept the corner saloon,
were, equally, descendants of a royal house. My scepticism was so precocious and acute, I even refused to
accept her more circumspect designation of Great-
grandfather McGinty as "an Irish Protestant gentleman."
When she insisted he had been driven to emigrate for
the defence of his faith, and because he loved liberty
better than the English Crown, I discredited her story
entirely. I have always been the victim of my own in-
verted pride, which so scorns subterfuge that any unflattering account of things (particularly things relating to
myself and my background) strikes me with a plausibility I seldom acknowledge in a more pleasing construing
of the same matter. It is only during the last five years
that I have been convinced, after documentary proof,
that my opinion of Mr. McGinty as from Dublin, and
a Catholic, was without any foundation other than my
own juvenile contrariness. Yet I have never met an Irish
immigrant to America with the fine taste for art and
learning my mother persistently attributed to him, although his cultural credentials have not yet been produced.

The most known of him is that, on his way from the
Celtic nowhere of his origin to another nowhere in the
pioneer land in which he was to die, he halted very
briefly in the East and married a German woman—Eliza
Hyer—whose antecedents were so totally obscure she
might as well have been an immaculate conception. She
was a Lutheran; he a Presbyterian; later, after the trek
across mountains into Tennessee, both became Method-

11

ists. She spoke English with an effort; he, one supposes, with that burr of the north which smacks as much of the Highlands of Scotlands as of the Lakes of Killarney. Presumably, when you are journeying over roads that were Indian "traces" less than half a century before, and living, by campfires, on parched corn, conversational interchanges cease to be important. Bishop Asbury, during his great campaign to lighten the lot of dwellers in the territories by giving them access to "free grace" which would be eternal, spoke somewhat harshly of the physical aspect of travel in his day; and in the time of my great-grandparents improvement had been only relative.

I hope the McGinty-Hyer pilgrims had the faith required for their consolation, for I feel certain, if they had set forth with much gear and many slaves to hearten them, some rumour of it would have been handed down. Iron knives and horn spoons may have passed out of use by them; unexcised tea no longer had to be smuggled; men in the wilderness were giving up moccasins and doeskin shirts and going about in store cottons, more like white people. But wardrobes continued to be in part of homespun, and women without pretensions wore calico sunbonnets made over a durable frame of white pine slats. And if Daniel Boone and Colonel Henderson were no longer trying to persuade the Indians out of any right to the country between the Tennessee, Ohio and Cumberland Rivers—the tract so useful to the Transylvania Company—men in my great-grandfather's era were quite as land mad as their immediate predecessors. Great-grandfather himself, looking about at the quantities of everything still left free for everybody, and either bewildered by the profusion or too reduced by exhaustion and difficulties to care for selectiveness, arrived at a place called Palmyra Bluffs and decided to go no further.

Palmyra Bluffs, on the Cumberland, near Clarksville, exists at this moment as a few stores, scattered and irregular lines of houses, a somewhat neglected wharf. Just what it was like around 1825 I don't know. Probably it has altered less in the same space of time than some other villages. Doubtless charming people live there —this is Tennessee, the South, where all are so charming! But when I was a child, attending school in Memphis, and would visit Clarksville of a summer, and was going toward Palmyra on the train, on a journey in which every revolution of the wheels of the railway car stressed the approach toward a Paradise, I was aware of Palmyra Bluffs chiefly because the familiar conductor always poked his head through the doorway and made a perfunctory announcement.

"Palmyra!" he would shout, then mutter disparagingly; and turn back hastily, without waiting to see if anybody wanted to get out there—nobody ever did. And I would thrill with a secondary, altogether derived interest in this sequestered spot, telling me that but a little and I should be able to sight the Mecca toward which my heart sped! Train schedules between Clarksville and Memphis were such that Palmyra, as if it were a mirage visible only during certain hours, on some shotts in Morocco, invariably appeared before me in the light of a setting sun—a dour, red light, with, curiously, an infusion of peace. And when the Pullman stopped and I glanced from the window, it was like seeing hell transported to Arcady.

There was a station of sorts—very poor sorts—and a general store or two with doors open wide, often prematurely illumined for the night. In the porch vestibules of these emporiums, loafers would have congregated—never, however, more than a *few* loafers. The stick-whittling, apple-barrel variety! A couple of girls, elaborately pompadoured and befrilled in their long dresses, would be strolling, arms interlaced, down the station platform, giving backward glances at the train; answering some jocularity from a member of the train crew coquettishly, with giggles. They—these lorn little belles —had been waiting all afternoon for the train to pull in: it was the event of the day. But nothing had happened. Soon we from the outer world, so much envied, would have disappeared. You could hear the leaves, as the river breeze wandered among them, sighing as though disappointedly. Beyond the village the fields lay withering under a sugary powdering of dust. Water was not visible until later, nearer Clarksville, where the Cumberland's sinuosities emerge openly, showing the green of the banks and the blue of the sky. Yet it was the presence of the hidden river which kept Palmyra alive. Something dankly vitalizing was borne upward from the shore on every current of a slothful wind. In the stagnancy of an atmosphere which buried ambition, vivid breaths, out of the damp below, rose like new courage on the stale air; as from some magical spring, secret and unperceived, at which, nonetheless, those thirsting, after the heat which still lingered under the crimson sunset, could slake themselves. In France, when we used to come up from Perpignan on the train which stopped at Arles-sur-Tech, and discover ourselves, in an hour, transported from the August dryness of the coast, with its sand and sirocco, to heights gushing moisture from real mountain freshets, I sometimes remembered Palmyra. The place my great-grandfather McGinty had come all the way from Ireland to find! And had found in the company of a wife he had married before there had been any opportunity to become genuinely acquainted with her!

Until 1779, when James Robertson sowed the first corn crop for this region, only trappers had any knowledge of the district—Mansker and other hunters, who, in the winters, imitated the Indian; and, in spring, loaded pirogues with skins and hides and descended gently the river flowing past Natchez. In those days, they traversed, alternately, the land of the Frenchman and the land of the Spaniard. In 1775 DeMumbrune had a cabin at Eaton's Station. Two years later a party explored the Cumberland extensively. A trapper named Spencer is supposed to have spent the whole of a certain cold season in a habitation he had contrived from the hollow of a tree. James Robertson came from Watauga. Robertson, John Donelson and certain friends were persuaded by Colonel Henderson to go west to commence the exploitation of the Transylvania Company's immense tract to which both the governors of North Carolina and Virginia had denied him his title. In 1778, Robertson, with eight others, following the trails left by Indians and wilder things, crossed the mountains through the Cumberland Gap. French Lick was a trading post, by the grace of the Chickasaws, who were then, temporarily, on good terms with the French. Robertson, when he arrived at that destination, began the disinvolvement of the country out of non-Anglo-Saxon hands. Simultaneously, John Donelson, in his boat the *Adventure*, moved some of the womenfolk of the Robertson party west, by water. On the 12th of April, 1780, a contingent from the Donelson expedition (Moses Renfroe and his company) disembarked and separated from the others at a point they called Red River, landing on a bluff above a tributary of the Cumberland.

Even when my great-grandfather arrived at Palmyra and began to gaze about him, there were plenty of virgin acres to delight the greedy eyes of a settler. He was almost penniless, yet he could help himself. He secured a lodging for himself and his wife somewhere, and inaugurated his bargain purchase by immediately beginning to clear ground. I had my own taste of pioneering, in Brazil, and I know a little of the heartaches that go with it. The aches in legs and arms, too (no woman attempts such work!), when you are felling trees, burning off brush, upheaving stumps or merely making as much havoc as you can with an axe and leaving the rest to rot. What great, obstinate roots are thrust into your precious soil by the things which were there first, and have a prior claim on nature for their sustenance! And yet what mad expansion for your ego in the vanity of *possessing*, though it is only a courtesy ownership, as much of the earth as you can see at once—as if all the six counties of Ulster had suddenly become yours!

My great-grandfather McGinty built his own log house. Sawmills had already been introduced, so he may have had a plank, not a puncheon floor, and real partitions, instead of curtains of bearskin or deerskin, dividing its dim interior into two or three rooms. They were a marvellous innovation when they came, those sawmills. It was like a miracle to watch the boards pour out of them as cleanly and rapidly as an expert gambler can deal playing cards! The very smell of the sawdust must have been an intoxicant to men who had attacked whole oaks with mauls and wedges and the patience of those resigned to labour to the end! In Brazil, I spent a year and a half where my feet were on earth whether I was under a roof or in the open. I hope it has helped me to understand. When I was seven, my cousin Elizabeth and myself yearned, above all things, for stilts. John, my uncle's houseboy, with the price of them in his pocket, went with us into a dingy street, into a yard so stacked with wood we little people felt hemmed in by buttes, bluffs, precipices, threading a way through canyons. From inside a shed with a corrugated iron roof, rose a slithery, whining sound, interrupted by clatterings and bumpings. Everywhere sawdust was scattered like the golden aftermath of a supernatural snowfall. Over it all hung the fragrance of a pine forest. In just half an hour, we were able to stalk proudly forth, mounted, like giants, on tremendous legs which, though they seemed affected by incipient paralysis, yet bore us along familiar sidewalks at an elevation impressive even to grown folk.

In the mountains of Tennessee, to this day, cabins go up higgledy-piggledy, without flooring; and with the chimneys outside, that used to be plastered with clay mixed with hay and hog bristles, fashioned almost as they were when the generation preceding my great-grandfather's had the additional task, once the dwelling was done, of protecting its labours by erecting a stockade. My great-grandparents, compared to some, enjoyed civilization. If they bought pigs—which seems probable —and Mr. McGinty was made homesick for the old country because of them, there was a cow, as well, to console him. Butter was not a mere euphemism for bear fat; though most of it, of course, had to be sold. And if coffee was still, sometimes, a distillation from parched rye and dried beans, this was not a deprivation to an Irishman, who would, at least occasionally and for a treat, brew some real tea, stewed to death on the hob on the hearth!

During the eighteen-twenties, Tennessee, by then a full-fledged state, was filled with political agitators proposing to put that region on a sound financial basis. After the War of 1812, in 1814, there was a general suspension of specie payment in most of the United States. And afterwards, for two decades, state leaders were largely preoccupied with plans either to relieve current "depression" or to prevent depression's return. The arguments put forward often have a ring of modernity; but this doesn't indicate pioneering was over with. It went on.

Before the war, I read, in *The Making of a State* by James Phelan, who was referring to that other struggle, called, in the North, "the War of the Rebellion": *few in practise drew a sharp line of demarcation between the exactions of business and the amenities of social life. The custom of indorsing notes indiscriminately for friends was universal, and refusal frequently brought about a rupture, at times a personal clash. A bill too often presented aroused anger and indignation. A gentleman's credit was supposed to be above suspicion, and, resting upon this supposition, liberties were taken with the goods of merchants and the bills of doctors that would now stamp a man as having no credit at all.* Mr. Phelan's history of Tennessee was published in 1888.

But I doubt the German woman my great-grandfather married was in a position to invoke this indulgence of caste. With all her immediate, practical absorptions, I doubt she knew it existed. She was too busy to make the attempt! What with milking, churning, slaughtering pork, boiling fat and lye down for soap, dripping tallow for candles—always an economy—cooking, cleaning house (every pail of water was lugged from the spring), sewing and, above everything, having babies, I doubt she had the leisure for very much thought. Of the children, four survived the miscarriages and stillbirths that had to be got through without medical help. And if my great-grandfather was not, as my mother averred, *devoted* to books, the names of his daughters are at least a tribute to literacy. They were Eliza Roxanna, Fredonia Francesca and Angelina Budette. I have been given to understand five of the six names assembled had been taken from novels, and that at least one of them was derived from the works of Sir Walter Scott, who was very popular in that day. My great-uncle was called Ewing, after a famous and self-immolating exhorter for Calvin, who preached the word of predestination around 1802. It seems indicative that the girls, at their primitive christening, were given, for patron saints, frivolous heroines of fiction; whereas the boy, at his baptism, was dedicated by implication, to a man of stern interests. Fredonia was my grandmother. She died the week I was born.

She was almost young—only sixty—yet, compared to her own mother at her death, an old woman; for the German girl who had nearly come to grips with starvation must have been under thirty, with the blue in her eye only a little faded by premature fatigue, and the braids of her hair still yellow-brown. She had been ill of a "fever," or it might have been "consumption." People in her predicament, in that age, in her surroundings, had none of the extravagant interest in diagnosis with which modern doctors and their patients amuse themselves, though it may not be possible to offer a cure. And if she was of peasant descent, she probably came prepared as well as you can be for the toll a wilderness takes from women. They die young there, as a matter of course. They are almost, you could say, forewarned— it is only instinct that ignores.

But Great-grandfather McGinty seems to have lacked a complementary resignation. Left to look at his acres and the fine log cabin which was the work of his hands; and his three daughters (not much more than babies); and the son whose career had been so stalwartly initiated; he fell sick himself, of sheer bitterness and discouragement; and succumbed to the inevitable—anticipated it!—dying long before he was forty, but already in a state of inertia—hopeless!—religion supplying everything but a really adequate reason for going on!

Charles II, when he made his grant to nobles to whom he was indebted, had not so much as glimpsed, at the distance a bird flies above the earth, these miles between the Carolinas, Virginia and the Pacific (fatuously described by his romancing geographers as stretching "to the south seas"). He had simply, in contempt of the Indians, appropriated them on parchment; later, with a few words, bartering away the destinies of people nameless to him, whose circumstances and very existence could not enter his imaginings. Can we wonder, when we listen to zealots haranguing today in Union Square, that vindictive passions sometimes seem to run off with the argument? Need we be astonished when some voice informed by a wretchedness of centuries describes the monstrous inhumanness of the aristocrat? Truly, if he is not a monster strictly speaking, his ignorance of adversity can reduce his wisdom to that of a child of six when he ought, otherwise, to be a grown man! Until suddenly a revolution, or something else, puts a stop to that daydreaming in which he is self-intoxicated to believe power is in his own personality, and unlimited; then necessity compels the primitive in his nature to renounce a few delusions.

But daydreams and delusions are not the exclusive prerogative of fortunate aristocrats and modern capitalists. My Great-grandfather McGinty, even without demonstrating his kingly lineage, claimed his right to share the pioneer's illusory expectation of certain success. On the first spring day at Palmyra, when he stood in the raw air surveying the tract he intended to make his, and the source of a fortune, he was the equal of Burr envisaging an empire. Unlike Burr's, his was to be the child of his thews and sinews rather than the illegitimate product of his brain alone!

But people in primitive surroundings, even when they are sophisticated (as great-grandfather, surely, was not), tend to revert—after a few bad years, a few failures with the crops, they begin to worship the Devil. They commence listening! When they hear the air coursing from the hills, it disturbs them; for they watch even the weather for the sign of a threat! The very ripples flowing over the stones of the river may mention matters not to be spoken of aloud with safety! While we are most afraid, we can't afford even the word—*fear*! The smell of danger every breeze carries has to be ignored, or morale will collapse.

Gazing at this world we pretend to call "ours," we take note of it stealthily. No one ever lived here before! How have we dared—? Space here is not a liberation, but a load fallen upon us, beneath which we will be

21

buried! I can never feel really intimate with people who have not been poor. Talking to them about essential values, life, fundamental significances, seems, paradoxically, like searching literature for great meanings in the company of those who know only the alphabet! Not that this is any guarantee of congenial company to the Left! *Blessed are the meek: for they shall inherit the earth. . . . Blessed are the poor in spirit: for theirs is the kingdom of heaven. . . .*

My Great-grandfather McGinty, on days when even the rains had forsaken him, must often have cursed by every sign in the zodiac; and said to himself he possessed too much! He must have prayed, on occasion, that he would be able to return his lands to nature, in exchange for any cranny at all in the snugness of a street in Belfast, however humble it had to be! If men owned the powers of gods, maybe they would never love one another! In the wilderness, where you are helpless, you begin to feel sentiment even for fleas and lice, who at least are gregarious!

Cover yourself with your deerskin when it blows cold; when you are devoured by the heat, open your calico shirt at the throat and make the best of it. You are lucky if you have anything to put into your belly. If you are hungry, and your children, as well; go after food, tireless until you have provided it. You may be a Methodist who has professed "grace," or a Presbyterian stayed by fatalism—whichever you are, you shed conscience when you come to these parts. White men are not as Indians, whose religion has reconciled them to earth. Don't reflect—reflection would defeat you! Even when you are like the rabbit, who screams as the steel molars of the trap scrunch through the bones of its little haunch; or like the bird, who, as the snake uncoils, squats wingless on the bough lapped narrowly by a sleek current of disaster; or the deer, whose spring above earth has only made the arrow more certain of its target in blood—don't cry out! No one will hear you, and you will only end by frightening yourself!

Your log cabin is built. There it stands, so irrelevant to the surrounding, it is as though, into this quiet of hunter and hunted, you had introduced the future—something visionary, not yet present, not truly actual! Maybe you have before you what inaugurates a new world—you will never live to enjoy it! Not you! You may have lifted the roof which will hold off the burden of that illimitable sky, but you cannot rest from your labours, which, if they are not altogether to the glory of God, are to your own glory, which must suffice! If only you can stick through another winter—one more winter! And through one more spring! At night, when stars and planets blaze softly from the river, and a twig creaking with beginning frost sounds as loud as a pistol-shot, sleep itself is a betrayal. Yet sleep you must—the sleep of a man with a broken heart! Of a man who is desperate and has flung off caution; and must never again fear!

When Moses Renfroe and his companions disembarked from the *Adventure* they believed themselves founding a community in which Moses himself would become the first patriarch; and they hewed the logs for their blockhouses and prepared well for days to follow. Until, suddenly, as if they had to die of their success, all were massacred. There was a single wretched woman —a Widow Jones—who escaped. It was twenty miles to Eaton's Station—new then, too. Twenty miles, green and infernal! At any moment that stump in the abandoned clearing, that shadow cast into a thicket black at midday with the trees overhead, might take recognizable shape! Every breeze whispering was a sneer at distress! A wild turkey gobbled in the distance, and the grotesque music was, all at once, a wild voice more terrible than all because it was at least half-human! Why, she must have asked God, am I allowed to live—I, who was not the worst sinner? Just the same, she continued: dreads like hers are so simple, they admit of but one answer. She gave it as if despite herself, with a resoluteness which was a conquest of her flinching and terrified flesh!

Fifty years of other sufferings, and a whole generation that had been born, matured and lost its youth, were between the time of my Great-grandfather McGinty and the ordeal of the Widow Jones. But in his day there were still Indians, their relentlessness broken and become mere slyness.

My grandmother, when she was a little girl, saw them, and remembered them forever. She recalled how they came, with the mask of pretended peace on their faces, to trade at the farms. Housewives—her own mother—would stand in the doorways of the cabins, arms akimbo, and reject the moccasins and beadwork they offered. When you were a little girl, and had been told you must suspect them, with their lurking and loitering, you had only to hear the guttural Indian voice, and you were like an animal beset by horrors provoked by the familiar-unfamiliar odour of blood. Without having seen death or understanding it, you smelled it and knew it! You crept to your mother, drew the folds of her wide petticoats over your head and wanted to be closer, closer: cover yourself with darkness! Afterward, you tried not to be alone, lest your nameless panic, provoked again by any chance word, take definite shapes you couldn't bear! And your virgin mind braced itself to endure the last outrage of real comprehension—!

My grandmother remembered wolves! And how she would go all over gooseflesh when one howled at night. She and her sisters and brother would have gathered, after a poor supper, about the fire that ran like red wind storming up the chimney, until the little house with its log interior was ablaze with consolation; my great-grandmother would be too tired to talk—she would have dropped to a homemade hassock beside the children; and my great-grandfather, weary, but with the fidgets, would be greasing the rifle he loved like a daughter. When abruptly, from the solid night, miraculously degutted to provide this kind warmth, a wolf, remote, solitary, would begin mourning; his long, faint howl sorrowful and sounding disembodied. "Wolf!" my great-grandfather would comment shortly. And Angelina, Fredonia, Eliza and Ewing would look at each other without speaking, and pretend they were not afraid. The girls, tousled and dirty after a day of play interspersed with helping Mother, would push their hair out of their eyes and bend together over the pictures in the almanac they had spread open on the floor. *Wolves*—ugh! Sometimes one was killed: brought in heavy and limp; the wound in the side of its head crusted and blackening; tongue swollen and lolling so that its fixed jaws had a terrible lear. I wonder if they had ever heard of Red Ridinghood! I never cared for that story. It was nasty, with no cathartic effect. There were no princes or princesses; and the realistic attack offended my sentimental conception of grandmothers as invariably benign.

How many Irish lies had my great-grandfather to tell himself to be convinced of the grand reasons he had for being where he was rather than in Ulster; and how many of them could he actually believe? Oh, well—he had his wife, his youngsters, the cow and pigs! Life is the same for poor men wherever they are! And if the creatures depending on you meet with accidents—a sow one year, a calf the next, the baby the year after, and then the wife!—nature takes care of you, and you harden. Until you regard yourself with amazement, astounded to find yourself a superman! Think how trifles upset you when you were young! Now you are iron! Give you every conceivable occasion to suffer, and you feel nothing whatever. Once you had a heart, pulsating emotion—you were as soft and easily hurt by what others said or did as the sheep dog that cowers and cringes when you shout a hard word to it. Now what beats under your wishbone is only dull, serviceable lead, its action mechanical! Or is this idea of self-conquest just another self-deception? You consider yousrelf invulnerable, and go about your business as if superior to life's hazards; but aren't you, really, skirting a crumbling crater, and far from safe? One misstep, one shove from Fate, from any unexpected quarter, and you are overboard! When my great-grand-mother died, my great-grandfather tumbled into a lake of pitch—into darkness, into the cold heat—the bitterness of his own terrible, unsuspected melancholy! There he was drowning in the black obscurity, and had no idea what was killing him! All he knew was that, now, at last, he really *was* dying, because he *wanted* to die. It was a way of returning to the grey, tender mists and emerald vales of the north: a way—the only one!—of escaping America, that had got its hooks into him and would never, in this life, let go! If only he had been King Charles, and comfortably able to dispose of the new territory by merely writing his name!

But *my* Indian was not, it appears, either one of those Great-great-grandfather Thomas ran afoul of while really fighting the British, or an Indian encountered by his son when he and his wife and a few slaves made a caravan over the Blue Ridge Mountains in 1829; and he was certainly not one of those morose government charges who alarmed my grandmother. *My* Indian, at first conjectured to be a wraith removed from one of the paintings in the parlour and set down in an imaginary outdoors, was finally identified—he was flesh and blood! Lithe and living and almost stark naked as I remembered him, he was yet of my own era, not attributable to some half-forgotten bad dream! In 1896, when I was three years old, a Wild West show exhibited in Clarksville. It was the year we left my mother's home— the house that had belonged to Grandfather Thomas, who had bought it from his friends the Lewises (for whom my Uncle Lewis was named), who had built it around 1848, before they quitted Clarksville. We went to live in a cottage—how my mother hated it!—which had, opposite it, vacant lots; with, beyond, fields, in the summer, so filled with daisies they looked like foam on a South Sea. There, one week, tepees were erected about a large central tent. And when my nurse, Ella Ray, took me for an afternoon stroll, we stopped to stare at the Indians—like the etchings by Frederic Remington in the folio my father had!

It was at this precise moment *he* presented himself, looking just as he might have in some village near Sycamore Shoals on the Watauga, when Colonel Henderson

27

and Colonel Hart and Daniel Boone avariciously persuaded the tribes to meet them in council in 1772! Like Dragging Canoe! Like Oconostota! Like Hiawatha! Passing before us from one tepee to another, his bronze body, with its liquid muscles, moving with a gliding strength and sureness not even Zane Grey could convey! Though there was the loincloth, this was my first electrifying glimpse of human nudity, and I was smitten as by revelation! Very likely, I never again belonged entirely to Queen Victoria, who, while she was Empress of all India, was a reigning sovereign in Clarksville, too! In the beginning, when I would mention my Indian, nobody knew to whom I referred; until Ella Ray and my mother, comparing notes, arrived at the only sane conclusion.

And I still possess the gift he made so casually of a David by Michael Angelo, a youth by Praxiteles—his thin, eager face inclined from us toward the tepee into which he was trying to disappear—modestly! Because he was embarrassed without war paint or feathers! Swift as a minnow through bright water, he dived through the sunshine—apocalyptically swift!—to escape our observation! It was an annunciation—as if the Angel Gabriel, radiant as a comet, had descended from heaven before me! From that moment forward, gentlemen in hard derbies and choker collars; gentlemen in little short-tailed jackets and tubelike trousers; gentlemen in morning coats with spats and lavender gloves, never completely deceived me as to what constituted beauty! I was faithful.

I remained so years later, when, visiting the pueblos and reservations in the Southwest, I failed to discover one survivor in the least resembling him. Either they had fattened on ease and were blandly indifferent, or they had starved and grown ugly with reticent cunning.

And they were, universally, clothed in such fashion as would have satisfied Ella Ray, who was Mrs. Grundy's own sister, though black. Until nothing but the corroboration my elders had given to my story allowed me to accept him as having existed—as more than a figment of fancy I had confused with Mercury, who had wings on his heels; or with Phaëthon, the lovely brown colour of whose body was the scar left after a challenge to the Sun!

2

HOW constantly, how perpetually, I, as a child, was troubled by the problem of the snob, it has taken me half a lifetime to recognize! I was first crushed by feeling it insoluble when we quitted a really grand old antebellum home, occupied by my mother's family immediately on the close of the Civil War, and went to live in the cottage I have mentioned—ignominiously, I thought. Though I tried to take comfort in the fact that the home place, which had gone to my aunt, was still *almost* our own, I was dimly troubled by something spurious in such weak bolstering of self-esteem. When we went to Russellville, Kentucky, then on to Evansville, Indiana, things seemed to get worse! My mother, for example, had to sell her saddle horse! But it was during three winters spent in Saint Louis that my maladjustments became formidable. For there we boarded; though the friend who harboured us soothed her own vanity and ours by calling us her "paying guests." Futile euphemism! Not even the fine house consoled me—it had previously belonged to western millionaires. The sort whose naïve taste for luxuries, baroque and almost ludicrous, is now a tradition. There were pool and billiard rooms, sculptured Italian marble mantelpieces; the master bedrooms had blue, tufted-satin ceilings like great testers on four-posted beds. I remember my first sight of the manorial hall with moose heads on the landings of a square staircase with a profusely carved balustrade, and a rotunda glittering with multicoloured, jewelled glass. It was night—gas candles in the crystal chandeliers were twinkling brilliantly! I was stricken, dumb! I had believed such grandeurs the exclusive property of large hotels! The place was "Yankee"; we were boarders; my mother said it had been built by "parvenus." I was oppressed. I vaguely felt we faced the world with false pretences.

Miss Virginia Elizabeth Stevenson, a teacher at Mary Institute, and the niece of Sam Houston, was a fellow lodger—a bright-eyed, rabbit-toothed paragon of an intelligent schoolmistress, with a frizzled bang like Queen Alexandra's. A privileged kind of bluestocking, with a great regard for "the intellectual life," as it was esteemed academically in nineteenth-century America, she had a didactic way with the young she believed calculated to inspire them with a humility equivalent to an unappeasable rapacity for learning. Greece, Italy, Browning and Elizabeth Barrett, the New England of Emerson, Thoreau and Margaret Fuller, and an old England bounded by Shakespeare, Stratford, Dr. Johnson, Wordsworth and Oxford (Cambridge was almost upstart in her view of the world) were the symbolic or actual shrines at which she sacrificed in the name of an esoteric respectability. And when she made mention of the soldier and statesman who had been "Uncle Sam"—she did so fairly frequently!—and of herself as a southerner, she successfully divorced culture from anything a man can get for himself, through his senses, in the ordinary course of living.

True, when she narrated anecdotes from the days when her uncle had thrown in his lot with the Indians; and told in turn of his exploits in the Creek War, his sober retirement to study law in Nashville, his adventures as a schoolmaster, his ascent to a height of power won by his oratorical talents, his governorship of the state, his marriage, its dramatic collapse (temporarily annihilating a public reputation already spectacular), his second essay in enjoying simple sanctuary among red men; and, finally, described eloquently his glorious re-emergence from obscurity as the liberator of Texas from the Mexican yoke—it was as good as an Alger book! Except that Miss Stevenson never properly allowed him the Alger rise from honourable anonymity; but presented him, always, as the man of lineage who had claimed from Fortune his inalienable right. As *she* saw Uncle Sam, he was anything but a pioneer dark horse, remarkably endowed! Her challenge was never more than implied; but I used to take it seriously, and suppress the McGintys. Poor Fräulein Hyer was absolutely unmentionable! My childish soul was grateful indeed for a governor of Virginia among the Thomases; and I was even driven to seek solace in a silent résumé of those among my father's ancestors who could best bear mustering! There was Governor Hutchinson of Massachusetts, another Hutchinson at Bunker Hill and William Larned Marcy (what shades of the past were disturbed, I wondered recently, when I noticed Allan Nevin, designated him "a self-made man"!); and there were others among Marcys and Seeleys. And then I would remember unhappily my father's people were Yankees, which permitted them no more than pinchbeck distinctions. And I would clutch again at the Thomases!

If only Great-grandfather Joseph Thomas could have got himself killed at New Orleans, with his reputation as a hero-in-arms unsullied! Whereas, actually, he had grown poorer, not richer, in his old age, got humdrum, and taken to schoolmastering! Sam Houston, when a stripling among gentlemen pioneers who prized their sabres and horses and the education of action more than anything to be had from a book, may have tackled school-mastering as an experiment, while he was hard up, and his fame may have survived it—but *I* knew, from authorities like Kingsley, that the Army, the Church, the State (and never in this world a *school!*) provided gentlemen with professions!

There was nothing to be done about it! Great-grand-father had simply lingered too long alive! When he had closed his Kentucky experiment (it had lasted for seven years) and descended into Tennessee, and built himself a large square brick house (it had been pointed out to me as a place used as a Confederate hospital during the Civil War), his had been a gesture of foolish miscalcula-tion for which I was paying! As for his wife, Miss Duval, with her French father and her mother from Cork; her close connection with John Philpot Curran was no con-solation to me whatever after I had noted in the *Encyclo-pedia* that he was a "descendant of one of Cromwell's soldiers" and was "educated at Middleton *through the kind help of a friend!*" For one thing, Roundheads and Pilgrim fathers were, in my imagination, inextricably identified as the same breed—both a species of Yankee, with no real grace! Almost with nothing in them to the manner born! Nor did the boast I had from my mother that my great-grandmother knew as much Greek and Latin as the most scholarly man at Dublin University

33

help very much: it was not then my ambition to compete with men in a knowledge of the classics!

I recall no picture of great-grandfather, but I am well acquainted with the personality of great-grandmother, as she appeared in a daguerreotype made sometime after her husband, Captain Joseph, had been laid to rest with his disappointments in the cemetery—now abandoned!—on the Providence Road, near Clarksville. I once accompanied my mother and aunt on a search for his grave; and it was as difficult to discover as overgrown Roman tumuli. His was a sad sort of Valhalla. I have thought since, it might have been pleasanter to die in Winchester, and lie by his father among things which have the reassuring but un-American air of having been where they are for many generations without suffering contempt. . . . Great-grandmother—an old lady, in the picture—is sitting very stiffly upright, wearing a curiously unyielding brocade dress (all bones and buttons and flaring sleeves) and a peaked lace cap with dangling ribbons. The third-hand account of her, as it came down to me, constituted my earliest acquaintance with a bluestocking. Even today, with her bony, regular features, her blond hair that never turned grey, and her tense, compelled placidity, she gazes at me, from her shrewd, light northern-French eyes, indomitably. So indomitable did she seem to me in my childhood that I did not wish to be like her! Not in the South—where women had either to be as respectably yielding as Murillo madonnas, or as becomingly reckless (though also respectable) as Lola Montez! Her uprightness, and that look of unflinching realism she had got from the French (certainly not from the Irish) repelled me. For I, in my own manner, was beginning to be realistic, too; and already understood that

34

women got what they wanted only by graciously, melt-
ingly, affecting to abdicate. Great-grandmother Sarah
looked like someone hard-driven to asceticism, and so,
so, so—almost unbearably!—intelligent! The sort of
woman who had never permitted a man to feel superior,
as, in the course of nature, he certainly should! If only
that tired, unflinching scrutiny had been relieved by
a dash of kindly humour, not weary satire! Toward the
end of her life, in a final grimly sensible attempt to sal-
vage something from threatening bankruptcy, she, also,
taught school for a while! She and Great-grandfather
Joseph had not been much rewarded for their long devotion to General Jackson's leadership!

What a hold the man had on popular favour during
that period in which his career was first launched; and
how many anecdotes, verifiable and apocryphal, relate
his courage and daring at a time in which the white man's
tenure in west Tennessee was still uncertain! He had
fully identified himself with the locale and its interests,
as his rejection of the Jay Treaty and his vote against
Washington in the House of Representatives indicates.
Andrew Jackson was present when a constitutional convention was called to meet at Knoxville, on January 11,
1796, to discuss the admission of the territory to the
Union as a full-fledged state. He was one of the first
men elected to Congress under a new order of things
by which Tennessee, on June 1, 1796, acquired the full
privilege of statehood. Already, however, Tennessee was
too crowded for men of ambition, none prepared to
tolerate any leadership not their own; and contests for
supremacy took an acrimonious and highly personal
turn. Sevier and Jackson seem to have shared a dictatorial cast of mind; and when they came into open conflict

the irregularity of Jackson's matrimonial venture left him wide open to insults from an opponent who seems to have been notably lacking in fastidious gallantry. The charge against Sevier—that he was profiting illegally by his disposition of land in the West not really his—was not brought against his competitor; yet it could be said of both that neither, in this respect, overlooked the opportune occasion. Probably Sevier considered his portion of the spoils from primitive real-estate dealing amply paid for according to an unwritten law. He was the best Indian fighter Tennessee ever had.

His brother, Colonel Valentine Sevier, who had been an original settler close to the spot lost by the Renfroe Expedition (almost in Clarksville as it is now), had defied discouragement from the massacre of his three sons, overcome by Indians while in a boat on the Cumberland. The ruthless determination to survive and possess again these tracts which had cost blood must have been refired in John Sevier also by this terrible personal grievance. My great-grandparents, though the fever of pioneering must have been in them when they left Virginia, were never required to make such calamitous, final sacrifices on the strange soil as would have caused them to dedicate themselves unequivocally to holding it. They were always uneasy in Tennessee, like birds of passage come to rest for a little while only—perpetually nostalgic, looking back.

Their attitude might have been different had they arrived fifty years earlier—for instance, during that winter of 1780-81, when food and ammunition, in the Cumberland settlements, was exhausted; and an overflow from the river ate the corn from the fields—the precious crop of which every blade and kernel had a richness that might preserve a man's life! It was bitter that year. Where the

36

settlers were—six hundred miles from anywhere else!— the cold was like a sickness. The game which refused to perish fled toward the hills as toward arks. General Robertson, who, like Sevier—like Billy the Kid, in the seventies—when he killed an Indian, did not think a man was dead (though General Robertson was a stable and kindly character whose record, handed down to us, shows us much worth!)—General Robertson felt a cautious and desperate responsibility for those under his leadership, together with pangs for himself and his sons. He decided rash measures were the only recourse, and volunteered to set forth for Virginia or Carolina, with whoever would accompany him, and return with gunpowder and seed for a second sowing. One of his sons responded to the example; and those two and a few others to whom history seems less grateful, departed one morning, like doves dispatched in a flock to search for an olive branch.

The women, of course, stayed behind, where snow fell in settlement enclosures and lowered the stockades by many inches. How shrink a day, that its painful passage may seem like an hour? How make months into weeks? Always it is the women who wait! You can't change that by becoming an ardent feminist, as I did at fifteen! I don't believe it was the hard work that sent so many pioneer wives to early graves that divorce laws would have been unnecessary for relieving the males of monotonous fidelity. Many a man who had said his adieus to some girl-bride must have found, on reappearing to greet her, a broken woman of middle age. A physician has told me we are as old as our hearts! The drama of farewell bears such a specious resemblance to celebration that it is not until after the leave-takings that the wilderness conquers and annihilates. Undoubtedly, during those absences, rites of propitiation to evil spirits were performed, and deities worshiped more familiar to the Congo than good Presbyterians and Methodists have cared to admit! Usually a slave or two had been brought along, and could instruct in voodoo. Religious observance in Tennessee is tinged with voodooism to this day. To persons in extremity, God is great by right of might only cruelly. When it was unavoidable to leave the protection of the blockhouses, and go into the fields, very likely the youth with the rifle, when he accompanied his mother, was provided by her with a charm. At night, people listened—like my great-grandfather from Ulster. Fortunately, that year, He who had inscrutably exacted so much from whites who would have grovelled for His favour, did not spare red men. Though the settlers, in these months, were without defence, the Indians were too much reduced by the general illness of privation to take advantage of the fact. Until Robertson and his party, who had got what they wanted in Kentucky without crossing the mountains at all, returned and were welcomed like messiahs!

But on the fall of first darkness, when Robertson himself had just lain down in the luxury of security, inside Fort Freelands, the cries of hoot owls nobody would have recognized as four-footed broke the sweet silence after victory. Some of the pious, shivering, wrapped their deer hides closer around them; but they refused to stir. Women who had recovered their men, held them in their arms, covering a world—shutting out that other world deliberately; refusing it existence; determined to forget it! How beautiful this daring! Surely they had earned it!

It was moonlight. When you glanced from your pallet, through a loophole, into the sky, you were pierced by astonishment—almost aghast before such glory. Snow, on this night, had disappeared from the ground; blenched still by the fall of radiance. But nobody saw or suspected black, furtive lines deploying in antlike trickles among trees magically blossoming. Let us be glad, God! Careless! Let us, if we can, even pretend to be glad!

The gate, bulky and stayed by chains though it was, gave way at last before the prolonged force exerted by warriors, who, though they were savages, were the injured, too; and had their own god to sponsor revenge. A man, inside the blockhouse, roused, and glimpsed, through an aperture, the yard under him become a pit brimming with animated horror. Where men are at peace and merely "sinful," let Christ be invoked—this was a mission for Jehovah, the vindictive! Be calm, you hard-pressed fellows; Colonel Robertson is here to lead us, and we have gunpowder! Gunpowder—proof to the whites that they enjoyed divine patronage!—made men invincible! *To him that hath shall be given.* In the end, the brilliant avalanche from heaven buried only the attackers. And in that same year, in April, after the Battle of the Bluffs, the Cherokee Nation went into a time of mourning; and moved west again; carrying its sadness of a people enigmatically betrayed by its own elemental, unshakable belief.

Expounders of the gospel of economic determinism—those for whom it *is* a gospel—will see behind these dramas of migrations, only a hunger drive, forcing action from the dispossessed. Yet I think another, equal urge sometimes discontented our forebears—the ones not satisfied to call home a castle even when it happened to be comfortable. For these, the glorified brutality which was the heroism of the border, where it was common for runners to carry, as if it were a brand flamingly ignited by their own fear, warnings to isolated homesteaders to gather in the nearest fort in preparation for an Indian raid, represented an answer to a different necessity. Sir John Millais painted a not very good picture entitled *The Boyhood of Raleigh* depicting an old, hard-bitten veteran of buccaneering as he squats on the beach and narrates, to his audience of two boys, past exploits, with that evident relish in the retrospect which is probably the true reward of adventurous suffering. One of the children listens with such a primrose-by-the-river's-brim look on his face as accounts for his future: it will be safe and conservative. But Raleigh (a little sentimentalized according to the Victorian pattern) attends with his heart before us in his eyes; obviously sighing in absorption as though each breath of intensity were the last he would draw. Which goes to show Sir John Millais a more than passable novelist, though a mediocre painter. His picture, without subtlety, does illustrate a distinction to be made between individuals who will cross vast and perilous waters without any sensible need to do so, and those who, early, adapt themselves to the usual disappointments and inevitably die in bed. Ego incentive—power expression; not a little acquisitive instinct, too—prompt the gestures of the first, as well as of the second; but the Raleighs feel, additionally, a distrust of vicarious living. After an original, proud declaration of self realized—*I am!*—comes the avid, complementary assertion: And I must *know*, for *myself!* I will break open this enigma of being, and discover its secrets! I, I, I—and none other!—will understand and experience *everything!*

This drive toward experimentalism on the grand scale

40

is one of the things that has made America what it is, for good or ill. Romanticism—a presumption, in the individual, of free will and a divine right to expand personality! The sky's the limit, boys! Unhappily, pioneer imaginings are dreams of youth, appropriate to adolescence, when there is no incongruity in beguilement by histrionic aspects of change brought about by a new scene. I will go to China and become a Chinaman! I will go to India, and be a mogul! I will live in a palace —that makes me a king! No doubt most pioneers, when they left home, *were* young. Once plunged into this existence they had elected, they never found time to grow up. Pirates, mutinies, Indian wars—during every hour and moment of their lives, they were called upon to be *doing* something. It would not *always* be this way, some may have decided, when tired of dealing perpetually with one elemental crisis after another. . . . Next week, next month, we shall be able to settle down with a good book, hear first-rate music, begin to figure out what it is all about! But the time never came; they never got around to that proposed interlude for contemplation and reflection. They haven't up to this day! Raleigh was privileged. He never broke entirely with an established society that patronized, for its own benefit, the fools who risked their lives abroad; and, in the end, he received an education through defeat, denied to the successful men who set the key for our civilization. I think that is attested to by those lines he wrote when he was about to die—lines so bare, so plain, so austere with deep feeling, they show him done with ambition's makeshifts. Such humble, meagre, authentic speech would hardly be possible to one of our generals of finance.

My great-grandfather Thomas never languished in a

prison to which the very sovereign he had served so well condemned him; but I think he knew his own prison of the spirit. The men growing old in Tennessee, who had come there from Virginia or North Carolina, and not been forced west by inexorable poverty, must have reached a period in life (Americans do, occasionally) when, gazing around them at the crude land to which they were committed irretrievably, they asked themselves in bewilderment: What have I? Then came the real conviction of failure—steamboats had begun to ply on the rivers, the cotton gin functioned—and such a disgust with gadgets as nothing could ever make good! And they were homesick—though perhaps their longings were for a world they had never seen. True, the wilderness had retreated like a subsiding tide—but it had left nothing to replace Greece, Rome, Tyre, Sidon. To be sure, there was Memphis—but how altered and dwindled! My great-grandfather had already tried Lebanon, in Kentucky, which had its name from the cedars; but he had been disappointed out of all hope. Everything that could be said to have sprung from the travail of two or three generations was before him—and how utterly anticlimactic! He commenced building about him barricades of exclusiveness, of intellectual snobbery—making them of anything he could lay hands on, be it Shakespeare's sonnets, the verse of Catullus, or Anacreon's odes. He had come into the state a strong Jacksonian; but in these years—the eighteen-thirties—during which Jackson's popularity was on the wane and the Whig party was receiving new nourishment through the decline of his autocracy—my great-grandfather lost interest in politics. He was, by this time, what would be called, I suppose, reactionary—which simply means his faith in benefits to be derived from change, per se, had weakened. It would also not be possible to absolve him entirely from an accusation of resenting democracy somewhat.

After all, when he had emigrated from Virginia with human chattels, he had come, like the snail, with his spiritual home in feudalism borne on his back. The Constitution of 1796 shows the bias of its framers, who were landowners, supporting an entail law, while not naming it that. The General Assembly of that day had tyrannical authority, and its membership was drawn from a class able to pay for the education of statesmen. But now, even as early as eighteen-thirty, old attitudes were being broken down.

James Phelan quotes an incident of the eighteen-twenties which is more than a straw for indicating from what quarter the wind had already begun to blow. It was during a gubernatorial contest between William Carroll and Edward Ward, when feeling ran highest in Montgomery County, where Clarksville is situated. The *Nashville Clarion* printed a satiric letter in which the following reasons were offered as objections to electing Carroll: . . . *he is of humble but poor parents . . . it would be a shame for the son of an old Revolutionary farmer to rule over 'the quality' of the State . . . he has never learned Latin and Greek.* Furthermore, the letter points out, as a boy he plowed and was *handy at reaping, log-rolling, and country weddings, all of which is coarse and vulgar . . . he is not rich and did not stay at home during the war . . . he does not carry himself with sufficient dignity and austerity, but will heartily shake the hand of a ragged fellow soldier, thus doing away with the distinctions of rank.* The *Clarion* was a Carroll paper, and Carroll was elected, over the wealthy and better-

43

born Ward, Carroll receiving forty-two thousand two hundred forty-six votes against Ward's eleven thousand two hundred. For me, the anecdote significantly emphasizes a fallacy of democracy rampant in the present, arrived at through misapplying logic so as to insinuate, as a substitute for the original premise, another not inevitably covered by the first statement. In this way: *Carroll is of humble but poor parents* comes to mean practically everything laudatory, and precludes further examination of his qualifications for public leadership. And *he has never learned Latin and Greek* provides all required for a damnation of the classics and a permanent dismissal of them as unimportant.

If my great-grandfather confused with his devotion to learning a degree of crass self-interest he would have done better to face, he was no more dishonest in this than the men who put him at bay because their inferiority complexes were not understood by themselves, and would never have been admitted. Poor man—he missed a comprehension of what constitutes the real defence for a snob in eras which exalt the handicaps consequent on privation. He sought merely whatever could be utilized for constructing the ivory tower into which he must escape to exist. Though he was not the single cultivated individual in a still sparsely populated district, he was justified in considering himself an exile.

For most, politics afforded a refuge from the disappointments of pioneering. What people had hoped to change—in life, in human nature, in unmalleable surroundings—by the sweat of their brows, and had not been able to change, they resolved to alter by legislating. And another pioneering began, to be continued vocally, and on paper, at far less cost to the individual than the old. Jackson's ascent to fame and the presidency had been an inspiration, and there were plenty of aspirants companioning him, and subsequently. David Crockett, John Bell, Felix Grundy, James K. Polk, Hugh White, Newton Cannon—in no time at all, Tennessee and the Mississippi valley had been converted from a semiwild region, dominated by foreign intriguers, and inhabited by the bold and simple manipulators of rafts, canoes and pirogues, into Mark Twain's America of wretched little villages and a few moderate-sized, moderately prospering towns with Main Streets and courthouses; while water itself had taken fire from the steam craft upon it, which were as grand as showboats and passing daily. The bombast and high-flown rhetoric always associated with political campaigning in America, in the South, soon reached a peak; as rising Whigs and their declining opponents vied with one another in vituperation. My great-grandfather's first residence near Clarksville was provided with a low line of outbuildings pointed out to me as slave quarters. When he erected them, and assumed himself monarch of all he surveyed, he must have had it in mind to resume life spaciously. He was not then, apparently, aware of the empty prospect!

When I was a child, I played a game (the only one I remember inventing myself in which playmates participated) which I called "God and Goddess," which consisted, chiefly, in imagining; and in fancifully endowing one's self with a power superior to nature's. We played it the year I was in Evansville: the back yard of the house my parents had rented was the Garden of the Hesperides; a permanent mud puddle in a bit of vacant, adjacent ground was the River Styx; and I ascribed to it magical properties, which you took advantage of whenever you liked, since, to do so, it was only necessary to dip a switch into the shallow, semisolid depths, hold it over your head and say "Abracadabra!" and it became a wand. I was most frequently Mercury; and Juno and Jupiter, stolidly embodied in two telegraph poles, were revengefully jealous of the facile generosity with which I aided, constantly, all mortals in distress. They direly resented my assumption of equality with them, and the preposterous ease with which I made the transition from Olympus, where I consorted with my own kind, to an earth over which I flitted freely without anybody at all suspecting me of godhead. My great-grandfather was, I believe, impractical; though a majority among pioneers are made practical through necessity. Now, however, with steam and inventiveness (a good deal of the latter from the North), and the assistance given by nature, as slaves in the South continued to reproduce (buying female slaves exclusively must have sometimes represented economy), the silver tongue of the politician seemed to offer more than men disillusioned otherwise could ever hope to win with hard work!

There was, really, scarcely a backwoodsman who did not envisage himself as a statesman. Lincoln and Andrew Johnson were exceptional because they succeeded, and not because they had unusual ambitions! In short, politics had carried the life of action—pioneer life!—into speech, where attainment could be perfect and extravagant. And there the discouraged in those tiny Mississippi ports—those miry little single-street hamlets on the Tennessee and the Cumberland!—discovered escape. Through oratorical propaganda! In an orgy of words! For they, too, needed a Russia; though they were so naïve they never propounded their wants in any clear doctrine. The most incurably maladjusted still clung to an attenuating dream of a great feudal-aristocratic commonwealth which was to spring, like Minerva from Jove's brow, from the swamps of Mississippi, the pine flats and bayous of Louisiana, the Indian-ridden forests of Arkansas, the mineral hills of Alabama, and mountain fastnesses in the Blue Ridge and the Cumberlands. Those who looked backward on less pleasant memories called attention to the new railroad charter (Memphis Railroad Company, 1831—railroads from Nashville to New Orleans, from Memphis to Virginia, from Memphis to Charleston, and to Cincinnati, and to Louisville, were discussed simultaneously) and dedicated themselves to "progress." Politicians were the spokesmen for both groups, and became the South's mythmakers. Orators stumping the country at election time made a gift of articulateness to masses otherwise mute and unlearned. If Roman Catholicism had received more encouragement in the South, there might have been a rudimentary development of truer aestheticism; but the democracy in religion of the Protestant churches abhored any informing of the public mind through a perceptivity originating *above*. Evangelists like James M'Gready, Finis Ewing, William and John M'Gee—pioneers and plain men themselves—were dead against intellectual hierarchies. The "Christian life" was concerned only with elemental emotion, its appeal confined to the unreflective. When expression was demanded by people a little more aware, politics was the single outlet.

Actually, I believe, the condition of society which encouraged the political speechmaker, exalting him to a position of exclusive leadership, spelled death to culture of another kind. I think it is this which was largely

47

responsible for the South's sterility in fields of art—responsible indeed for a century of shallow thinking, characterisic of all America. A tradition of southern oratory was established and maintained, and some of its exponents were deservedly notable. Yet, however much we may admire, *as* orators, the very best of them—men like Henry Clay, Judah P. Benjamin, Jefferson Davis—the stimulation of culture in a profound sense is not the politician's mission. As politics have been interpreted in this country, the orator (who is bent, first, on the manipulation of the crowd for the support of his own dominance) is the enemy of the artist; and the foe of any who would arouse men to search out values which have an aesthetic foundation and are, therefore, permanent. He is bound, while he would strengthen his own position, to distort or discourage an awakening consciousness of matters which might contribute to the realization of "truths" different from those he presents as the alpha and omega of human understanding and a final goal for human endeavour. No, political debating falls far short of the expressiveness of a full art, but, by way of a substitute for aesthetic articulateness, it was the only thing the pioneer mind was ready to receive—prepared to digest. And this statement goes not alone for the "low-brow" son of labourers who had settled in the Tennessee or Kentucky mountains, but for a class with the means to nourish "intellectuals." "High-brow" and "low-brow" had been impressed with the same pioneer stamp.

How ridiculous we are with our legend of a South of lovely women born to luxury and grace, and of dueling gallants for whom all existence was the bright interchange of wit with courtesy! Dickens, when he visited us, though he lacked a key in sympathy and could not interpret us, reported us accurately enough. The South, like the Middle border, the West, the Southwest, has passed through every phase of pioneering; and these can be as terrible as Stations of the Cross. The author of *Gone with the Wind* assumed the go-getting Nietzsche-anism of her heroine a development in circumstances without precedent before the Civil War; yet the demand of nature she answered so indomitably may have been made on her mother and grandmother. She was forging no unique way out of unduplicated difficulties—merely reverting, with the repetition of conditioning, to a near past. Even by the time of my great-grandfather Thomas, deeds, in America, had a meaning synonymous with the acquisition of cash! And beyond Virginia and the Caro-linas there had never been an "old South." The interlude between pioneering and the Civil War was too brief for its evolution in any genuine sense—no decent inter-val in which a culture might have developed and taken root had been allowed Southerners.

Surely my great-grandfather himself, glancing about at last, in a sort of reconnoitering of the results from what he had undertaken, noticed the lack! Though good solid residences were springing up in the fields where the tobacco leaves were now as broad as green umbrellas, something else was missing! Were there not, after all, things to esteem which were neither put into the mouth nor used to clothe and adorn the body? At the very least, men who were fine horsemen would not ride less brilliantly after learning to spell correctly!

It is wonderful to read of the days when the trappers from the Great Salt Lick, as they abandoned themselves, in their pirogues and dugouts, to currents like magnets drawing miles of water from the North into the Gulf, saw, as they floated gently on, buffaloes pasturing over the bluffs; and brush on a shoal or mudbank stirring in windless air, as a head with horns, a brow like Jove's and shoulders draped in a very thundercloud of mane, started from a willow thicket. Until a herd was distinguishable, where wild grape, blackberry and bamboo vine had been trampled under! And the bull in the forefront, with a wrecked canebreak behind him, halted, in ruminative anger, to gaze, with kindling jealousy and half fear, on a silent legion of his cautious enemies! And the hunters —it might be weeks before they reached New Orleans— drifted on, quietly, their craft lapped by their own watery reflections, where nothing else living was visible; though, in the distance, above a dangerous huddle of foreign wigwams, smoke—like some vine of life struggling to be green in an Atlantic of solitude!—crept toward the sky! Then, after the smoke, nothing—! Until, dropping below Natchez, the swamps commenced, and seemed endless, sad as silence; the trees in perpetual shrouds of grey moss, in which a breeze, wavering, only stressed an infinite lethargy. There is terrible self-containment in a swamp! Whatever enjoys existence there has become immune to men's destructive intrusions. Among brackish lagoons, the fringed hands of the palmettos rise in spreading warning, rigid as gestures from the crucified. Things growing in a swamp have an old, bitter look, and refuse to shed their leaves. Even water hyacinths and Cherokee roses, purple and white in the spring, seem like flowers of mourning. How dark the cypresses! Below their mortuary foliage and the plumes of the cedars, will be shattered trunks, charred and soot-striped, or actually smouldering with a damp fire generated in bogs. . . . In New Orleans, when the trappers

50

disembarked, they bartered with Spaniards who betrayed, with their difference, these simple minds sobered by hardships, and unable to grasp the secrets of fellows who had to glorify a foreign Pope!

But in my great-grandfather's day, when the steamboats, carrying tobacco, tallow, corn, beef, whiskey and cotton southward, already went, without convoys, through regions now inhabited by people under one flag; and voyagers returning to waiting women brought sophisticated gifts home from the Creole capital; there was no longer any personal adventure in trade. And at this point, in the due course of developing perfections, the adventure of the mind should have begun!

It did begin, after a fashion; but with what dreadful poverty of interest! What horrible paucity of fostering imagination! Yes, even the dwellers in first settlements had made little pitiful essays in getting themselves educated. Schools initiated in one-room cabins, where classes were held in the heat of the summer (because a pane of glass was as rare as a diamond, and solid wooden shutters which had to be closed against cold, in winter, excluded necessary light!)—schools of this kind persisted somehow! They persist in this present! In the mountains, where literacy is still at a premium, you find them in plenty! And as early as 1788 Martin Academy was incorporated by the North Carolina legislature—one of the first real educational institutions in Tennessee territory. Samuel Doak, the president, was an ex-Revolutionary soldier; a fanatical Calvinist. In 1785, Davidson Academy in Davidson County was incorporated, and received from the state a donation of lands near Nashville. By an act (1806), Congress set aside one hundred thousand acres of public property in one tract for the use of academies. Blount College, in the East, was founded. And one female academy—Fisk's Female Academy, at Hilham, Overton County. Until, actually, by 1829, the public was sufficiently respectful of learning to sponsor a definite plan for public instruction to be carried out by the state and supported by taxpayers. After 1830, it could really be said that Tennessee had a common school system—at least in theory! Cumberland College was admitting scholars in 1809; and in 1838, while my great-grandfather was still alive in Clarksville (he died the next year), the General Assembly voted, to the University of Nashville, eleven thousand five hundred and twenty acres just appropriated from the Indians.

At a first glance, you would say the cause of education had advanced by strides in no time at all! But it needs no more than the briefest survey of the state as it is today to see how much was meant by this in terms of true cultural growth! With all due respect to institutions that are contemporary, and do credit to the region, not very much! Though, very shortly after the arrival of first immigrants, and as soon as there was any respite from attacks by scalping parties, schools and academies sprang up, offering instruction in theology and a smattering of the classics to the sons and daughters of people who had been ladies and gentlemen elsewhere (or had not been, but were determined their children should be!) nothing happened, actually, which deserves to be recognized as a cultural event!

And how strangely remote that world of books, to girls and boys whose parents had rejoiced at the sight of a man nailing clapboards on his cabin walls, because they beheld in him the forerunner of a civilization! In the time of Robertson, the name of Robert Gilkey was preserved to fame in the western settlements on the basis of no more personal distinction than that of dying a natural death! Fifty years had gone by; but computing time as it is required to measure the rise of a nation, the fall of a race, even the evolution of a community from provincialism to metropolitanism, what do fifty years amount to? Read Haywood for colonial history; read the few books on Tennessee which our contemporary libraries offer as authoritative sources of information under given dates; and decide for yourself how significant the cultural "progress" of early Tennessee!

And when I was a child, and lived in Clarksville, then in Russellville, in Logan County, Kentucky, "great men"—so acknowledged by the populace!—were neither the few scholars who existed, nor creators in mediums like music, painting or poetic words; but were politicians! Political haranguing remained, diversified by religious exhortation, the mode of expression which won audiences, and was approved! Cultural standards, formulated under pioneer influence, had not altered since they had been obstacles in my great-grandfather's search for contentment. Already, when he took his books of Greek and Latin to bed with him on that last night, the shrewd, who could exploit the ignorantly hopeful by feeding them on fine phrases without scruple as to precise meaning, outnumbered those who went to the arts for exquisite statements relating to vital truth. And in my day, the ghosts of successful Indian campaigners, hard-bitten veterans of Mexican war, and stalwart circuit-riding dispensers of a primitive Christianity that had been athletically interpreted, still regulated the cultural preferences of their descendants, also "men of action." Before these, any least incipiently awakened interest in the arts was bound to go down! The society of Tennessee and Kentucky, as that of most of America, had been designed for and by extroverts of a most unsubtle variety!

This came to me when I was only six or seven—a dim apprehension! But it destined me to the lot of the unorthodox, which, unless you can make yourself into a complete escapist, is never enviable. It is amusing and pathetic to remember how my mother's delusion of snobbishness identified the appreciation of the best of bad painting (Bouguereau, Cabanel, Perrault, Schreyer, Daubigny—and who was it made pictures of great crises in lives that were history? and who was the depicter of innumerable monks, friars and cardinals at their games of chess?) with distinguished lineage and an inherited right to rule.

As if founders of aristocracies—successful barbarians! —had ever thought twice about art, until the arrival of the propitious moment for a judicious display of power, when they could exhibit the artist as one among their dependents whose talents they controlled, even as they owned him bodily! And why didn't I suspect it while I was still a devoted reader of *The Little Colonel Series*, and trying to convince myself I was a genuine Loyd Sherman, preparing to command with charm even my elders, and proposing to control those of my own generation by merely petulantly stamping my dainty foot? "I will never stoop to anything clandestine," I wrote, when I was eleven, to a small boy who admired me—we were communicating in notes he advised me to keep secret from my mother. My scruples mystified him; he did not recognize a direct quotation. Neither he nor myself could have discovered the seductress in the person of the prig! But a certain high-mindedness went with Corinthian columns and self-immolating black mammies —at least in that period. It may even have survived prohibition and the hip flask! For though arrogance and a passionate, tempestuous nature were the birthright of a southern woman, offerings to Venus were accompanied by cautious genuflections to Elsie Dinsmore, too. If you were a girl, and under an obligation to yourself to bring as many little boys as were within hailing distance to your feet; the performance, after all, was only in the character of a demonstration which was not to cost much; since at bottom you were abjured, indirectly, to bear in mind such cold doctrines of practicality as have made for workable marriages over the whole globe.

Techniques sacrifice romantic moods to emotionally sterilizing power-control. In thus gaining access to the emotions of others, you cut yourself off from your own feelings. While I was being gently inducted into the way of life befitting a potential southern belle, I was acquiring, primly, properly, and through example, the terrible emotional handicap of a technique—one the pioneer woman, in her vicarious conquest of circumstances with which only men might deal forthrightly, had employed from the beginning! There is something Napoleonic about the women of the South, who can simultaneously exploit the myth of themselves they themselves have fortuitously created, and remain guarded against its most dangerous implications!

If only I had been capable of profiting otherwise by such disguised encouragements to scepticism as converted what was actually attack, in sex, into apparent defence! But I remained vulnerable—wide open to suggestion—and thought I had to stand behind my mother, and unearth, if I could, patents of nobility for the McGintys, along with the Marcys, Seeleys, Thomases, Currans and Duvals! Her conception of my grandfather as a sort of Lorenzo di' Medici in America, in the nineteenth century, was one I tried to carry on, also; so that Miss Stevenson's superiority complex, when I encountered it in Saint Louis, seemed a challenge flung toward the heart of things; unanswerable, while we *boarded*—though *she* boarded, too!

It appears odd to me now that my susceptible awareness of condescension from her never caused me to contrast her constant circumspect boast of lineage with the admirable, delicate reticence of old Dr. Gatling, the inventor of the gun, another who shared our doubtful status as "paying guests" in a millionaire's mansion. He died the year after, and left, even with me—a child—a sense of irony, mingling with recollections of his old man's courtesy, gentle good humour and unflagging, tolerant pacificism. I remember when my mother, elaborating on his story in privacy, after our first introduction to him, told me he was the author of what was, then, the world's worst engine of war, how my child's mind rebelled against and rejected the paradox!

Incredible—as incredible, though in a different way, as Mark Twain, when I saw him, all perfect and complete and as I had expected him to be (I knew his pictures), entering the Saint Louis Club for a reception held in his honour. One to which my mother had been invited, which she was too timid to attend. But we sat in the window of our house, which was opposite, and observed everything—his deliberate, somewhat jaunty carriage, his satiric, kindly, hawklike face in its rampant auriole of snow-white hair! His very clothing—white from head to foot!—impressed me dramatically! We watched him walk, with his hosts, up the long flight of stone steps, indoors, where he was lost in the crowd that had assembled to honour him.

The only man who might have explained to me what I really inherited in being American! What it was that had come to me through the lives lived by my grandparents in the yet cruder days of early Tennessee! The one vital American who had preserved art, in his own person, in the environment least friendly to the artist. And I never saw him again—not even later, when he came out of the club! I was too tired to sit up and wait!

3

TRAVEL! In the days when that Montgomery for whom Montgomery County was named was raising troops in Clarksville for the Nickojack expedition which was to set an example to the Chickamaugas in cruelties practised by themselves (this was before 1800), travel was by pack horse; and the few roads that had begun to be opened in the eastern part of the state could be traversed by wagons safely only if they were driven by practised wagoners. How slowly the miles unfurled as the caravans crept along the mountains, so perpetually, drearily, monotonously grand and unknown. Then the descent, toward the West, into rugged placidity; and, beyond Clarksville itself, something in the immensity which was unexplored that stunned you—a glance forward toward an endless horizon when you are at sea. Not that incoming settlers cared to imagine. I can see the children, revived by sleep after yesterday's weariness, dashing ahead of their parents and pausing excitedly with shrill, speculative cries above a small, broadening canyon, a little valley desertedly offering a stream of clear, fresh water. . . . "Ma! Pa!" Little barefoot girls in long dirty homespun dresses jump about excitedly, clapping their hands in anticipation; little boys as hard-faced and dishevelled as incipient gangsters in the slums of New York, and four times as brown, dash behind, boasting to their elders their first information. "We've found it! Water, Pa! An' there's pine trees that's good logs!" (I haven't the slightest idea how these young immigrants talked in the late eighteenth and early nineteenth century; but it may have been as the folk in the mountains talk today.)

And Pa and Ma and Big Brother (perhaps one slave was there, tacitly commanded to reflect, with vicarious abandon, moods of hope and discouragement as they affected his owners)—Pa and Ma and Big Brother, older, so more sceptical, refusing to hasten their pace, and even lagging purposely, resisting the misleading optimism of the inexperienced, finally arrive. They stand gazing. Fresh running water (you can hear it in the quiet), grass that need only be burned off for a cornfield to emerge, tall trees perfect for logs! The cabin can be built with the slope to the rear to be a windbreak through cold seasons! Ma, who, this morning, feels too battered and bruised to endure more riding, and has kept to the ground with her younger sons and daughters and the slave, wants so much to stop here—stop anywhere!— that, while she discreetly fails to comment, she feels as if she had cried out. When Pa, roughly hugging the baby, clambers from the horse he and Ma often mount double, and, also mute, squats consideringly, to crumble in his fingers a lump of the clay soil, her repressed emotions rise in her to a shriek unuttered. Where is this place? Are they still far from a settlement? Has this land already been claimed, or is it the property of nobody? It can't belong to the Indians *now*—they have been pushed west!

"Poor!" Pa remarks, an exhausted note creeping again

59

into his voice, as he lets the red dust sift from his hand. "This is too fer from anywhere!"

Ma understands him. A tract of land in the wilderness is not always what it appears to be on a morning of smiling and bright spring wind. Besides, enemies may lurk in this very undergrowth. The family will camp here an hour, where scatterings of charred sticks are reminders that others have anticipated them, wait for the party of Carolinians, outdistanced earlier, to catch up with them, and go on. To Clarksville, to Nashville—though there are, officially, no Indians in this vicinity, it is unwise to journey without company. The children, bewildered to find their rapturous bad judgement despised, join with Elder Brother in a search for faggots for a fire in which to roast the meal for johnnycake ("journey cake" I understand it was called originally). And Ma, sinking soddenly to rest on a pile of stones, thinks of the day they left Raleigh as if it were years ago. In the wicker saddle baskets slung over one of the three muddied horses, pigs are squealing. In a sack on another horse are the few household implements. No, it wouldn't do to settle here—in Clarksville or Nashville you can buy nails. Nails, and maybe a bell for the cow! The cow, thin, with hollowed flanks, moans, in the sunlight, after her last lost calf, and tugs her halter miserably. On the trails through the mountains, she has lost weight; and has cost more trouble than all the family put together.

If anything happened to the cow—! "O Gawd, dear Jesus Christ in heaven," Ma prays to herself, "keep Molly safe!" And she orders the slave sharply to take the iron pot to the brook and bring it filled. She could almost hate the slave, with that look of meek, irresponsible resignation on his face! For he has only to do as she tells him—what are trials to him?

I must have learned in school of the famous gesture of disgruntlement in which the settlers who had brought such treks to an end on the Carolina border, and were still Carolinians by law, defied a neglectful government at home by declaring themselves, independently, the State of Franklin. It was their retort to burdens of taxation not to be borne passively while goods due the Indians for appropriated tracts were being withheld, fomenting further bloodthirsty friction between red men and white. The rebellion, led by John Sevier, advanced to such overtness that a committee was actually elected to draw up a constitution for the separationists. Sevier and his friends outbraved Governor Martin's manifesto against them, and failed to be seduced when an act of oblivion, to favour loyalists, was passed in Carolina. The rebellion, indeed, endured over years; the Franklinites unappeased until 1787, when Martin's successor, Governor Caswell, tactfully dispatched Evan Shelby to the settlements to arbitrate a compromise with the Sevier factionists. And even then protest continued to simmer in a feud between Sevier and John Tipton, who was more conservative. Until Sevier in his obstinacy, rebuffed by Shelby, whose support he had solicited, was tempted to dream grandiloquently of downright conspiracy—an alliance with Georgia, a pact with the Spaniards! For Bonaparte's mark was on the age!

The spirits of those whose fancies had embraced empires were still abroad when my great-uncle Ewing arrived in Clarksville; though nothing there but a line of straggling residences called Franklin Street commemorates a competition between founders of democracies. At this time—when there were no railways, before Nashville had become the capital of the state, while a future for Memphis was still in the hands of that super-real-estate agent, John Overton—the town's business activities had begun to centre in a square crowning bluffs from which you had an open view of the country—a view once of tactical advantage to military strategists. The residential section lay lower, facing the water. There was a Main Street, then, with wooden banquettes (or so I have been told) such as we used to see in New Orleans. Poor great-uncle Ewing! Poor little Dick Whittington, who was an orphan, fourteen years old, and had come from Palmyra with his three sisters, who had all they owned in a carpetbag! All he could sell was himself. I think he tried to make it an honourable bargain. At which corner did he hesitate, on that first day in Clarksville, the carpetbag at his feet, the little girls pressing about him excitedly, expectantly, already burdening him with respect, regarding him as a father? And what stranger men, comfortably consequential, in their long coats and beaver hats, went by without noticing him? How many matrons, whose petticoats gave them the majestic carriage of galleons, scanned him ignoringly as they picked a way in the mire of semirural thoroughfares? And the pert misses, with their demure bonnets, and their modernly streamline gowns that remembered somewhat styles of the directorate—did they glance contemptuously toward his young, earnest freckled face? My great-uncle Ewing must have been terribly afraid of girls, with *three* on his hands! I can see him take from the pocket of his jacket of homespun the letter to someone, given him by the kind family at Palmyra—so good

62

to him after his father's death, so kind to his sisters, but God knew how thankful to be rid of them all! And read and read again, his lips trembling. He has another letter, he reminds himself gratefully—to people who will board the girls.

He got the job! It was that of printer's devil on the local newspaper, the *Tobacco-Leaf Chronicle*, of which, later, he became the editor. And he rented, on *his* salary, a cottage that would have been a proper habitation for canary birds. I have visited it, on a hilly street, where the rooms of dwellings are of different levels, and you step from the front door directly into the road. Such a road—a stroll along it is like mountain climbing, with the river beneath! There was a tiny back garden, too small to mention, unless you considered the sky seen beyond it over a hedge.

My grandmother Thomas (the one who died three days before I was born) seems to have been a woman who felt intensely, confusedly, inarticulately. She was not given to elaborate anecdotes. "We were very happy there," she used to say to my mother, of the cottage, "though of course we were very poor." And her voice would break. I envisage her from a daguerreotype, in a black moiré dress with a black lace fichu: her hoops make her regal; her sea-shell shoulders, frail and lustrous, are exposed elegantly. But her large grey eyes, wide apart, slightly prominent, always darkening with the quick, wordless excitability of the over-intuitive, show her as if estranged from her own elegance. Irish eyes? Or maybe they are German eyes. And she has thin, wide lips that smile or droop with all suggestions, helplessly. In her old age, they looked sealed and bitter. She seems timid, ardent, unconquerably secretive, though she is volatile. And almost, sometimes, I think her lips are forming words: *There were wolves at the·door! It was at Palmyra Bluffs, when I was a child—we really heard wolves!* Oh, I understand. She can't forget. Not even though things happen so quickly in America that she was able, before the end of her life, to live like a princess, if not a too exacting one! She owned baubles fine enough to be called jewels; she had a great house, servants, carriages. Until she had almost realized the fancies which were a maggot-torture in the brain of her father, when he came over from Ireland, his hope and his despair both still green from the drizzle in Ulster, and decided to make a new world and a new history of mankind which should begin with himself. Things happen so quickly—and just because of it, we go awry!

My great-uncle Ewing—he served in the state legislature finally—must have absorbed just enough religiosity from his parents to exalt him with duty. I imagine him as a grave, chronically embarrassed youth, wanly stern through overwork, and disdainful, privately, of the laxity with which grownups pursued their ideals and ambitions. Failed to sustain them—*he* would be *different*! Among my ancestors are two who began their careers on the lowest rung of the ladder in newspaper offices: from commentaries descended to me, I judge great-uncle Ewing did not, at first, receive much encouragement from his employers for his opinion of himself as a potential great man. Yet he must have believed in his own genius, as his dedication to success proves.

Lucky youth! Perhaps it was owing to three always awaiting him at home, and convinced with him of his superiority, that he was able to demonstrate unusual qualities. What a relief, after twelve, sixteen, even eighteen hours of bondage to his own insignificance (after being yelled at by everybody, blamed for everything that went wrong!), to return, at any moment of the day or night, to three misses in unflagging ecstasies of welcoming. Three misses as adept at making a house tidy and livable, and keeping hot a delectable meal, as though their ages had not ranged from twelve to fifteen! How his heart leapt when he crossed the threshold of this ménage of children where he was a patriarch; and there was a flurry and flounce of petticoats and aprons, and a stampede to greet him. And Angelina, the eldest, ordered my grandmother, the youngest, into the trundle bed which had been pulled from under the double bed of the other two girls. It was after midnight. Fredonia had no right to be up. And my grandmother, pouting, finally resisted with downright naughty temper, until she won her point. Brother Ewing's reception into the bosom of his family, though it occurred seven times a week, must be treated as an event. And I can see him— perhaps he is seventeen—struggling to preserve his masculine dignity, which is attacked by his own exuberance, produced in direct response to their delighted giggles.

I think Angelina must have unlaced his boots for him, and brought his warmed slippers treasuringly from beneath the stove; while Eliza, under severe supervision, but aglow with her own importance, carried the plate of supper, waveringly, to the kitchen table. And my grandmother, defiantly devoted, though already in her nightgown, insisted on and gained—though she was such a mouse!—the privilege of bearing, from the fire to his chair, a weak cup of sloppily made tea.

Beside the kitchen, there were three rooms in the cottage; but when great-uncle Ewing had an evening at home and could study, the family, saving candles, would gather in one. And he, with his chin stubbornly bent, and his eyes on a book, would be divided between a passion for informing himself which no girl could understand, and a mellowing influence on the tortured self-love of adolescence when Angelina, commanding her sisters to quiet, made flattering remarks about him in a whisper quite distinct. However, all men who are successful through a rise from poverty have the souls of fanatics; so I don't suppose he was an exception. Those three beings who were both goads for ambition and obstacles to achievement, were never able to divert him for long from whatever it was he had set out to do. They might pout, sulk, or coax him with demureness, the half smile they provoked from him, in the end, was sure to become a rather desperate and really angry frown. Until Angelina would lay down her knitting; Eliza would make a grimace at his back, and Fredonia, fretting under the suppression of high spirits, would lead the way out.

When John Bell was defeated by Polk in the state elections of 1835 my great-uncle Ewing knew all about it. He had followed the course of public affairs after Newton Cannon became the first Whig candidate in the history of the state, and denounced General Jackson. He had read closely what Polk had to say of the Federalist origin of the Whig party—and had decided to be a Whig himself. And when a Whig dinner was given at Island Springs, near Nashville, in October, 1839, he would certainly have attended it if he hadn't been too young. There was a mammoth Whig festival held in Clarksville sometime in this era; it showed pretty certainly what proved true later—that the Whigs were to be the winning party. My great-uncle Ewing therefore, either because of deep, sincere convictions, or because he had an instinct for success, was converted to Whiggery with a fervour in accepting it that went with his acquired Methodism. And he became an editor of the *Tobacco-Leaf Chronicle*, and, some while after, of the Nashville *True Whig*; and sent his sisters, a little tardily, to be educated at one of the new female academies, where they were taught singing, got a smattering of French, and learned painting on china, and to make pictures in hair. And when the time came for them to marry, he saw to it that their unions were honourable, and probably resented it that the men they chose were not overly rich. But he never permitted them to dance! Until he had turned each one over to a husband, he never forgot his responsibility to preserve her morals, or that she owed respect to his still youthful authority. In his heart, secretly, he thought all three sisters beauties, which made him anxious, in a way, to get them off his hands. And when my grandmother stood up after a Methodist church service one Sunday morning and married my grandfather, who was Episcopalian and almost *High*-Church, great-uncle Ewing was proud of her, as well as jealous. She wore a green silk dress; and a leghorn bonnet with ostrich feathers was tied with a bow under her chin. But he hadn't relinquished his right to advise her, either as maid or matron. That his own father had come all that distance from Ireland to preserve the unity of Protestantism, only to have his daughter connect herself with a family cherishing a faith nearly as worldly and depraved as Roman Catholicism, made him feel bitter. If he hadn't had other axes to grind for himself, and if Fredonia hadn't been so infatuated, he might have put a stop to it. But there would be one less to feed now, and—! (*He remembered the wolves!*)

Yes, pioneering remained pioneering, whether or not conducted under the flattering shade cast by a family tree! There would be one less to feed; he would have to forget the exquisite sense of accomplishment and possession with which he had listened to Fredonia (my grandmother had a lovely, sympathetic light-soprano voice) the first time she had risen from an assemblage of the town's élite to sing, with all the grace of the sophistication she had acquired in Nashville: *Woodman, Spare That Tree!* He could be thankful young Dr. Edwin Thomas wasn't a mere day labourer!

Already, in a similar mingling of relief with less regret, he had parted with Angelina, who had not made much of a catch. Taking a cue from her brother, and deprecating the growing materialism of the era, she had consigned her svelte form and brandy-coloured eyes to an undenominational preacher, impressing it upon him that he had an undeserved bargain in her dour good looks and the "intellectuality" she was beginning to cultivate. For a man with no income at all, she was a chance in a lifetime. But she made him pay, and pay through the nose. While she also paid; and bore him children—endless children—until their poverty was more like squalor. Only three survived; and one, a daughter, hanged herself. Aunt Anne, in her middle years, became a widow whose frustrate gentility was like a wasting disease. She hated Ewing; and hated Fredonia. All that seemed left in her from the gay period in the cottage was the blackening memory of something wrested from her—a nostalgia which meant illimitable pain. Her son,

68

whom she had made the proxy for her own deceased aspiringness, wrote a little poetry—published, actually, a blank verse narrative: *The Hermit's Tale*. Because of some inexplicable fascination for me in the light blue jacket graven with a gilt vignette, it is the first book I remember myself to have treasured. At two, my mother says, I angrily insisted upon claiming it, renamed it, calling it my "Testament," and always carried it to bed with me. The author, a first cousin (though so many times removed), reduced to a condition which precluded art, clerked in a country dry goods store, and finally took poison.

Such incidents make the history of a family—my family, any family! Hence, the history of a country; and especially the fickle history of a race of pioneers! Eliza, plump, blond, azure-eyed sister of Angelina, Germanic in appearance, Irish in temperament, married the brother of my own grandfather—both the boys had studied medicine. She and her husband were another pair of adventurers, who, as soon as it was respectably convenient, set out together, down the east coast from Virginia in a sailing ship, across the Isthmus on mules, and by another boat up the Pacific to California, following the magnetic story of the gold! In a novel called *Migrations* I commemorated them fictitiously. And the tendency of the supposed "realist" to overcompensate for possible sentimentality seems indicated by my drawing of a heroine no man could admire with understanding; whereas, my great-aunt, whom I saw when she was over eighty, preserved, through practically every calamity that can beset a female human, a glance sparkling as a glacier but as warm as her heart, a tongue as quick as the saucy wing of a sparrow, and, even at that age, more gold in her hair than she had usually been privileged to put into her pocket.

She was living alone; her husband had died; her children (of which there had been a round dozen) had died, too; or were somewhere else; when my mother, moved by pricklings of conscience, took me with her on one of those duty visits which are the admission from younger folk that they, also, may one day grow old. Because my great-aunt Eliza boarded among strangers, a long way off, we went in a carriage. And I remember a yard dark green with late summer; and the tiny porch of a grey, paintless cottage—as small as *the* cottage and not half as nice!—and, inside, little dim rooms cluttered with vases of pampas grass, peacock feathers, crayon portraits and painted tin fire screens closing cold hearths. It was not at all the kind of house I then considered suitable for a member of our family, and I was rather shocked.

But if great-aunt Eliza felt neglected there, or out of place, or thought our delayed attentions perfunctory, she was humorously cordial and did not show any pique. We stayed, I think, upwards of an hour; while she, deprecating the proneness of the aged to interminable reminiscence, was yet encouraged to narrate this and that anecdote from the far, far past. Until my mother, whose eye, all the time, had been on the onyx clock upon the mantel draped with the fringed, plush lambrequin, interrupted apologetically to say we must be going—*though* Aunt Eliza's stories were so fascinating it was difficult for us to *tear* ourselves away.

"How I run on!" Aunt Eliza commented. "You young people are generous to spare me so much of your time." And as she pursued us hospitably to the gate of the garden that wasn't hers, and waited, smiling a little pathetically, for us to settle ourselves in the barouche, there was a curious expression on her face. I vaguely interpreted it as the ruminative one of introspection. Now, as I recall that glance of whimsical resignation, while she stood there against the background of the *wrong* sort of house, I think the look was a peep into the future.

"What a memory!" my mother remarked to my aunt, as the Negro coachman flecked the span with his whip and we started off. "She's really wonderful! She's quite lively!"

"Yes," my aunt agreed. "She's almost pretty with those pink cheeks and that lace cap. She could write a book about what she has seen and done. What a constitution she has!" But when we turned and gazed over our shoulders, toward a small, stiff figure walking very slowly back into the porch, and leaning on a cane, I thought uncomfortably, and almost furtively, she didn't seem as strong as they supposed.

Poor great-aunt Eliza! She had been to the banks of the Sacramento and seen men swarming there over the hidden gold, as blindly industrious as bees making honey! She had given birth to her numerous children, tended the injured (for my great-uncle, when doctoring people, had only her help); she had baked bread for twenty miners at once; washed clothes; met snows in a tent; and joked at her weakness in the heat of the tropics. Fatalistically, she had gone about her own business and aided others with theirs, during epidemics. She had watched men crazy-drunk going wild over the gambling, as if it were a last desperate love affair. When the gold betrayed them, they shot each other, or themselves.

And why? What had she to show for it? She had not even been rich! For some years, I wore a ring made of a nugget she had brought home as a souvenir; until I lost it, on Jones Street, in New York, when some friends, lending a hand during a removal to a new flat, unwittingly threw out some trinkets, thinking they were disposing of an empty box—to be quite accurate, a tobacco tin. I had put great-aunt Eliza's gift and a rather handsome sapphire together in it while I was cleaning up. Unhappily, a lorry passed, collecting trash. I suppose you call that "living in Bohemia."

"They have their memories to console them," people say of the aged. "What a satisfaction to have had a *full* life!" And why, pray, ought they to be consoled by recollections of so much wasted effort? It *is* wasted— John, James, Mary, for whom so much was sacrificed, are going to die, too! Experience, we are told, is always enriching; but who will utilize this plethora of long-accumulating wealth? If it were possible for anyone to be made wise or happy through another man's sufferings, suffering for everybody would have been over long ago. Everyone knows how helpful it is to a man on a thin diet to be reminded he once had enough to eat!

As for the race—these average people have not, with their unsung heroisms, kindled any flames that will never be extinguished. And what of this aggregate of human beings—this collective abstraction? On what basis does it claim these irrevocable tributes? Unless we are able to exalt the human spirit in some extradimensional sense not to be accounted for biologically, genetically, and so appear to demonstrate for ourselves that we are more than we seem, our unadvertised joys, our unheralded sorrows, inasmuch as we recognize them and are conscious, must be put down to loss. "The dignity of suffering," and "the beauty of human nature," we declaim, protesting stalwartly what must be, otherwise, a victimization by blind force. And perhaps we are right in insisting, even without proof. At any rate, we must go on believing, against every destructive argument of reason, or else give up. Maybe what is begun at birth and is named "development," and regarded as a process of "maturing," is only a slow unlearning of nature; so that we must recommence and learn again in the inferior terms of an educated awareness—and can never really complete the business in the short span of one life. Nothing in our store of three-dimensional knowledge is the key to what makes superior people (whose deeds add something qualitative to the sum of our observations) so different from merely small-souled purveyors of common sense and self-seeking, that they are, actually, another kind of being, and should be recognized as such by the scientists.

Fortunately for her, great-aunt Eliza had Methodism. This beginning of nations, this settling of states, this travail of generations, which were to bring forth, at the end, only one more ridiculous mouse, was accepted by her as teleologically justified. When families multiplied—and even had they been abolished, as has sometimes been proposed, and humanity reorganized under a new constitution!—this meant more to her than the multiplication of mice—thousands and thousands, millions and millions of mice! (All labouring together diligently with one purpose—their own survival!) Hers was a real day for Fundamentalists, in Tennessee and elsewhere; when the vital issue lay between persons addicted to baptism by complete immersion and those who believed in dedicating infants to the Deity with the symbolic signature of the Cross on the brow. And in Tennessee there are still plenty of people for whom Darwin, no more than the Devil, ever dies. If they seem tolerant of Einstein, Jeans and Eddington, it is because they have been erroneously led to hope science may shortly demonstrate what is obvious to themselves—that the world was really made in six calendar days. But more likely they have never heard of any of the above gentlemen.

Just the same, Episcopalianism was an entering wedge for scepticism; those temperamentally inclined toward speculation took advantage of its unwise appeal to liberal patronage.

THIS SOCIETY HAS ISSUED MORE THAN 200 DUO-DECIMO TRACTS, AND UPWARDS OF 60 CHILDREN'S TRACTS, ALL OF WHICH MAY BE HAD SEPARATELY OR IN VOLUMES NEATLY BOUND. ALSO TRACTS IN FRENCH, SPANISH, GERMAN. $20 BUYS A LIFE MEMBERSHIP, $50 A LIFE DIRECTORSHIP. MEMBERS ARE ENTITLED ANNUALLY TO 1000 PAGES OF TRACTS AND DIRECTORS TO 2000 PAGES, OR TO AN EQUIVALENT IN THE BOUND VOLUMES OR ANY OTHER PUBLICATION OF THE SOCIETY.

SOCIETY'S HOUSE, 144 NASSAU STREET, NEW YORK

This is an advertisement of the American Tract Society, taken from the *Christian Almanac for Tennessee*, for 1829. It suggests efficient wholesaling. Apparently we have here again, the Yankee zealot, discouraged by the adamantine surface of things in the North, carrying his missionary endeavours more profitably into fallow fields left undefended by the ingenuous southern pioneer. Even in my day, the condition of the public

74

mind still showed a compound return on the original investment. Yet there was the school bill: despite the intention of the pious to control the educational system, like a closed corporation, a few people *would* read—*would* insist on thinking for themselves!—and there was a leakage. My great-great-grandmother Curran, though she was born in Catholic Cork, was an eighteenth-century product; and even if her own daughter (with the conservatism of a woman) only straddled the fence, like Mr. T. S. Eliot, she initiated, without knowing it, what was bound to be, at least in one circumscribed direction (among her own descendants) the beginning of the end.

My grandfather Thomas was an agnostic almost from the start; later, virtually a free thinker, his Episcopalianism a genuflection of caution necessary to safeguard his hard-won prosperity against what must have seemed an anarchistic threat if rational materialism were applied, and society as he knew it made topsy-turvy.

Poor little grandmother McGinty-Thomas was affected by his example, and abandoned the primitive Methodism which had seemed adequate as a defence against wolves. Her Episcopalianism was the price she paid for the entrée into the more exalted sphere in which her husband moved. As a good wife, she respected his views and deferred to them, acknowledging her own naïveté. She, being a woman, was his intellectual inferior. She was like that—pliant; ready to yield her own uncertainty to his greater decisiveness. Always a Methodist at heart, she was probably incapable of realizing it and afraid to say so. Even though brave enough, when the Yankees invaded her house during the Civil War, to fix herself, revolver in hand, before her bedroom door, and, with her children clinging to her skirts, defy the whole Northern Army (which had already purloined most of the family silver). However, in my grandmother's era, all lovely young southern women were daring and courageous in the teeth of danger. That her presence of mind in a crisis was not exceptional, the history of every single family in the South proves. And courage relating to abstract principles is something else. Something people with a pioneer origin seem notably without. Or they are inarticulate in defending it. . . . They must secure, at any cost, the approval of the superiorly enlightened.

Some, if such approval is continuously withheld, will bite the hand they were erstwhile prepared to lick, and scoff at the whole mumbo jumbo of refinements and learning . . . only to grovel before a culture which has, as its mainstays, advertising, radios and motorcars.

My father played his small part, as an instrument of Fate, in leading the discontented pioneer out of a land of taverns, and coaching over imperfect wagon roads, into one of steel rails and carriages and congenial gadgetry. My father and *his* father, who came from the North. In 1839, while a scheme known as "the Pennsylvania Plan" was being applied to improve transportation in the state, sixty-seven thousand dollars, approximately, was issued to the Nashville, Murfreesboro and Shelbyville Turnpike Company to make over and extend old thoroughfares; while the La Grange and Memphis Railroad Company was encouraged in its operations with an appropriation of one hundred and twenty-five thousand dollars. The Gallatin Turnpike Company received forty-five thousand dollars; the Nashville Turnpike Company, forty thousand dollars—in those days, appreciable sums. Then came the formation of the Bank of Tennessee; one of the chief motives for its establishment being the further organization of a system of state improvement. But companies securing charters in this period were frequently unscrupulous, and communities jealous: citizens everywhere seemed reluctant to realize that transportation was not *one* problem on which future prosperity for the state hinged, but *the* problem above all else. In 1845, John C. Calhoun presided at a sort of state-boosters' convention held in Memphis, and the interest in new railways was sufficiently restimulated to produce eventual backers for the Memphis and Charleston Railroad. The first track was laid in Memphis, on April 1, 1852; but a whole book would be needed to recount the intrigues and political dramas which delayed and confused the road's construction, until its completion—at last—in 1857! "Progress," between this time and the period of greater upheaval following the Civil War, involved the state in an enormous debt. My father's father, who became an executive of the Louisville and Nashville Railroad in the late seventies, refounded his house below Mason and Dixon's line at the moment least propitious for the reception, in the South, of a Yankee; just when northerners, under the onus left by the carpetbaggers, were regarded most suspiciously; and the railroads, to gain in power until they became dominant in controlling politics in the locale, enjoyed the universal hatred of taxpayers not profiting by their developing aggression.

And who can say how I myself may not have been influenced, in my innocent association with those accused of squeezing the last drop of blood from the poor body politic, to feel that I, too, might be suspect—a

77

southerner by courtesy only? One of my first recollections is of a series of snapshots my father possessed which showed heaps of crude salt deposited on the Louisville and Nashville tracks: decoys, I was told, with which the farmers—the financially disinherited!—hoped to attract their own cattle to seek early and lucrative death. The pictures had been used as evidence by a company attorney in protesting damage suits; and, I hope, were not his own plants. More than likely, they were not. But at that time people in a predicament had to demonstrate their consistent nobility before I could see any reason to pity them; and I felt coldhearted and a little fearful when I speculated on the instigators of such a sinister subterfuge. And, after all, railroads hadn't been *sheerly* disadvantageous to the country!

Think of a certain Mrs. Scott, who, in an early period, had occupied four days with an expedition covering two miles! *My horse hath a horror of swimming Holston River every time I visit the country*, Bishop Asbury wrote; and continued, in the vein of a perfect *Pilgrim's Progress*, recounting what he had to endure, in danger and discomfort, to distribute "the Message." And when Sam Houston's mother led her family and a few slaves into Tennessee in 1807, she had to be as bold as Boadicea to get there without a catastrophe. Andrew Johnson, his mother and stepfather, leaving Raleigh one morning in 1826, with a two-wheel cart in which they rode in relays, "ride and tie," mounted on their few goods, before their arrival in Greeneville, where the benign look of the land decided them to linger, had accomplished an Odyssey.

For years, I was troubled because I could not accept an implied, general philosophy which insisted (though

78

not always explicitly) that things done to improve material conditions for ascendant races—ascendant groups—must, therefore, be just. But neither could I quite square the self-justificatory utterances of victims of society with my own firsthand observations. There was a phase in my development in which, it might be said, I defied my father's derogation of the Brotherhood of Locomotive Engineers; his savagely sincere, dreading contempt for "Red" Emma Goldman (later to become my own admired and enormously respected personal friend), in a spirit of challenge born simply of bewilderment.

No generation anywhere has more fitly interpreted justice, in the common acceptance of what it stands for, than did the French Revolutionists. They provide the single instance of rebels who could draw largely upon lawyers for their vocal support. Hence the Revolutionists were ably defended by arguments based on an exploitation of technicalities of logic. And the eighteenth-century mind was peculiarly prepared to appreciate the logical apology for the practically required deed. Because so many members of the legal profession, disappointed of titles, felt inspired hatred for the aristocracy, the Patriots were afforded opportunities for hearing special pleading at its very best. Among us, however, who take a complacent view of determinism, doctrines of necessity ought to be proclaimed without abashment; while the man of practical ability, calling himself a scientist, can equip us materially for any diabolically ruthless program to which we feel it convenient to commit ourselves. Curious how we remain dependent on old-fashioned, logical moralists for a different, plausible account of our motives. When we know we are only behaving "naturally"—and when did nature ever prove her preference for the just?

Oh, ineffable living in early childhood before there is any poisoning concern to demonstrate a righteousness that can never be made quite valid in those catholic terms which are to be justice for all mankind! At five years old, my data on the cosmos and on society came, in the main, from a perusal of Andrew Lang's, Laboulaye's and Bulfinch's anthologies; from *The Arabian Nights, Alice in Wonderland, The Adventures of Pinocchio*. My experience of geography embraced Clarksville, and Gutherie and Russellville, Kentucky. Once, exceptionally, my father had taken me to Owensborough, where he displayed to me—it was early spring—a vast, bleak sheet of water (yellow and grey and blown into foam) which filled me with satisfactory aghastness. "The Ohio! Next to the Mississippi, the largest river in America!" he explained educationally, in the pontifical manner of adults. The visit lingered notably in my memory because of eating, for the first time, in a hotel dining room. I spilled my soup on the tablecloth, and was humiliated by my father's insistence on my use of a napkin as a bib.

And when, on journeys between Russellville and Clarksville, we stopped in Gutherie to wait for trains, and everybody in the station hotel (it was overflowing with an ever-replenished assortment of colonels and majors by brevét) seemed to recognize us on sight, greeting us with an effusiveness I mistook for a spontaneous ovation, my comfortably elated sense of family importance was a pleasure I was not called on to expiate. I liked to hear my mother addressed, even by people who seemed strangers, as "Miss Maude." The number of solicitous inquiries made about my father, about our relatives in Clarksville, allowed me to bask in prestige as naturally as in the sun. There was usually some meal to be partaken of in Gutherie, and the food—until the day my mother very nearly swallowed a cockroach floating in a tumbler of pure cream—was itself an event. Oh, we were all friends in the South in those days—warm, cordial, hospitable!—and I had, always then, the precious feeling of being explained in advance. The proprietor of the hotel invariably urged us to try, without expense to ourselves, every dish on his bill of fare. How I loved Negroes! They were everywhere. With the hedonism of a child, I adored them constantly for what they contributed to a pure animal enjoyment of life!

Gutherie was most exciting at night: you heard, in the darkness which was almost complete outside the hotel, in what was, otherwise, the stillness of the country, the blasts of whistles, the shrieks and mournings of engines, the squeals of pigs and the despondent lowing of penned cattle. A most thrilling diversion came when you dared ask in a whisper to go to a certain place which well-reared children (it had been obscurely indicated) should not refer to in public aloud. Then Mother, disconcerted but compassionate, went after one of the houseboys (all those courteous, nimble Negroes in sleazy, black alpaca coats) and requested the key. He presented it; rushed back to the kitchen and returned with a stable lantern; and the real adventure began.

Then Mother and I, braver than Columbus, stole softly (so as not to attract undue notice) from a side door; descended three steps, to grass like wet mush, invisible underfoot; and mounted again the ten steps of a boardwalk like the one at Atlantic City (then unknown to me)—like the deck of a ship! Bare, dry, sound, unshakable, it stretched forward, through damp, black silence, below enveloping trees mysteriously talkative. The mild lantern gleams, shot ahead, anticipated us as with courage; though, when I glanced down the side of this jetty, and sensed a drop into unsubstantial gloom, I clung carefully to the handrails and held my breath. The leaves over us, divulged, retiring, made a sinister garden of emerald flowering which cut off the sky. If a star showed for an instant, it retreated at once. While from the abyss I conjectured, which we were straddling, rose scurryings, patterings, I never attributed, as my mother did, to mere "stray cats." Hadn't I once already, when startled by a lumbering movement in that canyon of shadows, peered dreadfully, as the lantern swerved, and glimpsed—so close to me I could have fingered it! —the switching tail and cadaverous haunches of a brindled COW? Down there, there might be almost anything! It was luridly relieving to see, in the distance, the glaring lamp with its tin reflector, shining quietly on a notice: LADIES; the moths, cowbugs and June beetles revolving about it in a teetotum dance. We might have been poor Pinocchio, after the whale had swallowed him, when he walked hopefully toward a small, far beacon in its belly, and discovered his father with a candle lighted studying before a little table.

And later, arriving in Clarksville, the clamour of the porters: "Franklin House! Franklin House! Arlin'ton Hotel! All heah yo' baggage!" so delicious with accomplished omen—familiar to me as a dependable chorus always chanting a happy event! (The Franklin House —forgotten Franklinites!) And I would be lifted into a marvellous hack my mother had already entered; and would dispose myself hilariously upon chilly leather upholstery, from which excelsior exploded with an effect like symbolism in a painting by Dali. Clarksville was called "the Queen City of the Cumberland"; reputed to resemble Rome and Lisbon. Certainly, during a winter I once spent by the Tagus, Lisbon never looked more fair. And there would be, where the track ended behind the station, the streetcar waiting for desultory passengers the train had unloaded who were not financially prepared for the glory of hacks.

It seemed homely and intimate, that car, so electrically bright and empty, bound by its trolley like a friendly hound held by a leash. I was sure of it (as of everything else in Clarksville—or so I felt!); and that it would follow us faithfully as we drove on, every face behind its rattling windows recognized by me. It as good as belonged to my uncle—if there were other directors of the street railway company, they were as removed as Sevier from the things of which I took cognizance. Three years ago, Clarksville celebrated its sesquicentennial; and in a paper posted to me (the paper so identified with the gawky, young ambition of my great-uncle Ewing) was a photograph of the house in which I was born:

A gaunt ghost of its past days of glory, the Gracey home stands abandoned, amidst mighty oaks on Madison Street reminiscent of the days which have gone by when glad voices and revelry ruled its halls. The home was built in 1840 by Dr. E. R. W. Thomas—which it wasn't, of course; but I am quoting from the newspaper.

I read this, and suddenly, without any assistance from the reporter's eloquence, I was overpowered by that lovely awareness of something finished which can bite your heart like fangs. And I was again in the derelict coupé, inhaling the musty scent from its scrofulous leather; bouncing and bounding on springless cushions in a rapture of foregone anticipations so keen they might have led Wise Men from nowhere toward a spot appointed for a miraculous nativity. Home! There was never another. And I imagined the delightfully ill-lit streets; and the dark air of the summer night, redolent of black-drenched lawns and gardens never too well kept. Occasionally, beyond a thunderous whispering from invisible trees, there would spring forth, preciously, from the shadow of the sky, an illumined veranda; or a figure in a window I could almost identify. And the whole scene, dramatically obscure, was yet so prescient with tomorrows certain to be ecstatic, joy bubbled up in me as from an inexhaustible fountain; tapped again on the instant of sighting *the* house!

As the horse jog-trotted through the iron picket gates flung wide for our welcome, *they* appeared—my aunt and my cousins!—an angelic host, on the bright, columned porch, before the brilliance of the stained glass door. And there was, even then, a curious confusing in me of pleasure with pain—it was too, too much.

Could it have meant more to Sevier, when, like a Stuart, with his lost cause, he held out, still, against the Carolinians; and offered Evan Shelby the vacated governorship of Franklin, like a veiled bribery, to insure his support? When the emigrant, on his way toward the settlements, squatted by the trail and examiningly crumbled the clay in his hand, did he know what he held? Or what he dispersed, as he flung it aside? He didn't —but if he had, what a muddling of historical measure would have resulted; what a fuddling of later attempts to sort things out and be precise about social justice!

84

4

AMERICANS have a way of distracting attention
from national shortcomings with a hasty reference
to the "cynicism of the European." As if Huey Long
and John Dillinger were not cynical. As if, when people acting from cynical motives gave a crude performance, no stigma could be attached to them. When we
lived in Russellville, and I was five and six, we were
in a house which had harboured, during the Civil War,
an impromptu banking enterprise. Jesse James and his
brother, at that time, had executed one of their coups
d'état on the premises; had wounded the banker in
charge; and had left, as a souvenir, as precious to the inheritors of the property as though it had been a shred
from Veronica's handkerchief or nail parings from Saint
Peter's left foot and they good Catholics, two bullets
embedded in a wall of the long double parlour. Even
my father was vain of our distinguished intimacy with
those bullets. He always wanted to exhibit them to uninitiate visitors. For that matter, he was not ashamed to
boast his accidental acquaintance with Gus Hyatt, the
famous lone robber of mail trains, who had held up the
Louisville express.

Luckily, my father had happened to board the very
coach in which Mr. Hyatt, after a spectacular escape

from the penitentiary, was being returned to confinement; and the conductor, wishing to curry favour with my father, I am sure, had manipulated an introduction, seeing to it that the guards companioning the apprehended prisoner desisted from interfering while Gus Hyatt and my father had half an hour's conversation. "An extraordinary man," my father said of him. "Intelligent, well-informed, courteous—you would have taken him for a gentleman!" And the trails of Gus Hyatt crossed those of my relatives on another occasion, when yet another escape was being made. One of my male cousins (I forget which), with another boy, rowing on the Cumberland, was accosted from the shore by a keen-faced, blue-eyed man, whose expression was resolute, if distracted. He wore convict's stripes. When he commanded them, in quiet but not uncertain terms, to pull for the bank, let him aboard, and transport him to the other side of the river, they meekly obeyed him. Sensations of dread and panic endured during the effort were rewarded later, when, tearful, tingling with delicious fear and incredulity, they were persuaded to confess to their elders, who were awed to respect: "We helped Gus Hyatt escape!" A government must be long established, its prestige ripened by inviolable traditions of centuries, before there will cease to be a question in the public mind as to whether a lawbreaker is to be considered a hero or a criminal. On the frontier, they were nearly indistinguishable; which is why paradoxes in our moral outlook bewilder the foreigner. The provincialism of American politics is a relic of pioneering, and includes a tolerance for wrongdoers which easily becomes laxity. Jefferson Davis did not think as a traitor, yet his dreams were a good deal those of Aaron

86

Burr. The Union of States was itself the outcome of a protestant view of absentee rule. For a man to take the law into his own hands is a prerogative of pioneering. When a set of convenient acts is interpreted, by those who would justify them, as representative of the functioning of some moral principle, it will always be possible to refer to that same principle in support of deeds directed against the original sponsoring authority itself. One needs to remember that Colonel Henderson acquired the better part of three virgin states by performing a sleight of hand in the presence of the Indian owners and making them a gift of fifty thousand dollars' worth of blankets and the contents of one Woolworth store. . . .

In Tennessee, as everywhere else, the government solved the problem of a prior claim by the Indians to the best tillable land, with the simple method of remaining blind to the encroachments of white settlers on disputed territory, until the vested interests of whites had become so imposing it was useless folly to propose an exodus. Then came the official apology for the obvious injustice, and the offer of a compromise as the only feasible way out of a dilemma. Then the winked-at infringement on Indian tracts was an admitted discovery which shocked the government!—and more beads, blankets, penny mirrors and other trash were produced as incontrovertible proof of the white man's love of right. And if, in the face of such testimony, his red brother remained unconvinced and recalcitrant, white brother—still, oh, so regretfully!—rose in his might (which now equalled the Indian's cunning!) and slew every brave foolhardy enough to attempt self-defence. There was enmity and confusion among the whites, also, because a custom of law gave sovereignty alone the right to trick, despoil and devastate natives; and individual whites, who resented it that a first profit from roguery went to people who took no physical risk, decided to revise custom; and to make their own separate treaties with chiefs, and break them at *their own* whim.

And Sevier, who had already saved the settlements more than once, went from a camp he had for re-enforcements at French Broad, crossed the little Tennessee and made a glorious bonfire of every Indian village between the Hiwasse and Tennessee Rivers; and was, to the Indians, as Attila to our earlier ancestors; though, in the eyes of most white men, he engaged in a holy crusade.

At Tellico, he even signed a peace treaty with the adjacent tribes; but, being a soldier at heart, knew what such things are worth—a scrap of paper! He went on; found an Indian stronghold at Hiwasse deserted and levelled it; and when he had passed through the Lookout villages of the Chickamaugas, they were barren wombs from which no member of the race which had constructed them would ever again emerge. Women, children, and the poor, lean domesticated stock from the Indian country, were herded and driven before the white men—the animals, probably, no worse off than before.

On the pine flats of the Coosa, the Indians had imagined themselves in a last security: here you entered, among bewilderingly regimented, identical trees, like a ghost, without footfalls. Here, soundless, almost invisible, men, prisoned only by air, could be secret as birds. In an unexceptional uniformity of green needles and red stripes of sun on myriad boles, you arrived, like a

Buddhist suppliant, in a Nirvana of serenity, at the empty heart of Nature herself. But in clear spaces, where wigwams were erected, human life, despite precautions, announced its presence wantonly; where corn—precious in a wilderness as anything a man can put into his mouth—was planted and worshipped. The whites advanced on these woods which were like another army, waiting; and made the dangers serviceable. Then red chiefs recognized the reliability of those who had prophesied evil.

The whites, as we count armies today, were a handful; but in their wake, burned corn kernels blackened like the teeth of witches; the canoes, weighted with stones, heavy as the spirits of defeated men, sank in the rivers; and the plague of hatred, worse than any other pestilence, wrecked and obliterated everything valuable to a savage—even things which had no warlike use! The founders of a new state were missing no chances—not an Indian was spared, except where, for some special reason, he could be an asset in white strategy. Sevier's triumphant recruits discovered one British agent, whom they were disappointingly obliged to kill forthrightly, when they had hoped he might be tortured. They dragged his corpse into the open. Alas, buzzards are not discriminating—even then, the buzzards of the South were pampered. The sky filled busily with wings, until it was like some pellucid, great lake, overcast by the black sails of pirate fleets. Red men, and such white Americans as could be got at, were disposed of with equal, economical relish.

Antique America! I remember my uncle's farm, to which the family were bundled every summer for a compulsory course in "sane, healthy," none too comfortable, outdoor living. (He was an amateur fowl fancier; breeding White Leghorns, Plymouth Rocks, Buff Cochins, and squabs, in such profusion, and under such indulgent auspices, you would, as likely as not, when you went to scrub your face of a morning, find an egg in the wash basin. Because the Renfroe party had been butchered in the vicinity, and the blockhouse put up by Colonel Sevier in the eighteenth century was near; and Creeks, Cherokees and Shawnees had once haunted the very neighbourhood, I considered the farm old; though the family's tenure of the property was a thing of recent date. How much older the forest, in which we had licence to stray only when we were accompanied by some male, or by the eldest of my girl cousins, with a Colt revolver slung on her hip, like a reminiscence of Pearl White, in those most daring days of the silent film! (A tribute to the Negro—among whites dependent on his subservience for their own inflated livelihood, the Negro infects every thought: either to menace or console, he is present through every phase of ordinary life, at almost every moment of the day and hour!) Lovely forest, through which, when we went to Red River to swim, we descended torturously! The summit of the slope it climbed was crowned with beeches as benignly aged and spreading as oaks in Surrey or Somerset; and, under the bluff, grew sycamores as hoary and large as plane trees abroad. Cedars, too, crowded, with their different green, interstices in the wood; and other greens were nameless—tangles as fresh throughout summer as if spring had been unending. The quiet delighted us children, who rejoiced in sundering it with shouts and halloos; those on the river-bank speaking upward to later arrivals, crying to them, from shores sombre with emerald shadows, in jovial yells that carried to the narrow slit of the sky. Even the birds, in multitudes, were mouselike; and might have been scraps of lichen, when they clung, silent, to the boughs—all but the cardinal, who appearing rarely, flecked and spattered the forest with blood. It was not until you listened intently that you became aware of a conversational agitation which was unceasing: the continual peeps and cheeps, no louder than sighs, ever-present, like the ghost whisper of the sea in a shell.

One day, when I was following several children with a grownup in advance of them, down to the water, I fell behind the rest; and sank experimentally to the bole of an oak which had been split by lightning, so that half the tree was prone, its shrivelling leafage jutting horizontally from the mud and granite cliff over a declivity which would have invited a suicide. Tempted, monkeylike, to new tricks, I had just wriggled myself forward on the wrecked trunk to the point which permitted me to dangle my legs in the chasm, when, glancing behind me into the few remaining upright boughs, I stared straight into the attentive, mindless eyes of a huge turkey buzzard. With his head, lean as a skull, red-fleshed and immodestly naked of feathers, and his drooping plumage, like a Japanese raincoat of dirty straw, he might, as he hunched there immobilely, have been only an effigy of a bird dead for a century. I fancied I smelled his carrion breath!—And I started in terror; and he, like some awful, drab banner, unfurling (with a noise of great feathers: the noise of wind while the storm is distant!), rose; and beat away gravely from me: circling and sailing with the slow assurance of a creature which has learned to bide its time. Until he attained heights he still made threatening; where he dwindled, and was secure—beyond the range of any gun. And I almost regretted him—as if I had evaded, by mere chance, initiation in ineluctable horror!

I sprang to the ground, and ran on; parting in panic the strong, shaggy ropes of wild grape curtaining the path (they were wonderful swings!)—long, swaying tangles of fibre, they looped the trees as liana does boughs in the tropics!—and was glad to glimpse the river, quick as light, alternately hiding and revealing itself. And to catch the laments of bees—little threads of discontented whining wove the silence. And to overhear again the voices of my cousins, gaily clamorous below me. And to see, above the surface of the adored, weak brown stream I approached, dragon flies ("snake doctors," I was taught to call them; and the Negroes insisted they were what that said!) darting here and yon like a thousand animate blue needles, making a search for mosquitoes into a pyrotechnical display. How glad, as, in my bathing suit (which disgraced me even at ten by having a skirt I removed surreptitiously), I plunged, with my recovered companions, into deeper, yet more primeval quiet, unshattered, though we plashed, yelled and employed ourselves industriously; filling and refilling a tin pail; dumping its contents on the precipitate bank until we had contrived a sort of antediluvian toboggan slide, down which we scooted at ecstatic risk. Sometimes, if it weren't for Mark Twain and Huckleberry Finn, I should believe I had merely dreamed an American childhood, in its curious intimate relationship with the archaic quality of crude country; so little is the placid savagery characteristic of our original scene represented in fiction and anecdote.

A highly developed civilization demands of those

who come under its influence that they yield, with some degree of disciplined grace, to the requirements of other individuals, or the behests of the many. People in an elementary society are not encouraged to yield, but must, if they are to survive, first cultivate resistance. Figures of men in the Tennessee mountains today are representative of the unyieldingness which is pioneer hardihood—pioneer strength, which is individualism in the narrowest sense; always reactionary rather than liberal. Tolerant generosity toward one's fellow men, in pioneer surroundings, may be fatal. Even when you have effectively persuaded the pioneer to accept progress along lines which will augment physical comforts, he still resists intellectual advancement; and remains, on the plane of a psychic evolution, dogmatically conservative. Americans tend to think of themselves as a vanguard in cultural progression toward complete modernity; actually, in this very present, they lag behind other peoples. You will not, as a rule, hear of an art movement over here until it is ten years old in Europe; we do not, as a public, adopt ideas and attitudes that have been intellectually current abroad, until they are already stale and old. The Swopes-Bryan trial of a few years ago would have been an unimaginable occurrence almost anywhere else in the supposedly civilized world. And where we are most justified in assuming our superiority, we are never quite as much in advance of the times as we like to believe. For instance, our transportation system! England has the fastest train in the world. In the matter of municipal conveyances, London was ahead of New York years ago: it is only recently that cross-town buses have begun to operate, and to supplant antiquated surface cars. American women can be so remarkably well-dressed at such small cost; but frequently the modes displayed for mass consumption have been introduced here from six to nine months after the heyday of their popularity with the best-gowned Parisian or English women.

God knows what my poor grandfather Thomas had to combat in the way of reaction when he was a youth in the fifties; such a little while after Sevier, under a cloud, and accused, by his rival, Tipton, of all kinds of unscrupulous illegalities, was ordered to lay down his arms! He defied those who ordered his arrest, and, refusing hiding, remained openly at the house of a friend in Jonesboro. Apprehended there, he was being conducted to Morgantown to stand trial, when he made a reckless failure of an effort to escape. Until, finally, in the very midst of the court session, he got free. Nathaniel Evans and James Cosby, who had left Sevier's own horse ready-saddled and waiting for him in the road, entered the courtroom and precipitated a demonstration in favour of the prisoner which so confused his guards and the judge that Sevier was able to dash high-handedly into the open, and gallop away. That settled his prosecution. Though the law deprived him of his right to hold office, his adherents were sufficiently numerous, and powerful enough, in Greene County, to elect him to the North Carolina Senate and, by suggesting physical threat, see to it that he was allowed a place in the Senate hall.

I mention this in passing, because it seems to me illustrative of an American tradition which persists, and particularly in the South. The Sevier-Tipton feud, with its termination in avowed contempt for law and juridical procedure, occurred while the majority of the settlers were still housed in shelters built of split saplings, while wild turkey, bear and buffalo meat were as common in the diet of the ordinary man as beef—more so. When rifles and spinning jennies were in the equipment of every cabin; and the gregarious impulses of various groups found gratification in quilting bees, corn shuckings and maple sugar stirrings; in deer-drives and foot and horse racing. When the books in circulation among those who could read were limited to the Bible, Watts's and Rippon's *Hymns*, Foxe's *Book of Martyrs*, *Robinson Crusoe*, *Pilgrim's Progress* and occasional spelling books. Yet, in my grandfather's day (even in my own), political feuds were identical; people in general inclined to be narrowly, circumspectly religious; and a lenient view was taken of it, if a man of action who had demonstrated any capacity for leadership became a lawbreaker. (In Russellville, Kentucky, for example, when men who were political opponents became ireful and tried pot shots at each other, they were seldom prosecuted and no great scandal resulted.) In my grandfather's time, commerce was evolving a life of greater complexity, but certain moral attitudes (unmoral attitudes, to speak technically) were unaltered.

A sensitive intelligence, after an impact with the crude ruthlessness of an unsentimental common sense that has been fortified by naïve, pious self-righteousness, tends to recoil; and to receive a permanent imprint of scepticism. Disbelief—a disgust with dogmas of all sorts—seems to have been the salient characteristic of my grandfather Thomas's mentality. Almost from the start, he exhibited (shall I say?) a peculiar furtive independence of mind. That is, he thought (and occasionally did) things not generally thought and done in his time, by his generation, in Tennessee; yet managed to hang on, and profit in a measure from the conduct of a society in which he was always a detached observer. In the end, he was defeated, and died intestate with just enough to his credit in the banks to settle his debts; when his children had had every reasonable expectation of inheriting a fortune. The concommitants of his demise, at sixty, though disappointing to his heirs, seem aesthetically proper for a man who had withdrawn consistently from every popular movement which had won his contemporaries.

I often speculate on what caused his aversion for politics, in that place and period in which politics was a religion; and wonder at the contrast between him and Great-uncle Ewing, who found such complete self-expression through being a Whig. Grandfather Thomas, though a Democrat by descent, and though he supported Democrats in the state and the Senate right up to the time of the Civil War, was against secession. And when Andrew Johnson reached the anticlimactic peak of his self-made career and was impeached (the tailor shop in Greeneville supplying some of the most infamous arguments of his attackers), my grandfather's conviction of his innocence was firm; though "Andy's" self-education, as it had progressed since days when his wife had corrected his semi-illiteracy by teaching him to write, had carried him further and further in hostility to the class to which my grandfather belonged—a class that had bulwarked slavery and prolonged feudalism. Continuing the paradox, my grandfather, who had inherited, from *his* father, a small number of slaves, but freed every one of them while Lincoln's proclamation was still a dream, had very little use for the Abolitionist "Left."

Ben Lundy, an Ohio Abolitionist, as early as 1821, was publishing, in Greeneville, a paper called the *Genius of Universal Emancipation.* "Parson" Brownlow was a contemporary of Johnson, and of my grandfather. In the mountains, where Negroes were of less value than when transported to the fertile valleys of middle Tennessee, where plantations could be laid out in the grand manner (though they seldom were), people were, almost from the start, brave with hatred of the slave owner. Indeed, the plasterers, tailors, bricklayers with whom Johnson consorted in his youth, proposed to hate the rest of the South out of existence. Poor Andy! When, at the end of the Civil War, Left Wing representatives in Washington began demanding blood, blood, ever more blood, and wanted to convert Lee's surrender into a Day of Atonement on which the proud—even the merely self-respecting!—should be brought low, the very mothers of sons who had served the Confederate cause sent, like Hagar, to wander, outcast, in a wilderness, Johnson's humanity overpowered his "principles." A faulty man, but sincere, he was, for all he fought against it, liberalized by his sufferings. Until the love he had in his heart for people who were fond of, and had been faithful to him, though his theories and theirs diverged, overcame the sternness of his ideas; and angels and the iniquitous were no longer to be distinguished as, merely, anti or pro slavery. And his sentiment for a South which held all his old associations proved itself something stronger than his theoretic identity with the self-appointed scourges of God who were descending from the North smugly to castigate offenders. It became less important to Andy that "the Apostle Paul was a tent-maker, Socrates a sculptor, Archimedes a mechanic," than that certain men in varying walks of life compassionated the victim of fanaticism and specific injustice.

Without waiting on Marx, people in the mountain villages, who were without slaves, had set out to proclaim a class war—Andy, it turned out, was one of the many whose devotion to abstraction was passionate and religious, who were to be hoist by their own petard. More than once, my grandfather showed himself an ironist, and I believe he appreciated this; and that the impeached president, long before the acquittal, had his sympathy on ironic grounds.

When you are very young, you are perpetually in love—not with a specific person (not necessarily!), but with everybody, everything! Your estimates of people and places are given with no more detachment than described your first sweetheart while you were still under his spell. (Mine was a choir boy, seventeen when I was seven; his legs like a stork's in short trousers, his voice like an uneasy frog's. He never suspected the habit I had of kicking up my heels whenever I saw him was a tribute from an exhibitionist—that I was really an Atalanta, before whom the apple was soon to be cast. I don't pretend to interpret Tennessee without any personal bias: my original acquaintance with it, extending through the beginning sixteen years of my life, was all a love affair—disturbed, at intervals, by deep unhappiness. Later, my retrospective summing up of the state has been tinged with "disillusion"—a reaction *after* a love passage. The reverse side of the original experience!

There are people who insist on remaining in love forever, even when a starving passion must sustain itself on self-manufactured, sentimental lies! Some—my mother is one—remain, to the end, genuinely enamoured of the remote past. For myself, I decided, some time back, that the only honest course for me, when I spoke of Tennessee, would be to give free rein to a bitterness inevitable when what has formerly constituted "glamour" in a surrounding has been recognized as the self-generated product of personal emotion. Now, lo, to my amazement, when I gaze behind me, I am regarding a Tennessee practically unaltered since those lost days of my infatuation! So, after all, there is a country of the heart—of one sort for my grandfather, of another for my mother, and of yet a different kind for me. And I am forced to acknowledge it exists, and that I consider it valid terrain. But all the more, with this admission, do I feel called on to assert my appreciation of the value of a scientific approach; and of the importance of those tentative conclusions about human life which proceed from scientific observation, and are a necessary corrective to opinions uttered by persons perpetually prejudiced by involvements of the feelings. Opinions formed either in anticipation of, during, or in consequence of, love affairs!

I believe I owe this regard for mental purity and detachment to my grandfather Thomas; and that it is because of him I often find myself allied, unsympathetically, even with behaviourists. He, like his brother, studied medicine; and though, unlike the same brother, he never completed his course, but compromised with ambition and became, for a while, a druggist in Clarksville—still, I think, his frustrations, which always favoured science, are responsible for the regard I have for liberally impersonal judgements of events. Though Grandfather was no more, in the beginning, than a pill mixer (his shop, like the surgery of an English G. P. only a kind of adjunct to his brother's practice, so that the profit on prescriptions could be kept in the family), I believe it was this experience of his early twenties which accomplished his final divorce from the Fundamentalists who surrounded him, whose bigotry antagonized him. Negroes, for instance, who have clairvoyant insight wherever tact is involved, to the day of his death, addressed him as "Doctor Thomas," when, by usual standards of a community in which the plain "Mister" is reserved for insult, the wealth he had transiently would, normally, have earned him a title of "Colonel" at the very least.

Perhaps, too, there was an influence on him from those early periodic forays he made in the East, when he went by coach to Philadelphia—at that time, Philadelphia, rather than New York, was the metropolitan storehouse for calomel, cascara, quinine and bismuth; as well as a centre of elegant fashion. My grandmother never forgot what she gained by her young husband's exploitation of his status as a buyer in wholesale—perfumes to seduce an emperor, literal bathtubs of cologne, dress lengths worthy of a Circe from the rue de la Paix. What marvellous opportunities were given males of that period to enact the benign and really godlike role before female wrens, doves and canaries who rarely left the home nest! And women, renouncing impatience with impetuosity, dutifully accepted, with the grace required of dependents, manna when it fell; or, in lean eras, the storm when it broke and sent nothing to the eternally waiting plane but thunder and devastating lightning.

Settlers had depended, for commercial relations with the outer world, on a trade with peddlers, who showed the courage of migrating birds when they came over the mountains with the pins and ribbons that were to supplement the homespun, or the occasional brocade some woman had brought west with her, and would don occasionally, to trail its flounces through rooms like stables. True, a dry goods store was opened at Ohio Falls in 1780; and one John Wilkinson set up another in Lexington, Kentucky, soon afterward; but the number of these emporiums increased slowly, and their stock, up to my grandfather's young manhood, would not have pleased men and women of fashion.

What changed everything, and caused the pettiest tradesman to expand his choice of wares in a way to appeal to people of means, was the tobacco. After the invasion of a hinterland by Boone and his successors, it was the one flower left by the Indians which blossomed perennially. The peace pipe had been smoked, over blood and bones, by peacemakers generous only to the dead: peacemakers who were destined, just the same, to live ever afterward encircled by its blue fumes! Even the Civil War was only an interlude—it did not prevent the tobacco from springing again. Tobacco has been the basis of most miracles performed in middle Tennessee; often enough, overnight, it has converted a cabin into a virtual palace. Tobacco is to that part of the country what herring are to the east coast of England. The rich fruitiness emanating from the open door of a warehouse is of the choicest of my juvenile memories. Tobacco and railroads I once considered the only appropriate sources of aristocratic income. (Both were in the family!) I was brought up to regard railroads and tobacco ours, as by a divine right shared with our own kind. If such intelligence as I possessed at seven or eight years old was sealed against revolutionary messages, my senses were wide to receive impacts; and I recollect that perfume of hogsheads, thunderously rolled through cathedral interiors, as a source of ineffable drunkenness —never duplicated, seldom equalled!

I have a daguerreotype picture of my grandfather, with his family—my uncle Lewis, who died at seventeen of "brain fever" (a jealous God's compliment to the brilliant of the nineteenth century, someone has said!); and my aunt Betty, who lived to be forty, but was martyred by domestic devotedness. Above his son in trousers like sacks, and the little daughter so matronly sedate in a frock with "drop shoulders" and a muslin apron fluttering satin bows, my grandfather (who was a short man) towers, idling dominantly, his arm resting on the back of the chair occupied by my slim little grandmother. In his pleated shirt with a huge black cravat, he looks, with his curly dark hair (and despite a rather fat nose) handsome, sulkily sweet-tempered and faintly unhappy. This portrait of a group was made long before my mother's birth, so it may have come from the drug-store epoch. But there is another picture, taken in the seventies, of the same people, matured, congregated on the veranda of the house built by the Lewises. Here are my aunts, all present at last, and grown-up, looped and girdled and hooked into bustled dresses which might have been portieres. And my grandfather himself, almost portly now, is there, too; in his broadcloth, with a high hat, against a façade so splendidly spacious it extends its dignity to the posturing group. He has a cockatoo on his shoulder; deer are present on the lawn. He owned horses, dogs, a Jersey herd and, as a private fancy, racoons, foxes, a pet snake and a circus-tamed bear.

It was the tobacco that had allowed it; the tobacco that had blessed him; the tobacco which had permitted him to purchase an estate. Tobacco made it possible for him to indulge ingenuous aspirations, and become an "art collector." It encouraged him to exceed his type in his ambition for his daughters, whom he proposed to convert into academic painters, literary creators, blue stockings. They were to carry on a tradition of eighteenth-century liberalism, which he had, vaguely, from his mother's mother, and from the Duvals.

Tobacco bought my grandfather's library he was too harassed to enjoy often; though he owned fine editions of most of the Greek and Latin classics, and of all the poets who, up to that date, had shown themselves worthy. It was owing to tobacco that he could indulge his interest in racing, and assemble rare folios on jockeys and horses. Racing, of course, was "a gentleman's sport." And the original Audubon drawings I, as a child, was free to pore over only if I had first washed my hands, had been his through tobacco; which had made him, in spare moments, an amateur "naturalist." Just as it had made him an amateur art fancier, as the Hogarth *Rake's Progress* (valued by his descendants chiefly because considered pornography) testified. The Doré Bible, the Doré *Ancient Mariner* (they tell me you can get a lot of money for a copy these days) I adored above all other books in the world, were by-products of tobacco. (How well I remember the mustiness associated with all those yellowed pages of my grandfather's books—a perfume like the fragrance from the potpourri of a dear mind! And a little green-bound series my mother had prized as a child—innocently pedantic, admirably instructive tales! Virtue was exemplified in a family of robins! And Miss Mulock's *Adventures of a Brownie*, with a frontispiece depicting the Brownie ice skating with the children. He looked rather like A. E. Coppard, the English short-story writer; though smaller, of course.)

Oddly, the district around Clarksville was destined, for a time, to become one of the great tobacco markets of the world—a centre, at any rate, for the distribution of tobacco of a certain type, which is dark, dampish and heavy; and has been popular in Europe. Africa and Bremen had free markets; while the purchase of tobacco in Italy, Spain and France was under government control. My grandfather, during a limited period of his life, supplied the government monopolists under contracts which were very profitable to him.

Edwin George, in *A Calendar of Sin*, was an invention; but, obviously, one suggested by incidents in my grandfather's life. If tobacco flourished, another sort of growth was less hardy. In the sense of an intention to reestablish in the southerner a regional pride which may be his salvation, the I-take-my-stand agrarians are certainly on the right track. But their imaginations, it seems to me, are overmuch employed with fable. They are spiritual isolationists, who bring to their proposed tradition of aggressive Dixieism, not only things anachronistic—not only attitudes sprung from ignoring many implacable actualities which must be dealt with before the South can be unified on a realistic basis—but views and assumed "facts" which are sheer literary romancing.

They were mostly descended from the more worthless of the poor white settlers, who, driven back from the seaboard, had herded among these wooded hills with the hordes of horse-thieves and criminals who had escaped from justice in the older settlements. The progeny of these people are even at this day (1899) a foul blot on American civilization. The women are coarse and desti-

tute of both intelligence and virtue, and the men rough, brutal in their instincts, and of no civilized use except as food for gunpowder, wrote James R. Gilmore, a lucid authority on Tennessee history in the Revolutionary period. He was describing the Tennessee backwoodsman; and it is difficult to say whether a reader like myself is left most stunned by his account of people who are linear inheritors of the laurels of King's Mountain, or by the smugness with which he dismisses an examination into their contemporaneously debased condition. His frank disposition of their use in society really outdoes Hitler!

Nonetheless, these folk, of whom Mr. Gilmore remarks, and quite correctly: *These people were the natural enemies of the respectable classes,* made up a fair portion of the territorial population. Their children, and children's children, were co-citizens with my grandfather; and have a numerous representation in the present. In their squalor, their ignorance, and their indomitable pioneer will to survive, they persist now, and are an electorate. Even as are Mr. Gilmore's prototypes in opinion, who see in the "enemies of the respectable classes" only the justly forgotten of God.

A friend of mine, on a recent visit to Dayton, Tennessee, made a pilgrimage to the William Jennings Bryan University, endowed (inadequately, at the moment) in compliment to *The Origin of Species,* encountering, on the campus, a lone student, surprised improving the solitude by practising hymns on a cornet. The student, to whose courtesy I am ungracious, gave my friend information of sixty enrolled students—"mostly consecrated Christians"—the majority of whom were, on their graduation, to carry the message of Darwin's iniquity to Java,

Turkestan, Benares and other points in the unenlight-
ened Far East. A library for the college had been improvised in the shed-roofed basement of a building yet
to be erected (the faculty is awaiting the arrival of
fresh funds); and in the stacks to which the librarian
cordially admitted my ungrateful friend, were no less
than three copies of the work that once rocked the state's
cultural foundations. Three volumes, containing book-
plates and inscriptions, showing them to have been Mr.
Bryan's own bequest—one supposes he was giving Mr.
Charles Darwin a sporting opportunity to be his own
hangman! (Céline's *Journey to the End of the Night*
turned up rather startlingly on an adjacent shelf; but
my friend spared the college authorities any embarrass-
ing questioning.)

When the North Carolina legislature met in 1785, and
arranged that taxes in the settlements, when not collecta-
ble as moneys, could be paid in raccoon and foxskins (official evaluation, one shilling and sixpence each—clean
beaverskins fetched sixpence; as did a pound of bacon
well cured); when almost no cash was changing hands;
when cornhuskings, logrollings and wrestling matches
were the rule of entertainment; when whiskey (also an
allowable substitute for tax money) was half a crown a
gallon, and as good as a ticket to Paradise—the details
of existence must have had a certain harmony within
themselves, in the lives of those who were exclusively
men of action. If people were hanged or shot, or, when
the judges were more lenient, branded with a *T* in the
palm of the hand, for stealing a cow or a hog, the moral
code which was being applied was proportioned to pioneer needs; and cultural standards were equivalent. We
may presume a hard-put woman, now and then, when her

husband was absent, sampled for herself what gave him such perilous advantage over her in making the best of situations that were a test for *his* physical endurance. Women did not gamble for the new land with the game of "rattle and snap" which was so popular in the settlements, and with distractions so few, can scarcely be blamed by sometimes rescuing themselves from calamitous insignificance by the exploitation of their primitive powers: in the court records of the period, a huge number of disputes about property are accounted for by the frequency with which the legitimacy of heirs is called into question. But leeway was given the indiscreet whose misdemeanours did not affect the disposition of tangible things; and there was really nothing in the management of group affairs that one can criticize aesthetically. That is, taking into account the circumstances, and the exhibited natures of the people. Samuel Doak, James Balch, William and John McGee, and similar divines, as men with a world outlook as circumscribed as that of their followers, and with, technically, more learning, were amply justified in their assumption of spiritual leadership.

But already in my grandfather's day, the cultural ambitions of those few among the leisured who were at all reflective, had to be gratified at a distance, or very artificially. No system of manners, no code of behaviour ever received a more orchidlike sustenance than the system in vogue and the code approved in middle Tennessee in my grandfather's maturity, while my mother was still a young girl. Pioneering, which is not, in a psychological sense, over with among us even yet, had scarcely accomplished its physical cycle, when there began, first, the Civil War; then carpetbagging, and the hypocrisies and cynicisms become flagrant throughout the country as an effect of the amoral good nature of President Grant's administration. Obviously, while Grant allowed the least scrupulous of his friends to manipulate federal politics, the pioneer's problem, of drawing that nearly indefinable line between a local criminal and a hero meriting disciples, grew ever more difficult. The proof is, we do not yet make the distinction. It seems to me the influential position of a man like Huey Long is testimony to the fact that it was not only in the North that people were, long ago, plunged into such ethical confusion as has protracted itself to this day. Time was lacking, before the Civil War, for a flowering of culture, out of feudalism, in any of the *young* states, west of Virginia. *After* the Civil War, conditions (for which, to be sure, southerners ought not to be held responsible) converted a hope into the dream of a dream—a merely wishful speculation on the true character of an ancestral souvenir.

For when you come right down to it, money, between 1870 and 1900 (I say nothing of later decades), was ruler; and that went for the whole country. Money, which could purchase leisure, but could not inspire anybody with a profound vision! Money, which has never generated anywhere (unless, inversely, in Karl Marx, or in Jesus) an impulse to be honestly expressive about anything vital! Money—and for people whom the Civil War had deprived, an obsessive fantasia of yearnings after luxuries sought for and lost!

I know a woman whose husband, under circumstances which left her self-accused, became, as they say, "temporarily insane," and committed suicide. And she was amazed, for a while, to find herself, apparently, nearly unmoved by something she had too often anticipated as a major tragedy: she was able to continue with her ordinary affairs, almost as calmly as if nothing had happened. Then, suddenly, though she was still notably unemotional, she began to run amok, exhibiting a nearly uncontrollable desire to hang herself by her bedsheets or fling herself from a window—coldly, frenziedly, in a mere attack of nerves. She did not recognize her own despair—the paradoxical despair which overcomes people of feeling when it seems to them, horribly, they have ceased to feel. I think this was a state of mind which had its frequent parallels among southerners immediately after the Civil War, when tragedy was so general, and so complete, it was defeat to face it—something not to be borne! A few, confronting the actuality, rejected it simply, by turning their army revolvers (no longer useful for anything else) against their own breasts. Others, discovering in themselves atavistic resources not previously exploited, became shrewd and merciless enough to deal ably with peacetime enemies, who were not only shrewd and merciless, but, in the bargain, sanctimonious about it. A popular majority in the South took refuge in a verbal extravagance which released tormented nerves—in escapisms. Where the only feelings valid for the time are inacceptable to instinct, it takes escapism of some sort to compensate men for the slaughtering of their decent self-approval, required for their courage.

I think the Yankee espousing the cause of universal justice, without consideration of caste, colour or local peculiarity, when he goes south (in a missionary spirit), and is met at the railway station by an irate and curiously biased constabulary, or by some vigilante body of brutally inclined citizens, though he be brave and his intentions admirable, is not as unqualifiedly right as he supposes. For, if he is right, he is certainly not imaginative; therefore, not entirely wise. The northerner who treks to the defence of the genuinely victimized Scottsboro boys, or goes somewhere else to report, accurately, abuse of labour by bosses bent on curtailing expense for themselves whatever the cost to others, has usually forgotten that this particular type of invasion—the intrusion, on southern territory, of Yankee reformers (often with a world to win and nothing they much care for to be forfeited!)—is an old story below Mason and Dixon's line, and one justly abhorred in the past. That cabinet of Johnson's, which split on this very theme of bringing the South to its knees, may be at least a racial memory to men lingering in darkness. The self-interest usually behind their obstinate benightedness may not, after all, constitute the whole story. Where missionaries are called for, they ought to be southern-bred, if possible. So many Biblical sayings represent psychological truisms—in the New Testament, certainly, there must be one to fit!

My grandfather reached middle age, my mother adolescence, while a shadow cast by defeat made the regional landscape sombre, and escapist proclivities were unacknowledged and desperate among persons who were sensitive and not crassly hypocritical. And in that era provincialism became a cult; and was holy. The influx of greedy Yankees, happening so soon after hardships, killed, in many southerners, the last vestiges of any urge to confront life realistically. Reduced—after so brief a respite!—to an equivalent of existence in blockhouse and stockade; and surrounded by victors come to make money out of the very conditions which had proved fatal to southern self-respect, southern pride and ambition; people who had been stripped naked (sometimes literally, as well as figuratively), the quivering wounds of the most vulnerable exposed to eyes the least calculated to take a sympathetic view, had no defence—no justification for assumed superiority!—except in the tall story. They were driven, self-protectively, to impress the Yankees by whatever means available. I think this is one origin of southern mythmaking, as we now know it, which has so often stood in the way of southern progress. Having begun with the intention of seducing the enemy, and rendering him fitly humble, southerners, like the Irish, have seduced themselves to vainglorious amoral slovenliness; and are, in the main, paralyzed for action.

I feel I may be more fortunate than some southerners: in my case, the anodyne for disappointments, the cure for factual deficiencies, though administered, like a vaccine, very early, refused to "take." Or maybe I am only unlucky! My Yankee blood has made the difference! And yet I could swear (though my datum is no more conclusive than the look of sharpened resignation and profound weariness in the eyes of my grandfather Thomas's last portrait) that disillusion came, on occasion, even to those in whom a Maryland-Virginia strain was pure. Though his daughters, far from regarding dancing as the pitfall it had seemed to Scotch-Presbyterians and Primitive Methodists, put on little pink and blue kid slippers (made to order at more per pair than my great-grandfather from Ulster could have spent on foolishness in a dozen months) and were sent under proper chaperonage to a professor of dancing while they were still of a very tender age; though they were conversant with French as the language of elegance, and knew, also, a little Italian; and though one of my aunts, with a talent for painting, was an "elocutionist" as well, and would recite *High Tide on the Coast of Lincolnshire* or *Annabel Lee* with such effect as wet every eye in a crowded drawing room—still I think my grandfather, when he forgot tobacco, and considered his fine house, his servants and his smart vehicles, and asked himself: What has this amounted to? received the answer, out of his heart: Nothing! At any rate, very little! I am not a Methodist, Baptist, Campbellite or good Presbyterian; yet I must have a belief, a faith, a tradition to hold by! Something better than ancestor worship; something more than perpetual harping on the sketchily verifiable glories of retrospective gentility! Something that will fill me emotionally, and allow me some pride in the free use of my mind! As it is, I may die worse off than those who, protected in a measure by blindness, cannot see themselves as I see *myself*—just another ridiculous mouse!

By the time my mother had recovered from the maidenly misery it was to learn arithmetic, Chester A. Arthur, or maybe Benjamin Harrison, was president, and the carpetbagger had paid something in his turn for the excoriation of southern pride. A sister of hers, married to a doctor whose inherited income made him independent of a practice, lived in the country, where her husband bred beagles as a specialty, and other hounds as a side line diversion. Hunts convened in the neighborhood. There were no pink coats—Tennesseeans, alas, have never done these things with quite that air of being to the manner born which prevails in Virginia. But there was sport other than the treeing of raccoons; and the hospitality which came after it (so I gather from a perusal of recipes in my grandmother's cookbook) would have been a credit to a hostess of the days of Queen Bess. My mother (who had not, like *her* mother, heard the wolf at the door, but in her physical nature seems always to have expected it) overcame her timidity to the extent of becoming a locally admired horsewoman. Hounds and horses, visible distantly, flashed through gaps between wood lots; or plunged, all together, in an animal cataract, rushing, galloping, with directionless tumult, all with one motive—escape! The riders bent on one thing—avoiding reminders that there had ever been squalid frontier villages where children were fortunate if they learned the three R's, and the reading matter available might be an almanac! Girls ignoring terrors that must have haunted women who gave birth to a first child, in the husband's absence, while there was work to be done in the fields, and no one by to act as midwife—only a half-witted black boy, got in exchange for a colt, able to help a little. Until, what with labour and responsibilities, and children so many, the woman and the husband (he had seemed such a grand lover!) felt with each other as mutually hating as beasts chained together. Poverty—makeshifts for existing that degrade existence! To people of my mother's class and generation, in the South, nobody had ever been poor.

The cult of France was not so strong in most families as in my own; yet education in certain quarters assured you you would find those with a knowledgeable respect for Matthew Arnold, a devout view of Ruskin, a comfortable if meaningless dependence on such stand-bys as Thackeray, Dickens, George Eliot and Scott, all vaguely lumped together as authors who had the support of the well-bred in England. Young ladies who played the piano, and had to get through a Beethoven sonata or two with their music lessons, when left to express their own tastes, preferred *La Czarina Mazurka*, or some charming little drawing room ballad—*My Lady's Bower* would be representative—the more artificial, the more successful. Chaminade was later, but they would have adored her—and Massenet. I doubt they had heard of Tschaikowsky, and, very likely, he would have been too Slavonic and strange.

There was no longer a male relative acting as professional shopper for the family; hence less distressing uncertainty as to what really *was* being worn in Paris. The most chic costumes were exhibited at spring "openings" held in dry goods stores on the ground. These were as fashionable in Holy Week as the Easter Day services; and were similarly inaugurated by a performance of musicians behind barricades of croci, jonquils, Ascension lilies and other symbolic flora. Indeed the wardrobes of my mother and my aunts filled me with despair and envy even twenty years after various garments had outlived a fashionable use, when they were sometimes unearthed from cedar chests in searches after anything at all to mend a soft cushion. A few of those who had been girls in my mother's day had gone in for advanced games, and had played tennis; but the most fetching effects of the designer were creations to be worn by others who preferred archery—a more leisurely pastime, giving ample opportunity for badinage exchanged with gentlemen present and appreciative when these young Dianas displayed the firm arm, the supple finger, and the steady wrist. There were, also, yachting costumes, in white flannel, with braided revers and many gilt buttons, suitable for the postwar adventure of going north for a summer on the Great Lakes.

There was no paucity of antebellum relics now, either.

Square, white-columned houses were appearing—reappearing—everywhere; until you could easily have convinced yourself the original Athens had been located in Georgia, after all! And that the invading Yankees, by destroying so many cruder, less pretentious, earlier erections, had actually performed a benefit. However, no use insisting these things were products of a soil in which a rich, indigenous culture thrived. There is a first admonition to scientific scruple in observing, which says that a tree shall be known by its fruits. Though, before the Civil War, and, occasionally, after, Tennessee produced talented politicians, some accomplished soldiers, and a few flamboyantly impressive orators; there is a notable absence in the state of anything like a cultural harvest worthy of remark. All over America, those last decades of the nineteenth century are distinguished by general cultural sterility, so that to stress, in particular, the desert atmosphere of one state, or the aridity of the South, would be beside the point; were it not that there is a persistent southern myth of contradiction.

In Clarksville, it was based on Cave Johnson, Gustavus Henry, Colonel John House, Hallie Erminie Rives, Martha McCulloch Williams, and Dorothy Dix. An additional boost to prestige was the residence in Clarksville, for one year, of Father Ryan, the impassioned perpetrator of a platitudinous tribute to the "Lost Cause." He was the author of a poem called *The Conquered Banner*. Clarksville's cultural history is, I believe, typical. Those well disposed toward Tennessee, but with no regional axe to grind, if they incline to disagree with me, may, I suggest, consult files of *John Trotwood Moore's Magazine* (which, incidentally, accepted the second long story I ever sent into the world, when I was sixteen; but, before the cheque for thirty-five dollars arrived—it was payment on publication—forwarded me a notification that the periodical was changing editors, and that my manuscript should be resubmitted). Mr. and Mrs. Allen Tate, John Crowe Ransome, Donald Davidson, Stribling and others, were not then improving the Tennessee tradition with another sort of writing; Joseph Wood Krutch had not lent the lovely clarity of a genuinely first-rate mind to the support of a negative thesis, in *The Modern Temper.*

To people like the Southern people, retired from the world at large, and in their family seats from each other also (this sounds a trifle obscure), *home had a meaning far more sentimental than it has for people who live in swarming cities, where a change of residence from one house or one street to another is a very common occurrence. Those homes in the Southern countryside had, in most instances, come down from a distant past* (from the time of Charlemagne, probably—certainly none was built as late as 1800!); *they were invested with the sacred interest of ancestral traditions and personal associations alike; and were expected to descend to a remote posterity of the same blood, who, in their turn, would look upon them with the same affection,* says Philip Alexander Bruce, LL.D., in a volume entitled *Brave Deeds of Confederate Soldiers.* As he shifts his telescope, first one way, then another, it becomes plain that time is relative; and that as many anecdotes to the glory of family can be accumulated in sixty years as in six hundred, if you are willing to employ your imagination with sufficient earnestness. And if you are not, and have a greater respect for modern author-

116

ities, go to vignettes drawn by Mr. Joseph Herges-
heimer, who treats of the political oratory of the South
as if it were a true art.

Call it an art if you will—it at once aims to stimulate,
for the sake of the direct power motive, the pulse of
a specific audience, and to trace, as with a graph, de-
grees of response to be practically exploited. To me,
political oratory (and no matter how ennobling the
orator's outlook) is only a debased theatricalness; lacking in everything to represent the artist's true ethic,
which insists on a scrupulous integrity in measuring
with the word the artist's own inner experiencing of
fact. But the south, if it has not encouraged artists,
has only been like the rest of America: genuine aesthetic
appreciations cannot develop among persons with a pioneer bias in thought; and to this very day, the average citizen of this United States (and I include many
"art lovers" and "art patrons") is totally devoid of
the aesthetic sense, pure. The circumstances of his existence are such that art, which evolves through an
awareness of life in terms which are the natural language of the sensitively reflective—terms alien to the
man centered on practical, and especially commercial,
achievement—exists to supply wants as yet unknown to
him. Wants which will remain incomprehensible until
the evidence of matters he will share, which will constitute what was formerly described as "a spiritual life"
(one devised for the exercise of the intellect and emotions), make art his necessity. Not, as it is now, his
diversion.

Certainly the determination of a certain class of
southerners to establish beginnings for another race of

feudal aristocrats had nothing whatever to do with art. That sort of aristocracy, until it reaches a last stage which is the commencement of its own decline, is entirely indifferent both to aesthetic niceties and to refinements of speculative thought. Then the feudal baron may permit the artist—like Little Tommy Tucker! like the minstrel authors of Beowulf!—to sing for his supper. Otherwise, it will be no more in the nature of the feudal aristocrat than of the Communist general to care for art deeply. When I, as a child, was sent to school for a year in Memphis, I was given, with my *History of the Confederacy*, a brochure which directed attention toward achievements in the state, and saw a photograph of the F. P. Gracey Tobacco Warehouse, situated in Clarksville, and mentioned as one of the largest extant. And when I was soothed in my vanity because my aunt had married F. P. Gracey's son, I was very near the core of this discussion!

Once, while we were living in Russellville, my mother, who had been out afternoon-calling, entered our yard (she was looking so pretty in her grey broadcloth gown with her ostrich-plumed hat and her furs and violets, that I remember it still), and discovered me squatting in the grass, digging violently and laboriously with a large tin spoon. Questioned on my preoccupation, I explained to her that I did not like Russellville and was digging to reach China, which I understood to be at the other side of the world. I think this began an adventure, which has always had a somewhat desperate character, and is not yet done. I was like a trapped rat, forging a way through obstacles with a new burrow! Like a convict frenziedly employing a pocketknife as he seeks for freedom through ten yards of solid masonry with a guarded continent beyond! I wanted to get out, and be able to arrive somewhere else—on the other side of the strange taboos and inscrutable injunctions which hedged and hemmed me in.

5

I HAD two great-uncles who fought (one was killed) in the Northern Army—they were the uncles of my father. When I was a child, and used to hear of the exploits of Captain Frank P. Gracey, who had captured, singlehanded, on the Tennessee River, a Federal steamboat called the *Mazeppa*, I felt very much humiliated. He was the grandfather of my cousins, but unrelated to myself. My own grandfather Thomas had remained, with considerable moral daring, a noncombatant; and the single brother of my mother, who might have retrieved me from my discomfort, had not lived long enough to become officially a hero of any kind. Yet I hope I may never fall into that consoling illusion of the self-righteous, and assume the sufferings of the vanquished in a cause I condemn, less than the agonies which have been undergone by "God's chosen," who agree with myself! For "the just" are that only relatively, through the coincidence of opinions held at the moment and approved by me; whereas pain is absolute—the human capacity for it individual, and apart from any mere theory likely to occasion victims.

"*The* war," I was taught to call it; there in the South, where we were all brought up to regard ourselves as little princesses defrauded of their heritage. The Alcott version of obscure worth and gentility—of happiness achieved through the excellent performance of homely duties that are woman's lot—though soothing reading, was appropriate to the modest aspiringness of plainer people in another latitude, never to ourselves! Mrs. Annie Fellows Johnston backed us; and I suppose good Miss Mulock, in my mother's time, was behind as many little pretenders. It is certainly true that my mother, when she went north to school in the winters, carried, into enemy territory, a banner of unbroken defiance. Girls who were southern, and in the North, felt, then, even more than they do at present, the obligation to be self-consciously and dramatically different from other American girls through every instant of waking life. When my mother visited friends in Boston, she was charging a firing line. When the Bostonese brother of the family that had entertained her came south one Christmas, arriving without requisite warm clothes, and was hilariously convicted of being the dupe of his erroneous preconception of an exotic race, he, too, while he hunched miserably over one of the only three radiators in a barn of a house, cursing a climate as damply morose as that of the British Isles, had to meet some of the tests invented for epic figures. Though eyes which flashed for the "Lost Cause" were not fired by the sun and the weather! "*The* war!" grown people used to exclaim in my presence, with such a note of indignation and suffering vanity in their voices as made me feel early the defeated were the martyrs and the true elect.

And why not, my God? For compared to the physical aftermath of hostile invasion, quibblings about "right" and "wrong" become impertinences! In the vicinity of Clarksville were buildings that had been reduced to a single chimney, like the monument to a bereavement; or to mere brick skeletons of foundations, tentatively secret beneath mats of ivy. I think no one not reared below Louisville can ever quite grasp how the phrase, "before the war," ran through a southern childhood, re-echoing, and reiterating, a nostalgia for ineffable things. Until it had become the poem not alone of what had been lost through war, but of what had never existed! Until it was a cry after a refurbished, better world! The very plaint of Adam's exile from original Paradise! Until the Negroes themselves, their naïve regrets a commentary on those who had betrayed dreams of freedom, spoke, like the whites, feelingly—the bondsman, under the departed regime, had been at least as sure of food and a roof as the cow in the barn, the horse in his stable!

I think what had happened to the south filled me, in my impressionable childhood, with a precocious half awareness of men's perishable ambitions. Premonitions of the bitter wisdom of *Ecclesiastes* were vaguely mine with every visit to the Barker house: a large, foursquare antebellum residence which, in halcyon days gone by, had been approached along a driveway leading from the river between sloping lawns, below huge trees. "*The war*," I gathered, was responsible for the curious fact that its welcoming white portico, facing the river, had been averted forever from the town's newly cut street; so that the family residing there had to meet life from a misleading, latticed veranda which should have screened a kitchen. It was inexhaustibly amazing to enter a barrenly commodious rear-front hall through a sort of back-front door, be conducted into a presumed parlour which was nothing of the kind, and, after formally greeting "Miss Sally" (to whom a garden was a "gyarden," in the purest Virginian), find yourself released for a rediscovery of the front-back of things; where, out of sight, yet strangely open in its concealment, would be all the signs of an existence that had been on a far grander scale. There, substituted for the spare exterior presented to uninitiate passers-by, was a true façade of almost celestial dimensions, with pillars as tall as the roof of the Vatican, and small-paned, floor-length windows (they were never French doors in those houses) giving on rooms that had bedroom furnishings but should have been used for presidential soirées. The virtual estate which lay behind everything, declined, in a rioting of weeds, through cropped stretches of grass where sheep were sometimes pastured, to the River Road (which could scarcely be seen); and to water, greenly still and sinuously coursing toward the blue Cumberland foothills, misted like the valley of the Thames.

Whenever I walked into the resounding, back-front entrance hall at the Barkers', I felt myself Alice, urged by an irrepressible, exploratory thrill, through the palpable mystery of the mirror, toward the near-faraway land beyond the hearthrug: moved from a day in the early nineteen hundreds into a period in which a dream of every settler from Virginia had just been fulfilled. Portraits of Janus used to make me think of that house, oppressive with intimations of a metaphysical drama of disparity. I remember hearing from my mother that Mr. Barker, after the war, had been the proprietor of a store; I hope his descendants will forgive this confession of my early, inarticulate repulsion to the idea—

it seemed beneath him, inappropriate! My conception of fitting baronial behaviour had been supplemented in detail by Mrs. Frances Hodgson Burnett. However, I doubt if even General Forrest, the state's supreme man of action, or Albert Sidney Johnston, who contributed so perfectly to the southern tradition of soldier-gentleman, or General Morgan, who was so daring, or Jefferson Davis himself, could have saved a South entirely victorious from a conquest by expanding industry. The struggle of the sixties was an overdue crisis. If men like W. L. Yancey, who were urging rebellion years before the explosion came, had been listened to, young fellows to whom the war with Mexico was a retrospective beacon for picaresque imaginations, might have had a sporting chance to delay history. . . .

Odd that the aridly practical President Polk (who, in all but the matter of his birthplace, was a Tennesseean) should have been the deus ex machina of that Mexican episode of picturesque empire brigandage! (He and my paternal relative, Mr. Marcy, the "self-made" Secretary of War!) President Polk, commenting, in his diary, on the most romantically high-handed bit of warfaring of which Americans can boast, might have appealed to the mouse, when he recommended that Alice take prophylactic measures to save from bad colds the dripping creatures who had half drowned in her tears—surely almost anything written by President Polk might be regarded as "the driest paragraph in history." (Poor man—his demise was brought about so wistfully! A martyrdom endured through sheer sense of duty to his own acclaim!) Nevertheless, the liberation of Texas meant to the young men of the sixties what the Great War does to many in our own times, who know its horrors only cinematographically. Such, even when technically reluctant to insist on an open stand for secession, were in the condition of a woman about to be seduced, and willing; who resists, still, not the seducer, but her own fearsomely denied impulse to capitulate. When crowds flee in aversion from the site of a fire, the scene of an accident, and horror tales are unread; when movie addicts show a conclusive preference for films without gun plots, murder or violent action, there will be hope for the pacifist—I try so hard to be a pacifist myself!

Personally, I am unable to believe in the detached quest with an origin in love of detachment pure; so am bound to presume even my grandfather's resistance to maelstroms of contemporary political feeling was founded at some point in a disappointment he had received from the view his neighbours took of him. Perhaps he had sensed, in first youth—in the drugstore era—social advantage was being taken of the temporary decline of family prestige. Terrible vicissitudes can attack families in an individualistic democracy: to follow the rise to affluence of one branch, the fall into poverty of another, the fluctuations of fortune which in one period withdraw, in another, return, public applause to the same man, is an education in cynicism. The fickleness and crass self-seeking of average human nature is never so flagrantly illustrated in feudal communities where prestige is unshakable. I used to despise interest in one's progenitors, and regarded it as a wasted, narcissistic pursuit; now I interpret differently what may be a last clutching at any straw for a clue to the enigma of one's raison d'être. If the curiosity exhibited has any philosophical character at all, investigation of a personal past may be a gesture of final humility. As the problem, at first stemming from what seems data on things specifically individual, extends itself, spreading circles toward the fringes of all known existence, one returns again, helplessly, to the particular—to a few certainties! It is as if, reaching into the sea, one drew forth, piecemeal, a heterogeneous débris: empty shells, tangles of weed, driftwood, bits of broken bottle—a little assembling of recognized facts and immediate apprehensions, drawn from vast regions unexplored and unexplorable! That people can accept their politics, their conventions, their convenient moralities as ultimate reports on a cosmos, always amazes me. Fancy taking judgments made in inadequate contexts, not simply as matters for which they themselves will die, but as "principles" which demand and enforce final sacrifices of the lives of others!

Surely such an attitude would not be possible to people who really believed in death! Recognizing the little time at the individual's disposal, they would give life itself every peaceable opportunity, in the hope that something significant might be revealed. With so much undecided, they could not afford to be petty or tyrannical, and cruelty would serve no purpose!

Did my grandfather Thomas, who dabbled in British positivistic philosophy—in British materialism—speculate in any such fashion, I wonder, in that period in which his gropings after a liberal view must have left him the only man not a hero in the eyes of a community which (after the Federal invasion, after the taking of Fort Donelson, the fighting at Fort Henry and at Dover, and, most of all, the surrender of Lee) would have no son not an Ajax or Achilles? In the struggle of two factions without mercy for each other, the man who reserves his allegiance for a third unrepresented is pretty inevitably

126

destined for uncrowned martyrdom. Besides, people beginning a war are made arrogant with the élan that comes when there is a glorious escape from everyday routine. Would-be peacemakers are bound to be unpopular.

Fifty dollars reward for the apprehension or delivery of my boy Charles, who is quite black, small stature, and about 22 years old. He has a shrill voice something like a woman's, is quick-witted and good-natured. He formerly belonged to Captain West of Mississippi and was raised about Chattanooga in the house. He got a pass, Sunday evening July 17th, to see some of his old friends, the white ones of whom he was so proud. Early next morning we were moved from our encampment to Bridgeport and he failed to appear.

L. W. PEARCE,
Lt. Col. Batt. Sharp-Shooters,
Anderson's Brigade.

read the notice of a runaway inserted in the *Chattanooga Daily Rebel* of July 22, 1863. "And what have you to say to excuse *that*, Dr. Thomas?" my grandfather's Yankee friends may have demanded, calling attention to the advertisement, and reminding my grandfather of his avowed disgust with slavery. "Those are dreadful words to see set down in a spirit of commonplace, like an appeal to the finder of a lost pocketbook or a pair of mislaid spectacles!"

Twenty-five dollars reward. Ran away from the subscriber his negro boy Simp. Said boy is 18 years old, 5 ft. 5 or 6 in., copper colour, and will weigh 140 or 150 pounds; had on when last seen a grey jacket and

127

grey pants. Said boy is supposed to be in the Army somewhere around Chattanooga. I will give the above reward to anyone delivering said boy at the camp of 44th (Blythe's) Mississippi Regiment, Anderson's Brigade, Wither's Division on the picket at Taylor's Store, Alabama.

JOHN R. WILKES,
Co. F., 44th Mississippi Regiment.

the righteous accusers may have persisted. "You would think Mr. Wilkes would pay more for the recovery of a strayed steer! Surely, if you are not wholeheartedly secessionist, you have cast your lot with the loyal Union men? It is only the coward who takes sides with neither!"

I don't know how my grandfather would have answered, in this hypothetical conversation. It is utterly impossible to make plain to persons who are colourblind to all but black or white that what is actually before them is grey. In any case, the southern advocate who was bellicose and vociferous in wartimes was no more a "rationalizer" on behalf of the program most in his economic favour than was his brother Yankee when favouring abolition. In New York or Boston journals of the period, the Yankee stands forth offering himself to pure service for an idea, with never an intimation that he may be, also, fostering a practical design. If my grandfather had dared to suggest that the existence in the south of institutions which were tolerant of a white man's possession of human chattels was less significant as commentary on southern character, than as illustrative of the ease with which average beings are persuaded, by custom, to accept and excuse any monstrous thing which serves convenient ends, it would have been indignantly denied.

If he had said: "I will believe you, serving your cause, capable of accomplishing that for which you profess to stand, *only* when you can inspire me with faith in yourselves as individuals," his reservation would have marked him at once as a traitor. Those who were Jehovah's appointed proxies would have turned in disgust on the man who *dared* hint the necessity for consistent, personal demonstrations of the disciplines which are requisite preparations for the service of God!

Yet before the war, economic rivalry between North and South was obvious, and there were ample data for making the issue clear-cut. If slavery endowed average people with a power over human beings, none but those morally supermen, completely benevolent, could be trusted not to abuse; then contemporary conditions in the feudal, agrarian south provided a motive for its continuance which northerners, equally self-interested, lacked entirely. The wisest person of my acquaintance gives as his test of a hero, the conduct of a man who is in a position to exercise an absolute power. Considering this test, and the human race realistically, you have an adequate condemnation of slavery without further argument. On the other hand, it ought to be admitted that even folk like the east Tennessee mountaineers, who were southerners as well as Abolitionists, cordially hated the slave himself, envying and despising him because, in their eyes, he "lived soft."

In a final issue of "Parson" Brownlow's Knoxville *Whig and Rebel Ventilator*, which appeared as he was about to be tried for treasonable utterances before the

Grand Jury of the Confederate Court, appears the following:

In regard to Slavery, we take the ground which experience and logic prove—and that is that it cannot any longer maintain itself, after this Rebellion, in the temperate zone, and that the African race, when emancipated, will disappear. . . . And the last conclusion was, for him, a note of hope. He had the true temperament of a rationalizer: instead of stooping to appeals to passion, he referred you to the climate—forgetting there are psychological climates which are universal; hence identical for Eskimos, Nordics and East Indians. *Southerners oppose emancipation because of the negro's repugnance to labour,* he elaborates. For practically anything will serve for bolstering an idée fixe.

It was to be expected that a resistance to democracy, strong even in the fathers of the Constitution, who would have been horrified by the suggestion of electing a president by popular vote, should re-emerge in the character of the southern planter, asked to share with an illiterate, alien and biologically competing race things that had been erstwhile regarded as the privileges of kings; but it seems well to remember that the Yankee —the emancipator of the downtrodden—enjoyed the moral luxury of advocating, *after* the war, reforms that, for him, were to be merely theoretic and without a cost! He has rarely given more to interpreting the Negro generously than does the little white girl in distress who learns early to run for comfort to her black mammy without once suspecting the alien heart of Africa beats out its own joys and tragedies in that breast most consoling of all! Arguments on the south, coming from the northerner today, still, in most instances, support his

unacknowledged self-interest; even as self-interest is behind the plausibility with which the southerner excuses
the peonage which has been substituted for slavery, or
the economic subjection of the share-cropper. A lust
and love for punishment—a fondness for dealing retribu-
tions which cannot have any result beyond the further
suffering caused—seems to me unvaryingly rooted in
the avenger's premonition that he, also, tempted, will
become as the guilty.

Slavery was abolished, but the change was not always
noticeable, since darkies were as prolific as ever and
almost as dependent. They were as ready as "befo' de
wah" to contribute verbally to the prestige of households in which, if the salaries paid domestics were a pit-
tance, opportunities for theft—not to be tolerated by
careful Yankees—were a boon to those inured to pauper-
ism. In my mother's youth, it was common for persons
far from millionaires to maintain twelve or fifteen servants; looking back on my own childhood, so largely
spent with the household of my aunt, I count nine constant hangers-on. Negroes make themselves twice beloved because of the good-humoured grace with which
they accept being, in effect, sworn at. There is a genius
born of social degradation which is as inspired as the
genius for conquest and domination! Only the subju-
gated know how to make the sun of compliment so shine
for their subjugators that they will ease the terms of
the injustice the improvident flatterer, living in the moment, undoubtedly prolongs for himself by his mis-
placed art. As for the white, his way of surviving what
is inescapably a tragic dilemma is to interpret it humorously: obliged to confront the consequences of an
unpremeditated ancestral crime, he evades a solution by

making the Negro a comic figure. For, though it is said Rabelais died laughing, it remains to be proved that any man, really, ever met his end because of a joke he himself enjoyed.

Probably circumstances which confer on individuals the exclusive power to dispense kindness are a more insidious encouragement to tyrants than are situations which permit unchecked displays of brutality. I am not, I think, tyrannically disposed, yet during the last, more prosperous years of the six I lived in Brazil, I had to fight self-complaisance whenever I opened the doors of our kitchen to the wives, children, aunts and cousins of our small domestic staff. Hospitality, I had determined, was to be unlimited for so long as the beans and manioc meal held out; and those who appreciated the luck which had cast a fool in their path, genuflected before me with such devoutness as only good appetites could have inspired. Surrounded by so great a respect, so easily purchased, it was difficult for me to enter the servants' quarters without being tempted to mistake the source of a nearly effortless generosity for the impulse which had fired Saint Elizabeth, stirred Saint Joan to action, or sent Bridget to martyrdom! Feudalism, to the Yankee, to the westerner, is a mere spectacle, chartering unmoral privilege; but to those with a social conscience whom chance has led to dwell in feudal pomp and state, it is a masque of the Devil, at which Satan is the messiah! You cannot voice the most insignificant wish without starting up a brace of sycophantish coloured people bent on insuring their own survival by ruining your decent character! Without the Negro to assist, the southern myth, in every respect in which it is falsely, magniloquently self-flattering, would have broken down

132

long ago! How absurd of the northern idealist to suppose men were to be made free by a mere proclamation! Fortunately, slavery was the development of mores which were dying at the commencement of the Civil War, and continue to die; but they are not yet dead.

As the behaviour of subjugate sexes and subjugate races—even of subjugate classes not yet conscious of potential power to be directly enforced—is, in a broad sense, indistinguishable, it is, perhaps, not surprising that ex-slaves of the female gender were better than their male prototypes at exercising talents cultivated in weakness; or that white gentlemen rather than white ladies responded to the effects. . . . In my grandfather's day, in my mother's day, a certain gentleman whose high standing was known all over the south, entered into a convenient relation with a handsome dark-skinned woman who was the family cook; provided her with a residence on his own property, and co-operated with her to produce a coffee-coloured progeny; the situation arousing only a mildly questioning, discreet interest in those who were spectators of these lightly veiled events. The tolerance of society was made easy through a gratitude natural to socially orthodox people anywhere when they are not obliged to recognize publicly the conduct of one of their own kind guilty of incorrect behaviour: Mr. Y. (and I tread softly—almost as if I were introducing into a Russian novel the well-known figures of old Prince X. and the inimitable Grand Duchess Q.!) embarrassed nobody by insisting on equality for his left-handed offspring; did not educate them; and was satisfied when the eldest of the brood marked with the bar sinister, found a vocation as body servant to his own legitimate half brother. You were at liberty, if you liked, to pretend the mulatto's light complexion the result of a potion given his mother by a voodoo midwife.

A contrast to Mr. X. was a certain congressman I will call Mr. P., who was known about Washington, and gave a similar mésalliance a notorious character by supporting his illicit ménage openly; until even gentlemen with a flair for gallantry regarded askance a man who not only kept a mulatto mistress in an aboveboard way, but sent a biscuit-brown daughter north to a conservatory of music and biscuit-brown sons to the best schools available to members of their race. My grandfather, I am proud to report, went to the last extreme of the cautious defiance of which he was capable, by defending, in the teeth of censorious, die-hard provincials, the gentleman in question, who was his personal friend. Mr. P.'s stubborn insistence on compromise justice, at one time, almost threatened the demolition of his political career.

I heard these things in my early youth from a lady temperamentally distrustful of individuals, but as uncritically accepting of social institutions (even those sanctioned by custom, and not dignified by law) as a child or an idiot. Though she had witnessed these things, her faith was not disturbed. My own (then of a narrow, almost puritanical sort, radically exemplary) was shattered. I conceded nothing that could excuse gentlemen who took mistresses from a social stratum so inferior they dared discount, in their involvements, all the usual obligations of duty which rob sex affairs between equals of original pagan attractiveness. And it never occurred to me that the women implicated, considering how little they had to lose at any time, might, as individuals, actually gain in their betrayal by masters who turned out good providers. I condemned "on principle"; and, in principle, was, I think, right. At any rate, I still regard conviction as the beginning of integrity; so that it is probably better to measure by a wrong standard purely accepted and unequivocally treasured, than to wish, merely, to *seem* right according to some measure of convenience which may vary from year to year, or even day to day. Though perhaps if I had inherited the house I was born in, and tradition with it, I would never have learned to be critical!

My girl cousins, who were the true heirs, invited to drive in flower-decked carriages reserved for "sponsors" at Confederate reunions, certainly did not take the imperfections of their progenitors to heart in the degree I did, who had never been called on to enact, in respect to the "Lost Cause," a rôle like that of a star in operetta surrounded by an exclusively male chorus. That grey-clad, straggling ranks of great ex-Confederates passed in the street with no more effect than had been produced by the funeral of the town barber, conducted to his grave by the Odd Fellows, filled me, then, with consoling astonishment. When I was very young, my heroes were monsters of perfection; and I should never have expected a Roland or a Bayard to unbuckle his sword! It was utterly beyond me, at that age, to find ways of squaring the bravery shown in the Wilderness or at Bull Run, or during the immortal Gettysburg charge with the fact that many of the veterans (after the toasts drunk with the speeches), on the dispersal of the paraders, when the ceremonies were over, were visibly drunk! So drunk, and so pathetic sometimes, that even my cousins smiled at their maunderings. My cousins who were young, too; unable to feel with old people a past persistent in the terrible, foreign present! Their own eyes, like mine, avidly observing the moment; yet blind as stone in a backward glance! We children, when we encountered these doddering gentlemen in a state which made it impossible for them to recite deeds of valour without becoming lachrymose, never suspected they might be weeping honestly for a greatness dead in themselves! I am glad, today, to think they could flourish again for a while in an inebriation produced less by alcohol than by sentimental adulation and the plethora of dedicated maidenly lips which, on such occasions, were presented to be kissed. Accurate justice demands too much concentration on data, too rich and elaborate an experience of life: it is unpopular because impractical.

In England, if you are mystified by the security of some reputation of dimensions not measurable by equivalent accomplishment, you have only to look a little way behind the celebrity to discover he had an ancestor whose onetime existence explains it all. The South, with the same system, put the emphasis on ghoulish credentials from battlefields—the right kind of battlefields! That was even more important than knowing the right sort of people. I, as a child, realized unhappily that neither my relatives in the Northern Army nor a double line of Revolutionary forebears would serve! I remember a Yankee visitor before whom my cousins sang:

> *I am a ravin' rebel*
> *And that's just what I am!*
> *For this fair land of freedom*
> *I do not give a——!* (dashes were still eloquent!)

and that I was silent, lest I be accused of false pretences. The Yankee was attractive. Indeed the "sex war," which made girls of the sixties so provocative to gentlemen in blue uniforms, is so insidious, and nature has such a way of circumventing theoretic obstacles, that even today, many conquests are made in defiance of all the barbed wire in the world! There may yet be a chance for somebody to supply the apologia for doughty General Ben Butler!

6

WHEN I was returning from the Southwest a few years ago, and passed from Colorado into Kansas, into prairie fields with the sun of noon standing red over them as in the Sargasso Sea; I looked out on cabins with their little verandas in which dark people had gathered, breathless for any coolness that might stray across shrivelling wheat, and felt I, like Coleridge's Mariner, wore an albatross. Something that had been beautiful in my own childhood had been killed, and if I was not the actual murderer, I had helped others destroy the bird of good omen—helped as a negative accomplice, by failing to prevent. An increasing number of dusky faces among white, lonesomely reviewing the train as it sped by, became like a description of the double anguish of two unjust fates. Of course the Negro has been the greater sufferer; yet he oftenest of the two emerges from his calamitous association with the "superior" race an attractive object—a sympathetic and engaging victim. Though such aesthetic compensation may not be a substitute for economic advantage; the average Negro is not, by an injustice of circumstance, converted into the simulacrum of a monster—a veritable monster, at times. He at least has escaped the traumas which make the distorted psychology of the Southern white lyncher. These traumas, it seems to me, must be an outcome of the individual's perpetual struggle between impulses early propinquities make natural, and inexorably cultivated social taboos.

I had scarcely been rescued from strangulation by an umbilical cord tied around my neck, when I was turned over to one Aunt Harriet, elected in advance by my mother as her proxy for maternal offices. Thus I, in common with most Southern children whose parents are less than abjectly poor, when I had been revived, after the ordeal of my own birth, passed straight into an enveloping tenderness and solicitude which had a dark-skinned embodiment. When I was only a few months old, Aunt Harriet died. She was succeeded by a stranger, cryptic as an idol and black as Ham. She was called Aunt Belle. At the very start she predisposed my mother to a prejudice against her, by disdaining, as badges of servitude, the nice white caps and aprons which had been provided for her. Aunt Belle, very shortly, showed herself a woman of mystery, peculiarly interpreting my mother's injunction to take me, daily, for a promenade, as encouragement to repair with me (dressed in my best cloak and bonnet), *not* to the street as my mother intended, but to the *attic*—of all unsuspected places! There, among empty Saratoga trunks, dusty bound copies of the *Atlantic Monthly*, *Century*, *Collier's Weekly* and *Harper's Bazaar*, and derelict hatracks and armchairs, she would remain with me, in hiding, for hours together. I wish I knew, today, what she and I did, in that mysterious seclusion at the top of the house, where shutters were always bolted, and only flying squirrels from adjacent oak trees, approving opportunities offered by broken slats and windowpanes, ever entered the dimness. If only my psychic censor, like an amateur vice commission, had not so carefully obliterated anything which might have illumined, with a hint, impressions of beginning memory, and the secret of those clandestine rendezvous were mine, I might be relieved of the burden it is to write many books!

Alas, my mother, in an era in which medicine, still identified with earlier humanities, was hardly a science at all, was an exceptionally literate person for any age; and, suspecting Aunt Belle of administering soothing syrup to me, and refreshing herself with snuff, dismissed her. I never had a real mammy afterward! Ella Ray, who followed, was "educated," and too young. And Mammy Duke, who, when she came to be our cook for a year while we were in the North, played up to my inferiority complex, and kept the cakebox filled with cinnamon buns, gingerbread and iced teacakes which she declared were for me alone, was, actually, just a loan from my cousins, several of whom she had reared single-handed. Though her stay with us seemed to me, at the time, a victory of conformity, I realized, after her departure, mine had been a pyrrhic triumph. All that was left for the consolation of sentiment, was a black rubber doll in a pillow-ticking suit, who had been named Jake, for a servant in Clarksville who had acted as chef on my father's fishing expeditions.

Jake was symbolic: he made me think of Wade, who had been porter at the railway station—"deepot," they called it—in Russellville; but had worked for us on Saturdays, assisting with the heavy cleaning. He was over six feet tall, and true black—something rarer in the south than most southerners admit. And he had a voice as good as Paul Robeson's, like a wonderful church organ in his chest, so that the least remark he made was a richly musical sound. At the age of five or six, when I considered myself privileged if I could tag behind him while he did his chores, I think I may have been in love with him. Negroes understand children so perfectly, and, unless the exception be some nursemaid standing on her highhorse for histrionic effect in enforcing authority, never condescend to them. Wade used to converse with me as formally and politely as he might have talked to a grownup, God bless him!

I remember him most distinctly in connection with events on a particular day, when something occurred, apparently trivial, which turned out to be full of portent and revelation. It was the first of May; Wade, squatting on the hearthrug, surrounded by the Dutch genre paintings, early American masterpieces, French nudes and dying-gladiator lamps which crowded the most ceremonial room in our house, was polishing a grate. I, stiffly overlooking him, was watching with a usual, unexplained pleasure in everything he did; and I recollect it was on this morning I especially noticed his hands, which were like sooty kid on their upper surfaces, whereas the calloused palms were pale and yellow-pink like a white cow's horns. This undertint of his skin, incongruous with the general sombreness of his complexion, held, for me, an intimate allure. Wade was not really black—not all over! I felt as if I had discovered, stealthily, something I was not supposed to know, and that I was closer to him on that account. Some doubt was silenced.

We had been discussing a variety of topics; Wade, as always, gravely, deferentially, encouraging me to dilate selfishly on fairy tales and dolls—whatever interested *me*!

Suddenly, still varying attention to his task with slow, reassuring grins at me, he fell into abstraction, and was mute. Until his persistent quiet, and the ruminative sadness of his face, began to vex my pampered vanity, and I turned from him injuredly.

"A penny faw yo' thoughts?" he demanded quickly, reminded, I suppose, of his self-imposed obligation to treat me like a small queen. And I halted—that remark still had, for me, the useful flavour of wit!

"A penny for *your* thoughts!" I countered—I expect I was sulky.

Wade hesitated; his glance straying toward open windows, where my mother's best lace curtains blew, in a gay mist, across azure heavens and little new leaves, as small and curled and crisp as chicory. "Out yondah's pretty, ain't it?" he commented, sighing. I looked with him—abruptly the wanton dance of figured net befogged my eyes as with strange, thrilling suppressed tears of joy. "Ah sho' love spring," Wade resumed wistfully, failing, for a moment, to apply the polishing cloth. "Seems like dis heah's de pretties' month dey is—mah month, Miss Honey. Ah 'uz bawn in May. You feels ha'f daid sometime in win'ah, but dey's always spring yawl kin look forward to."

"In May? *When* were you born in May? How old are you? I'm almost six!" (I think I boasted.) But the thrill persisted. That Wade—so huge, so dark, so cumberous!—laid claim to any month so bright, so light, so blue and golden, and so delicate, struck me with such a violence of paradox the crisis became metaphysical! That he *had* a birthday was enough to set him suddenly apart from other Negroes—most of them could do no more than speculate about such things inaccurately!

"Mah birfday come on May de eight. Ah's thirty-five. Das gittin' mighty ole, Miss Honey. Mah mammy tell me May's a lucky month—Ah sho' ain' had no luck dis fer! But when de weathah git like dis, Ah's glad Ah's livin'! Ah guess Ah's lazy cause Ah's bawn in May," he smiled. "Today jes' make you wanta git in de new grass and sprawl, an' lie dere dreamin' at de sky until you dreams yo' se'f to sleep!" Wade's marvellous voice was shaky; vibrant with emotion. And suddenly he was before me a new being, in this unsuspected guise of his. The cool surface of my small girl's mind, disturbed, reviewed this curious phenomenon—a Negro *feeling* in *these* terms!—almost resentfully! Thirty-five! My father was twenty-seven! Wade's age amazed me indeterminately—thirty-five stretched away before me into blank regions of the incalculable! I remembered a snapshot of my father, lying on his back on a riverbank, clasped hands pillowing his head, gaze fixed vacantly in contentment upon passing clouls. Below it, on the page of the album containing it, he himself had scribbled a line interpreted to me as poetry: *The thoughts of youth are long, long thoughts!* And imagination, stunned and stimulated by the same blow, fumbled rapidly for an indefinite meaning, in which were blended Daddy, Longfellow, Heine, and a familiar black giant, hitherto identified only with fish frys, strawberry festivals, extravagant funerals and such other ludicrous affairs as were, I had been taught to consider, strictly "nigger," invariably funny!

"*My* birthday's January," I stammered honestly, depressed to think myself permanently exiled from sharing the indolent beauties of spring. "I don't like January! It's too cold, and after Christmas, and it's not any fun!" And unexpectedly, without any reason, I knew I wanted to cry.

"Yes, Jinuary's cole; but yawl kin have fun in win'ah, too!" And Wade, instantly self-effacing and returning to tact, tried to cheer me with that ready grin, which he kept for me like an inexhaustible generosity.

I shook my head, and, something overpowering me which I have not named to this day, ran from the room. . . . *Wade, thirty-five, May, January (feelings like white people's)* . . . And though I don't yet understand it, often, if I happen to glance into a sky like a blue, unrippled lagoon, or feel a spring breeze, dulcet in trees, moving about me with limitless placidity, I sense, in a temperament in which enjoyment was once confident, a cicatrized wound.

Then it is I see again three cedars near the gate of the Russellville cemetery, three trees precisely like whole groves surrounding them, bordering drives, and shading the graves—cedars that might have been anywhere between Louisiana and Kentucky, or, for that matter, several northern states! My father pointed them out to me quite casually, one day when he was breaking my mother's saddle horse to harness, and had taken me with him for a drive in the new buggy. Almost, I remember his kind hand, grasping the whip, indicating them precisely—yes, I'm sure it was three! The mystical number! Correct for three Negroes! They had hung there, I gathered, long after the mob that had put them there had been dispersed—until the great, flapping, bald buzzards which were everywhere, had come, like vultures to a Parsee's remains, and carried the flesh off piecemeal! Until the authorities, cautiously quiescent during the event, had seen fit to take steps!

144

Sometimes you enter a subway train in New York and say to yourself: Out of this population of eight millions, so many are desperate and dangerous, the chances are that, of the vast percentage who are criminals, a few may be *here*! They are hiding, openly, under a deceptive commonplaceness, their perilous *differentness*! That jolly gentleman, like the benevolent father of a family, may be a *murderer*! Somebody *must* be, if pictures in the tabloids, of severed limbs found in trash receptacles in parks, are photographs of actual things, and not wax models the reporters and police have faked! What if it could be demonstrated to you that this *difference* was characteristic of the people nearest you, those you most loved? Those you trusted! Those who had never failed to offer you, specifically, unflagging and protective tenderness! Children are logical in drawing their conclusions from the data of their small experience. If they are confronted with apparent contradictions which cannot possibly be dovetailed and make any sense, they may be thrown into such confusions of judgment as will leave them for years bereft of all standards and values. The three cedars by the Russellville cemetery were without individual distinction. It became a game to locate them. If there was any sign by which they might be recognized—any "distinguishing mark," as the passports says!—it was slight, hardly perceptible! A mole like a fleck of mud on a man's right hand! A scratch on his chin he has made while shaving! A scar by his eye—his mother knows it!—it reminds her of the day he hurt himself when he fell from the barn roof in boyhood! Yet once I had located knot holes in the cedars' trunks, above the roots, what awful meanings were there signified!

To express what the cedars represented, no words came to me! I could only hope, after my initiation, that my father, when he took us for an airing, would choose to drive in an opposite direction! If he did not, and the turnpike, springing ahead of us through a homely disguise of sun and sombreness, began to point, like an extending finger, toward *the* spot of all others—I had no recourse but to squeeze myself deeper into snug half concealment between my parents (who were talking of something else!) and try to be prepared! And even then, when I could spy out the single, dying upper limb protruding from the foremost tree, there was no evading what I knew I *had* to feel!

Dandy, the horse, might take it into his head to pass the cedars briskly; yet he was quite as likely to amble lackadaisically. Deceitful trees, warm and sweet-smelling in the green afternoon cloudy with heat; their plump, vague silhouettes lay coolly, innocently, on the fine clay dust! Bees hummed in the clover, and in the pink shells that were wild roses blooming by the fences. And over everything spread a blue sky, as blandly bright as a serene heart! But the landscape itself was against me! The azure hills, the Negro cabins in gardens crazy with sunflowers, the scrubby corn patches which, for me, were clattering jungles luxuriant as cane in the tropics, the very slattern, zigzag fences with rails missing, beguiled with calm which was threat! For how could you know where it had been concealed—that horror which was nameless, which my father called real! —and where it was hiding? And even had I been at home, and happy by the sand pile in the yard, it might have stalked me!

And suppose, when I went with my cousins to visit

146

Mammy Alice, who lived in an outbuilding, once the kitchen of my birthplace, it followed me there, and I betrayed her, who had entertained us, always royally, and was our female "Uncle Remus"? For every rich indigenous experience of my childhood is a memory of the coloured race, which was the leaven in an otherwise too often desiccated loaf! Negroes never, on the surface, censor seriously; and never, on the surface, attempt to impress themselves on white people by arguing. Relations with them create the perfect illusion of a return to nature—the illusion of affections shared and accepted on an instinctive level, where questionings, disputes and explanations are superfluous. The white man finds these treacherously congenial—he is never reproached for his tyranny. Between him and the Negro, all is as in the Garden of Eden, in the first days of mankind!

Maggie, for example, was our servant for years: she was unflaggingly affable, consistently aloof. I had to grow up before I realized our interchanges with her had a cryptic character—that she was resigned to us, and tolerant of us, not really warm toward us. Yet I never, in my childhood, talked to her without receiving fresh exhilaration from her spontaneity and her unformulated views. She was mentally as simple as she was emotionally subtle. And when her skin, normally the tint of pale maple sugar, rosied duskily; and a vivid, naïve brightening appreciation in her eyes expressed quick pleasure in the beauty of some object totally non-utilitarian, I felt surprised by her enthusiasm, just as I had felt with Wade! For Negroes in the South are not supposed to respond to loveliness, but to rest content with Woolworth finery! And when my mother hung up curtains in the windows of the kitchen of our house in New Orleans, I was astonished. Previously, I had supposed such lower regions lay beyond the aestheticians' scope. So many fine ladies, precisely aware of all that went on in the parlour, would have thought it beneath them to show the same familiarity with what was done belowstairs! Kitchens were removed—in outbuildings, like the one behind my birthplace. The Negroes reigned there: you could forget them. There, in their hideous surroundings, in the happy sloth of those to whom ambitions have been rendered meaningless, they could waste the food contentedly, and gossip out their days. "Those new folks must be Yankees," Maggie once complained scornfully, petulantly contemptuous of people who had moved next door to our house. "As I was goin' out today, I peeked into their garbage pails, and dey doan throw away a thing!" And she was a genuinely fastidious young woman, lovely—like a refined model for Gauguin.

She wanted to improve herself in a completely imitative way, and took disparaging, repressed delight in gifts I made her of old party frocks. But her native exuberance, timid and trammeled though it was, shattered again and again the mask she wore on features that would have charmed equally a Leonardo and a painter of South Sea Islanders. She was engaged—but never married—to a young man from Martinique she proudly introduced to us as "French." I doubt she had more regard than most Negroes for the white fetish of technical virginity, but there was something virginal in her spirit, at once cautious and as open as an early summer day. She died, at twenty-nine, of tuberculosis, which we in the family ought to have contracted as punishment for blindly having allowed her to work for us in such a condition. For me, Maggie is history—not, of course, in that usual sense of names and dates impressed on the young! So much that is done to you as a child is done in the dark—your own darkness, and an equally Plutonian shadow in other minds! Until you mature without suspecting what has happened; unless you see, suddenly reflected in the mirror of an opposite observing you, not the expected, unharmed face, but a distortion! Is it possible those gone before you, of whom you so forthrightly disapprove, have, after all, made you into their own image; and you *are* this suffering monstrosity?

And now, perhaps, with the leap forward in awareness, comes an emotional explosion; and a torrent of revelation, bright as the glare cast from an erupting volcano! Too bright! Such flashes of vision, illumining your own character and your own past, are never sustained! The glow of acute apprehension subsides; until you know only you have wept, and for a reason! How then do more than stammer such words as come to you, which are like a plea for absolution for others, with yourself?

When my mother used to call on Mrs. Y., a lady of conscious culture, and an organizer of Browning Clubs and French Circles, I sometimes accompanied her. Then Mrs. Y., as she and my mother sat down in Colonel Y.'s library to confide to each other the latest opinions on Racine and Molière, would issue a gentle command to her grandson to take me outside to play. Once in the garden, and without any variation, we played "circus." I was the performing animal; W., the grandson, the ringmaster. And whether I was presumed to be a horse, an elephant, or a raging lion, I always raced round and round a certain weeping willow tree, which had been designated the centre of a tent. It was the single weeping willow tree in Russellville—the only weeping willow tree in the whole world, for all I knew to the contrary! W., who wielded a stout peach tree switch, liked to abuse a ringmaster's prerogatives occasionally by lashing venomously at my legs. I masochistically permitted it, and fled on dismally—around, around, around, around! Where everything was weeping, to allow myself to be made even more completely miserable, perfected an aesthetic mood.

Though white people were the immediate cause of the depressions of my childhood, it was the perpetual contact with Negroes which cultivated in me those appreciative melancholies that are, romantically speaking, worth while; for the musical background coloured people give to their griefs became, in a fashion more removed, mine, also. I think I never awoke in Clarksville except to the sound of some female voice whining, in a high, minor key:

> H'it's de ole ship o' Zion,
> H'it's de ole ship o' Zion,
> H'it's de ole ship o' Zion—
> Acomin' faw to ca'y me home!

Or *De Ole-Time Religion!* Or *Steal Away!* Or *Rocks an' You Mountains!* Or *I Got a Home in de Rock!* The room my mother and myself occupied at my aunt's opened on a broad rear veranda from which there was access to the kitchen, too; and Mammy Alice, who, because of her age, had been officially retired from domestic service, and, because of her energetic temperament, could no more remain idle than she could get on com-

150

fortably with whatever coloured woman happened to be the presiding cook in that huge and harassing household, used, of a morning, to seek expression in the open; and from daybreak onwards occupied herself in some manner which necessitated a great banging of buckets, clattering of brooms and slopping of water, at the distance of only a few yards from where we were trying to sleep. This devotion to industry was accompanied by song, and was a frantic exasperation to my mother. I, on the contrary, having been packed off to bed at half past eight or nine the night before, would be wide-eyed when Mammy Alice began her exhortations to the dawn. And I would be glad of her shrilly invisible human debut, which was a grateful distraction from another noise—remote, dehumanized, regular, terrifying—to which I had roused earlier. A sound which was like the faint, methodical, brazen gasping of an exhausted dragon! Or like the thump-thump of a stoically suffering heart! Or the thudding, back and forth, of a pendulum (I used sometimes to think of Poe's story), which I imagined swinging in the nothingness, in the deserted outdoors; describing, as its arcs contracted, the gradual encroachment of inescapable doom!

Literalists had given me the explanation of this mechanical breathing which, all night long, and every night, agitated a world otherwise emptily at peace; but their matter-of-fact dismissals of my panics had helped me not a bit. To know that this mechanized labouring accompanied every run of iron at the Helen Furnace on the Red River Road, only supplied fancy with an ominous envisagement of molten blood, glowing and sputtering, coursing painfully through cold, constricting arteries. Again and again, I would start from my dreams, to lie for minutes—hours!—under the clammy oppression of that Frankenstein respiration, which was everlasting, tireless. Nothing broke in upon it, unless a train, rumbling below the wooden bridge across Madison Street, spoke for me—with a shriek from a freight whistle, a moan from the express!—the very extremity of my own unnamable fear! But the train rushed off; my mother, beside me, preserved composure with obliviousness. And I could only fix the gaze of one starving in the direction of obliterated windows, and wait for the day. I hate the crow of a rooster more than any sound on earth! When grey light began its exposure of a two-dimensional world—everything in the room looked flat and colourless—roosters would begin disconnected, idiotic clamourings, initiating their own cold, vapid discontents.

Until finally, just as a first spark of sun glittered in the slats of the tightly bolted shutters—as though somebody outside had struck a match!—a quavering, minor *human* voice would announce suddenly, from the back porch: *Done found mah lost sheep!* the melody at once a threnody and a paean!

And I would feel a tingling all over me, ecstatic though still fearful, as if (the comparison of experiences came to me lately) I had plunged abruptly into a steaming hot bath out of icy indoor air.

Swing Low, Sweet Chariot was one of Mammy Alice's favourite songs, and for years embroidered for me these early miseries; so that when, recently, a professional musician remarked to me that it was "hackneyed" and he hoped "never to have to listen to it again" (or to any spiritual), I reacted like a good Roman Catholic to a demand for variety in the conduct of the Mass.

152

And always Negro singing, whether it is the monotonous chanting of stevedores loading cotton on a Memphis wharf, or a similar dirge to exalt labour coming from the lips of black men rhythmically descending cargo from banana boats in New Orleans, or the inexplicably spirited choir practice of some chain gang, or the voice of Paul Robeson fastidiously echoing them with *Water Boy*, or the Hampton Singers (though their arrangements of familiar melodies often seem to me over-sophisticated); the cathartic effect on my emotions is invariably complete and profound. And I wonder how many other Southern children felt as I did, when, sometimes, the vocal activity of Mammy Alice started a contagion, and four or five succeeding voices caught up her tricky improvisations on themes known to everybody, greeting sunrise together with the religiousness of poets! Then something my white rearing was already destroying and sealing in me, would protest freedom to feel; and I would be elevated above whatever I, with the perceptivity of a child, had sensed as false in the provincial atmosphere I distrusted long before I grew consciously examining; and life would become as good in every way as a living immediately in, and through, what is represented by the Bible's best passages.

I did not realize then, as I do now, after listening to the songs of native Zulu students from Hampton, who came to *Yaddo* to celebrate the birthday of Mr. George Foster Peabody (a gentleman who has faithfully interested himself, for years, in the advancement of education for coloured people), that *even* Mammy Alice, *even* Maggie, *even* Ella Ray, or Mammy Duke, or Mammy Florence (to mention old acquaintances) had been blighted a little, as I was blighted more fatally.

For the friends of my childhood, though they could be graciously natural, powerfully despairing, or capable of rich, spontaneous, instantaneous expressions of joy, were already under the shadow of a century of alien constraint. The Zulus still kept whole (they will lose it, certainly!) what the Hampton Singers have only in small part; what Negroes who have won deserved distinguished recognition in competition with white people, have scarcely at all. Samuel Coleridge-Taylor, Paul Laurence Dunbar, James Weldon Johnson, Roland Hayes, Paul Robeson, and others extraordinary in accomplishments which outbrave the handicap of a tragically anomalous position between two cultures, retain, with their talents, something diluted which is of the genius of the Negro race—but even that, most probably, will not descend to later generations. Beyond the faddy exploitation of Harlem by a few whose cult of sophistication itself contradicts a claim to interpret, there is no adequate expressed appreciation of Negro quality, so always born of a genius for the natural! So doomed to lapse where cultural standards are entirely of machine derivation! We, who think so little of naturalness, confess, by implication, our own perversions.

White Southern writers sensible of the Negro do exist —William Faulkner, Du Bose Heyward, Julia Peterkin— and are creatively capable of conveying individual Negroes authentically; but such writers incline to a single interest in manifestations of the Negro's sex life, presenting as it does, to the repressed white, an attracting picture of escape from taboos. No American has yet attempted a true and adequate philosophical evaluation of what the Negro embodies as a surviving example of instinctual living, persisting in an era in which instinct and intuition, as cultural instruments, are losing their refinement with their profundity. Curious that D. H. Lawrence, who expressed, in poetical absolutes, his intuition of a way to understanding not to be found in the shallow inventiveness of the machine age, though his search for a corroboration of the natural, as opposed to the mechanized, carried him half around the globe, never turned to the people who, more than any other, could have revealed to him, and without self-consciousness, the character of his own gods!

I believe D. H. Lawrence had a valid intuition about a deep and permanent (unfortunately, not abiding!) aspect of truth; but that he apprehended only its isolated significance; being temperamentally beyond realistic concern for actual people whose impulses toward natural living meet contemporaneous obstacles. Because he himself felt pride in living simply, I think not even his origin in the working class prepared him for an imaginative grasp of degradations resulting from poverty. Besides, as a creative artist, he had a religious refuge in his own temperamental endowments and convictions. And he was a romantic—no romantic with a developed aesthetic sense will endure preoccupation with problems of nutrition! Marxist romantics, were it not that the majority are aesthetically juvenile, and, as thinkers, too inept to distinguish the true stuff of their argument from interjected emotional matter which has another bearing, could never in the world release, as they do, religious-romantic feeling in such a connection!

And when I was a child, romantically inclined, it required the concrete association of witnessed suffering with absorbed effects from Christian-Negro poetry, to make me realize the Negro had a right to resent sympathy offered without any protest against his economic degradation. Aunt Polly and Uncle Charlie Dortch (he had taken the name of his antebellum owner) were Negroes who served my uncle-by-marriage; and I, in the beginning (even as the grownups), would have found it impossible to regard these incompetent retainers as victims of cruel social injustice. Mammy Alice, in a rage, once described Uncle Charlie in a venomous retort on his uselessness: "A little mo', an' yawl'd been a *varmint*, Uncle Charlie!" The characterization was accurate. He was squat, bandy-legged like a professional jockey; and his small, wrinkled face, vaguely aged, was perpetually twisted by a sort of reptilian squint. It was his habit to collect from rubbish remnants of medicine discarded by the family, and dose himself at random. That he never showed serious damage from this constant amateur therapy is either a commentary on allopathy, and an implied brief for Christian Science, or testimony to the hardihood of a body which always suggested rusty, bent, noncorrodible wire. Uncle Charlie did not perform even desultory stable work with particular energy or marked efficiency, but I suppose if he loved anything, it was horses: he talked to them a great deal, though he was conversational with himself, too. When not compelled to his indifferent labours, he was, as we children discovered, somewhat sly, and villainously dirty-minded. He was perpetually ragged, physically never clean, and had personal habits I observed which it would be repellent to mention.

Aunt Polly's appearance was a contrast to his, for she was like a perambulating telegraph pole, "split to her ears," as the vulgar put it. She compensated for her husband's furtive lassitude with her own vigorous industry, and was as neat as a pin, and soberly dependable in relations with her social betters. But she was also a scold and a domestic bully; often, to Uncle Charlie (they had married late, and I believe both had been married before) she must have been a scourge of God very like the Devil! The pair had two children, little girls: Arcola and Happy; small and ratlike, resembling their father. Their air of supervivacity was an effect of undernourishment on people with highly keyed nervous systems and no brains whatever. Arcola, the supreme Pollyanna of these exuberant, scrawny pickaninnies, had a harelip, like a child Quasimodo. There was a general presumption among adult whites that the whole coloured Dortch family of four people won its tolerance on earth by providing continual merriment. Mammy Alice herself, portly, vigorous despite rheumatism, and a proudly self-declared "pure African" (she verbally scorned Americanization), fostered the tradition which made it impossible to discuss the Dortches except with bitter facetiousness. I can see her today, as she would sit on the back porch after a meal, enjoying her own digestion and belching tributes to Black Draught (which was her favourite tonic and concluded all gustatory pleasures), while she discoursed with relish on latest evidences of Uncle Charlie's unmatched ineptitude.

One day—I was about thirteen—Aunt Polly, who was not a routine member of the household staff, was wanted by my aunt for an extra chore; my cousin E. and myself were commandeered to carry the order for her to present herself. We started off in the high cart behind the cob, but were without definite instructions as to the location of the Dortch domicile. Though the family had always been on the fringes of our existences, neither kindness nor curiosity had ever impelled any white person to make exact inquiries about how or where they lived. "Niggertown" was a strange place, unfamiliar to the point of picturesqueness. Driving through it, I had what I now recognize to be a literary experience of a foreign race. Seeing Negroes at home rather than at the places of their employment, was like seeing Italians in Italy after having met them only on Bleecker Street in New York. A similar excitement in anticlimax came to me the first time I found myself settled at a café table and gazing directly at Notre Dame. After a long acquaintance with the Paris of the Medicis, the Paris of Madame de Sévigné, Madame de Staël, Madame Roland, Madame Récamier, Stendhal, Balzac, Hugo and Daudet; the Paris of Delacroix and Géricault, Corot and Courbet; Daumier, Renoir and Degas; Monet, Manet and Cézanne, there was—*this*, I thought! All these usual-looking men and women going about their ordinary business! In a way, they were disappointing me simply because they were real! Though it wasn't exactly for sadness, I felt like crying. Poor Paris—so commonplace (despite Notre Dame) that the existence of that other side it was concealing became pathetic, like some desperate gallantry! And suddenly I fell in love with it all over again because it looked so unheroic! For men should be measured by their honest dreams, and not judged merely according to the power of their deeds! In the matter of deeds which will have the lasting effects intended by their perpetrators, we are all defeated at the start—we are as good as dead as soon as we are born!

158

"Niggertown," I remember, impressed me wistfully with my very first view of it. Initially, it was a shock to realize Negroes possessed more freedom than a right to somebody else's kitchen, back veranda or rear garden! Staring from the cart, with an interest which embarrassed me (which I made stealthy), and seeing, as we drove by, the rows of ill-conditioned little houses brightened by occasional sunflowers, calycanthus bushes, or clumps of golden glow in nearly bare yards, I was mutely amazed to find black people at large. Glimpsing, through cracked windows, and darned tatters of Nottingham lace, faces decorously familiar to me in a context of servility, in another surrounding, was like being permitted, by some entomologist, to watch the domestic manœuvres of ants, kept under glass which defended their illusion of liberty. The sight of a woman in a wrapper and bandanna, pursuing a rickety baby as it ran away from her through a garden, became thrilling when I recognized in her a certain reticent housemaid, never before encountered divested of cap and apron. I even noticed, though without remark, the wells, pumps, and tottering lines of privies which told of the absence in "Niggertown" of usual water pipes laid from a central reservoir. And when an "uncle," venerable, hair white as lamb's wool, leaning on his gate and sucking his corncob—the last pipe of the day, and the day's summit!—deferentially emerged from his voluptuous self-absorption to render expected homage with a "Howdy, young mis'tises! Howdy!" I felt uncomfortably like a spy. A curious, subconscious process, like moral arithmetic, had begun in Russellville some years earlier; and continued; while I went on adding two and two and two and two—computing sums I never named!

It was the beginning of winter, that day when my cousin and myself went in quest of Aunt Polly; and, learning that she and Uncle Charlie had removed to the country, drove along smartly, between dead hedgerows, gullies a wreck of dry weeds, and fields stripped of tobacco and now only flat, uncompromising earth. Though the afternoon held grey suspense, and snowflakes, like afterthoughts of repressed misery, fell occasionally, we were at that height of physical enjoyment produced when good health is stimulated by a first dash of cold in the air; and we sang and giggled. We were happy—indeed we had no reason to be anything else! I think, even had there been cause for tragedy, we might have been happy simultaneously! Wretched occasions, in that period, usually elevated rather than depressed us—they were oftenest high drama! The very alive, for whom there can never be too much life, experience even sadness with insatiable gusto; and in those days, when the bitterest wind only whipped the blood and made it more speaking, I rarely felt my chains. There were few motorcars in our part of Tennessee then, and the spanking trot of the cob, while we owned the roads, put us into the mood of Roman charioteers, arrogant and free with space. And when my cousin burst, with a trill of hilarity, into *Red Wing*, and I joined in, we children reached a peak in rowdy defiance to what was presaged in these sudden winter amplitudes, sullenly ignoring our joy. Nothing checked our flow of animal spirits, until my cousin drew up with a last flourish of exuberance before a very ancient two-story, log house, gale-swept and wanly derelict—a city home in its dimensions, but with materials of the frontier, already in decay for a century.

"Aunt Po-ol-ly! Aunt Po-ol-leeeee!" The rushing silence seized on her gay voice, hurling it through a shutterless, glassless upper window. "Aunt Po-ol-lee! My mother wants you!" The sound which replied came from the sawing and creaking of a broken-down gate, and from a rattle of loose shingle on the roof of a collapsing tobacco barn, so bent in the middle it was like a camel kneeling. Must we climb out and knock? We resented errands. It was Happy who appeared, so unexpectedly it was as if she had crawled from among the stilt foundations of the swaying old building. She wore an adult sweater, dirty-brown, riddled with holes, and fastened with safety pins across a chest I knew to be a basket of bones. A greasy woolen tam o' shanter, too large for her, had been pulled over her "ropped" wool, and it half engulfed her face which the cold had greyed until it was the colour of a withered plum. As she raced toward us, knock-kneed, spindly, her ribbed stockings, so worn they looked moth-eaten, tied at the knees with twine, she hugged herself, shivering: and commenced from a distance a jumbled and incoherent excuse for delay. "Mammy say—" she shouted; and went on unintelligibly, sputtering and ejaculatory; her half-dancing movements, inanely jubilant, contradicted by her obvious physical misery.

Suddenly Aunt Polly, like an heroic jumping jack, sprang into view in one of the upper orifices that were windows; behind her, dimly, the vacancy of a despoiled hayloft with rotting floor boards. "Uncle Charlie he sick," she yelled. "Look like he got pleurisy's why I ain' been to work today, tell yo' mamma; but Ah'll leave Happy an' Arcola to mine him so he doan git no worse, an' come right 'long," she apologized grimly.

"Tell her ain' no need to fret herse'f—Ah'll be dere a'most 'fo yawl git back." And, brusquely polite, she popped out of sight again; leaving us to Happy's rambling chatter which recommenced; and to the rush of the small tornado which had free passage between the piles on which the farmhouse had been reared.

My cousin flicked her whip, and once more we started off, the brass harness on the cob jingling like sleigh-bells; Happy, foolishly ready to celebrate anything and everything, ran, for a little, gigglingly beside us, until pursuit was hopeless. Again we tried to be boisterous. I don't know what went through my cousin's thoughts, but I struggled with vague, unaccustomed depression. Why, for instance, hadn't we offered to give Aunt Polly a lift to her destination? In those days, when a certain type of vague reflection crossed my mind, I tried to forget it. I wanted so much to be liked, and I had already been made aware that the mention of certain topics put grit into every interchange. Abruptly I felt, all about me, a dread, a chill, a mystery created by the unelucidated spectacle of poverty! And in that instant, though my own predicament was blind, and I was nearly wordless, I began to wear the albatross.

I remembered an incident in the far past of a child of thirteen—something that had happened when I was only five or six; once, when my mother, righteously excited by a theft of clothing, marched me with her to the remote cabin of Aunt Elvira, our laundress, whom she held responsible for the disappearance of two "brand new" blue and pink flannelette nightgowns belonging to me. Aunt Elvira lived by the railway line, and indignation made my mother dangerously adventurous: despising the turnpike, she took a short cut across a trestle, where crossties, to my short legs, seemed miles apart. Until our hair-breadth progress concluded with what was, for me, a triple reward; and we found ourselves in the kind of crazy little garden I have loved ever since; where sunflowers, large as dinner plates, the seeds at their enormous cores so heavy the stalks like trunks of young saplings barely supported them, mingled with bleeding hearts, lady's-slippers, wonderful touch-me-nots (Aunt Elvira demonstrated to me how the pods protested and exploded like firecrackers with the least pressure), and mad jumbles of red ramblers and undistinguished little pink climbing roses; and there was honeysuckle, and tuberose, and passionflower (the cross and the purple-fringed, royal napkin flecked with blood were here explained to me for the first time), until, for me, with my nose as useful as a dog's, breathing in so many perfumes became epicurean drunkenness. And there followed, after the garden, which should have belonged to a cottage made of sugar and marzipan, our introduction into a strange little shack—it was no more! —filled with bitter aromas (woodsmoke, Negroes' bodies and boiling laundry supplied it), and as steamy as the Marsh Woman's Brewery in Hans Andersen's tale. And it was revealed to me that a house actually existed made snug from top to bottom by amateur wallpapering, utilizing numberless copies of the Louisville *Courier-Journal* pasted end to end. And Aunt Elvira's husband was discovered apologetically doing nothing (my mother dubbed him "the gentleman of the plush rocker," after a story of that name). And we were entertained with an Oriental deference and elaborateness of humble hospitality; and shown Aunt Elvira's patchwork quilts, all as gaudy as her horticulture, and each one, I suspect, a

163

masterpiece. Until, as we prepared for departure (my mother with a large bouquet), I was presented with a small and hideous China dog, which I had tactlessly admired where it had reposed on a shelf, amidst souvenir mugs and coloured pictures of Niagara Falls; and could hardly believe in the good fortune which gave me ownership of a thing so rare and astoundingly precious!

All these experiences—in sum, an Odyssey—a Nibelungenlied!—yet my mother, when we arrived at home again, was still annoyed; and rated Aunt Elvira because my pink and blue flannelette nightgowns had not been produced! And many bitter things were said about the Negro race; still more bitter things felt, forcing, ultimately, a climax of drama which is the sequel to this story. For Aunt Elvira, class-conscious though she may have been, was race-conscious to an even greater degree; and was afflicted by the self-righteousness which invariably torments people who feel victimized by prevalent social attitudes: she could not endure to have it hinted of her that she, a respectable coloured woman, had stolen anything! Not even the solidarity with which the poor instinctively defend their poverty against the arrogance of the rich, restrained her tongue when she had to meet a positive accusation! She had *not* stolen; to prove it, she blurted malicious suspicions as to the culprit's identity. Her reckless charges were passed on to a local policeman; and the guilty party—a white boy of twelve— was caught in a state more than red-handed: he was actually wearing one of my nightgowns as a daytime shirt!

Both nightgowns were, in fact, recovered—not that my mother would ever risk pollution for my well-bathed skin by allowing me, ever again, to don these desecrated garments. Even after long stewing in a clothes boiler, they were considered unfit, and given away. And I will say for my parents, that the thief, who belonged to a half-starving family Aunt Elvira herself sanctimoniously condemned as riffraff, was never prosecuted. Yet often, and for many months thereafter, I inclined to rouse in the loneliest hours of the morning, just before dawn, trembling and frightened by some dream I had had about a little poor child who was hungry, wearing a dreadful flannelette dress like the robe of an angel, but stained and roughened by many washings that had turned it a bilious, yellowy blue suggesting tobacco-stained spittle. I knew too well the definite stand my parents took in distinguishing between "right" and "wrong"; and there was nobody to comfort me!

> *O Pilate's wife she hed a dream!*
> *O Pilate's wife she hed a dream!*
> *O Pilate's wife she hed a dream!*
> *Go git dat water an' towels!*

ran the refrain of an improvised spiritual which fascinated me throughout a whole spring, once, in New Orleans, when it was repeated and repeated, with a variety of applications, by a gang of Negroes who were laying water mains along the street in which we lived. In my own heart, they were instituting a whole revival meeting. Twenty pick handles were flung into the air as by the gesture of twenty united, unanimous arms; twenty pick heads descended with a single reverberating thud into the packed mud of Louisiana; and each time this occurred, I, like some proselyte witnessing Mrs. Aimee McPherson's graphic demonstration of the three hours' agony (every nail in the Cross accounted for with the blow of a genuine hammer), was fixed again to my turmoiled conscience. For Hans Andersen's Little Match Girl, Hans Andersen's Little Gerda, Hans Andersen's Little Mermaid, had taught me to cry; and there I was, conceptions of general suffering as pervasive in my very adolescent imaginings as the signs of an undiagnosable disease; while I stood, like some Kuan Yin who had not a single godlike attribute, by the river of my own tears; which flowed out forever into a world which was a hecatomb. . . . Wondering, wondering, what was to be done, and why even the very nice people I knew seemed to care so little!

7

EVERYTHING had to go! I suppose this happens to everybody; and that self-pity makes for aesthetic disproportion, and is, socially speaking, in poor taste. However, I am relying on what may be a myth of physiology, and excusing myself on the basis of my presumption that the human body is renewed in its every part once in (roughly speaking) seven years; and that I therefore dare commiserate someone already more than six times removed from my present self, and a quite different person. Anyhow, on a day when Slaughter (his strange name!), the coloured male servant of Mrs. R., in Russellville, invited me to catch a robin by putting salt on its tail, and the charm not only failed in effect, but made me a butt for the merriment of grownups who caught me at this experimental magic, faith in Tennessee—which was the world—suffered the first of a series of shocks which, cumulatively, would have caused rifts and cracks in the foundations of Rome. The first effect of Slaughter's exploitation of a trusting nature was the demolition of the Easter Rabbit's prestige. When Mrs. R. invited me to be the guest of honour at an Easter Hunt the very same year, I attended, defended by a new scepticism, and suspected Slaughter of having masqueraded, like Baby Bunting, and capped his deception by filling a nest under a lilac bush with twenty vari-tinted eggs. After that, though a dying protest continued to rack my soul, disillusion was progressive; and was speeded hopelessly after a momentous visit to Buena Vista Springs.

Buena Vista Springs (like Idaho Springs, like Crystal Springs, like hundreds of nearly identical rude spas scattered throughout the south) consisted of a huge whitewashed, two-story frame hotel, encircled by low verandas and galleries which gave it, not dignity, but the air of a racing stable; this relatively sophisticated main structure, surrounded by outbuildings, facing as it did miles of uncultivated hills and primitive farm land. "The waters" were sulphurous; and the efficacy of sulphur, as a cure for almost every disorder (particularly disorders of the blood to which people are said to be prone in the joyous months of April and May), will have been impressed on a generation of Southerners who were, in their childhood, readers of *Diddy, Dumps and Tot*. For Diddy, Dumps and Tot, "bawn an' raised" on a plantation, where master and mistress were thoughtful of children and slaves, had, each spring, to suffer dosing with sulphur, generously disguised with molasses—it was the seasonal tonic! Presumably, while I was still very young, it remained a custom for heads of households in which the girls had reached an age to make them welcome in society, to betake themselves and the marriageable portions of their families to spots where sulphur was available in a context of formal gaiety.

Which explains the popularity of Buena Vista, spilling over, when we arrived, with anxious duennas and misses who had come with the balloon-puffed sleeves and tulle-flounced trains of their dance frocks hopefully pressed and ready for the triweekly "hops" and the Saturday-night cotillions. Eighteen ninety-eight should be remembered, chiefly, for something called a "Spanish-American War," convulsing Tennessee and the rest of America with such patriotism as caused even boys I, at five, knew by name, to buy themselves uniforms and shout and drill before my very eyes, with an enthusiasm finally involving them in mild risks of annihilation. It was a year of national victories, national catastrophes; but it was also the first year I had malaria—an ignominious year, when illness robbed me of most of my small store of self-assurance; and my mother finished the virtual annihilation of my amour propre by shearing me like a sheep of curls admired in my hearing by every adult from Russellville to Clarksville! Alas, though the hair grew back, it never again crisped and crinkled in the same way, and no one ever again attempted my favour by addressing me as "Gold Elsie"!

As Buena Vista first struck me, it was anything but the site for a catastrophe. I had never, then, lived in a city, but neither had I ever before been allowed liberty beyond the confines of a town; and I had only to venture some fifty yards from the hotel to find myself in woods where the curious barrenness under the trees, as if the earth were a floor well garnished, astonished me; and to feel (though I lacked explanatory allusions) something never revealed to a European, and impossible in England, where wheat, poppies and the loam from which they spring, are all enriched by the bones of men —the primeval character of crude country, where, even among signs of a human occupation that is immature, you are constantly reminded of a nature older than any civilization! Can I ever forget the intoxication induced

169

by the licence to make my own a sky belonging, otherwise, only to the tops of trees in forests where, a century earlier, strayed buffalo may have been wont to
scrape ticks from their hides on convenient stumps? Par-
ticipating with me in the ancient outlawry I sensed without interpreting, were racoons, possums, squirrels, foxes
—I had been told there were bears. My liberty, strangely
dreaded, though it was so welcome, caused the welling
up in me of emotions I like to fancy those of others,
accustomed, so many decades in advance of me, to stand
confronted by a great solitude; no resource theirs to
command except what each provided for himself with
his wits and hands! I used, in the end, to run away from
the giddiness induced by the gift of a life too utterly
my personal possession!

Then I was glad to return to the spring, where fastidious ladies, bearing their own tumblers, would be
gathered about a pump, from the handle of which hung
a tin dipper, secured by a chain—the drinking receptacle
regarded as adequate for children and Negroes! Then
I might even swallow, under duress (my nostrils safely
pinched together) a concoction which stank so horribly
that eggs sold by the least scrupulous grocers would
have been a pleasurable antidote! If I eluded my mother,
I gave my attention to a second font which gushed an
almost odourless, far more palatable, but less respected
mineral potion, purported to be tinctured with iron.
After the bearable taste of this, I decided on iron exclusively, and that I would manufacture my own medic-
ament; which I did; tediously collecting dropped horse-
shoes for the purpose, and sinking the nails I removed
from them into a tin pail of water, carefully guarded
and secreted in a barn. The result was satisfactory, for

there gradually appeared, on the surface of my rust-coloured solution, an iridescent scum, like bilge spilled from an oil tanker; and my faith in its qualitative virtue was fortified by the advice of a venerable black gardener who assured me it would "strengthen de blood." As this was the era in which Dr. Bell's symbolic old lady was ringing her glad tidings of "Pine, Tar, and Honey" on the back page of every newspaper (and with such vigour as has caused another writer to refer to her wittily as "Tennyson's own daughter"); while Lydia E. Pinkham, like some female Pope, was offering, as purchasable immunity from the consequences of Original Sin, indulgences to as many of the daughters of Eve as could afford a bottle of her remedy; my medical credo will be understood. For several weeks I drank my elixir privately.

But malarious humours, instead of yielding to the double attack of the superior venom officially provided, and my more original decoction, combined with them to precipitate a downright poison. A climax came when, in addition, on a visit to the springhouse in which the hotel cooled its dairy foods, I was tempted, by the way, to eat green persimmons; thus achieving, without all knowledge, a considerably increased comprehension of evil. Then "Gold Elsie," exhibited for so long by her fond mamma as a porcelain blonde, broke into boils! And a bluntly concerned country physician—the Kentucky version of Charles Bovary!—declared the malaria, out of hand, cholera morbus. I did not die, as was expected; but for several weeks he visited me daily with his lancet; and my yells, as successive boils received his practical care, were so amplified in that huge, echoing building that Logan County (and, probably, the whole world) had news of my rude awakening to suffering and indignity.

This experience of a malady profoundly humiliating to precocious vanity has never, thank God, been repeated; but it was an indelible narrowing influence as it affected my compassion for the afflicted. Years later, when my uncle went to bed with a carbuncle, his abject wretchedness, instead of arousing my pity, merely revolted me; while, for a long time, a usually constant responsiveness to the poetry of the Bible, failed me when I listened to the loftiest utterances of Job.

So I believe, are we all, as theorists, subject to conditioning factors in our pasts, so trivial, in the light of every abstract judgement of present intellects, we reject an investigation of them; and had rather ignore them in favour of more general, and far simpler, explanations of conduct, such as we find in Karl Marx. Though great prophets may be urged toward the cultivation of their talents sheerly in order to compensate for embarrassments engendered by calamitous bed-wetting at the age of three; to acknowledge a whole series of significant effects traceable to such an undistinguished infantile lapse, is, somehow, too, too unflattering to a humanity aspiring to despise its shackles!

Yet I am thoroughly convinced what clinched my position as a sceptic, and will colour even my view of Tennessee, began as an indirect outcome of boils; following as they did on the loss of my flannelette nightgowns, and Slaughter's derisive exploitation of my desire to catch robins and meet Easter Rabbits personally. After all, boils were half Job's compulsion when he formulated his philosophy: they were largely responsible for his individual ennoblement of the Jewish faith. And he, too,

172

before turning his defeat to any lasting account as a spiritual victory, had to undergo the trial of time!

At five, I had not yet realized the only way to withstand, for a while, time's inevitable corrosiveness was to become rock. Interpreting ignorantly, I remained rebellious, inwardly defiant. One day (the boils were in abeyance, so that I had an illusory sense of hardihood), my mother, after buttoning me into a fresh, befrilled frock with a sash broad enough, and blue enough to armour (*she* supposed!) the most acute inferiority complex ever contracted with a shorn head, unwisely persuaded me to seek, outdoors, the company of the five or six other obnoxious children, whose natures, like my own, were being warped by existence, among adults, in a hotel. I discovered them by shouts. All, save one child younger than myself, were boys. And they had congregated at the brink of a creek, where several were wading. I approached them laggingly; instantly, I was hemmed in, welcomed by remarks on my appearance which, from older commentators, would have been lewd. One boy— the eldest, taller, and therefore more insolent than the rest!—stood apart, teetering, invitingly barefoot, on the first of a line of partially submerged, very slippery steppingstones. At once, he charged me to show myself worthy of his contemptuous notice by crossing the creek after him. And, just *because* I was—contemptibly!—a girl, with patent leather slippers, a blue sash and other fripperies more appropriate to a French doll, I was to follow behind him quickly, shod as I was! And if I did not—! I knew the answer, even as he began chanting it: "Anybody'll take a dare'll suck eggs!" With the alternative of facing such anathematizing, my weak spirit rallied.

O God, to have learned of Job not to be provoked by a common strategy of mobs—always fond of issuing taunts that drive the ingenuous to attempt heroisms no mob ever essays! Nothing in previous experience had prepared me for the world's way of dealing with those foolish beings who take it at its literal word which calls for supermen! I did not foresee cruelty as the reward for those who charge heights, accept the pangs of enforced isolations—even heartbreaks!—yet fail, through no moral fault of their own! I had not then witnessed the showering of adulation on a single successful Lindbergh; the public's ungrateful ignoring of others who, traversing as courageously wastes as dangerous as the ocean between here and Paris, forfeited tribute by yielding up their lives!

Clark was the boy's name. I hated him; both for his own veiled caution, and because nature had given him the kind of hair, eyes, nose and mouth I disliked anyway. O vanity that can be exploited by the least worthy source of possible adulation! It led Napoleon to Saint Helena! I was victorious, as I made a perilous leap forward, and gained the first stone. Again I jumped; again, again, again, again! But at the sixth stage in my progress, because my legs were shorter than Clark's, and I had no knack for visual measurement, and had been simply going on blindly, I became suddenly distrustful of my own triumph. It was valedictory! Abruptly, the slimed boulders and my trembling members betrayed me, and I plunged! Mine was no inconsequential tumble—no partial descent! I went down like Lucifer, and straight into a hole; where I struggled, immersed like a good Baptist—sash and everything!—to my chin! *Let darkness and the shadow of death stain it. . . . Let the stars of the twi-*

light thereof be dark, I say with Job, of that day, and that instant of floundering which shattered my trust in my race! Yes, and though it may be the catastrophe, later, helped me to find my own god! If it was not the worst moment I ever had, it was the first of its sort!

I was rescued, of course; and, as if to further accent humiliation, by Clark himself, whose impudence was dashed as soon as I reverted to the frankly feminine and cried. However, once I was on dry land, and he confident he need fear no Nemesis for himself after my death by drowning, he was the loudest of the lot in cheering my departure in disgrace. And I ran, my very spine electrified by sensations of accruing shame; my soaked white dimity, like a sort of suppurating, blistering epidermis, sticking to flesh virtually naked despite it; my slippers squelching water; my wet sash, as if grief had dimmed and darkened it, trailing, like the dripping tail of a beaten puppy, after me in the dust! Ran and ran, through an open farm gate, and was in a field I had never before visited. There I felt a culprit's reassurance in a strange scene; until I was startled by the mild, torpid stare of a cow I mistook for a bull; and distrusted anyhow, because she was alive! Leaving her stamping, switching flies and ruminating languidly in the midst of her own dung, I dashed in an opposite direction; whimpering as I crawled through a barbed-wire fence that tugged and tore at my dress and almost refused to release me; until, somehow, I was in the woods, where all was green with summer, vapidly tender; and horseflies and deer flies, as thick as gnats about a stagnant pond, teased and half devoured me; and I began shivering; and sat down with a bump, as if I had plumbed despair with my bottom! And there I remained for a while, hugging

175

to myself as much consolation as was to be found in privacy; and contemplating stockings so mud-caked they were like the cracking hide of a very old rhinoceros. Until ants, whose devilish intuition immediately recognizes a creature reduced and helpless and unable to defend itself, began wandering over me with insulting insect-aliveness and impunity.

It was half past five—perhaps half past six—in the evening. Though gilded light flew upward to the treetops, the birds flitted like ghosts. Then ceased to flit; their faint chirrups of complaint merging in antiphonal, fairy-like cheeps and whispers, which were the swan song of my obstinacy. Silence and cold, rising from the ground inside the wood, seemed to be erecting, between me and a world which was still bright, a battlement, slowly becoming impregnable. I dared not linger.

Then came a second ordeal; and I could not meet it either, I felt, as, from a distance, and within the pale reserved for the outcast, I had a glimpse of the verandas of the hotel, where rows of ladies, like lines of Chinese toy, roly-poly mandarins with nodding heads, rocked and smiled and conversed with one another; their palm-leaf fans wafting air methodically, like the rhythmically fluctuating gills of a school of fish. Between these guests, and menials gossiping in humbler gregariousness outside the kitchens, I was fairly trapped. I almost decided to plop in the dust where I was and sit on forever—like the least militant of modern strikers, like Gandhi, like the Grand Lama of Tibet!

But chance came—a side door, little used, unexpectedly left open by somebody! As I raced, between Scylla and Charybdis, over a scrap of lawn, I felt myself following myself—the ultimate self of tragedy, pursued implacably by its own wet, ridiculous grotesque, whose boil-scarred face would be sure to avert sympathy! The absurd second self caused my stumbling as I climbed, panting, a carpetless staircase familiar to servants who manipulated breakfast trays. Arrived in an upper corridor, and seeing behind me dripping spoors I, as if I were an ill-trained dog, had left to guide whatever pursuing Furies, I bolted into my mother's room; and, sinking on all fours, crawled under a four-poster bed.

And as I crouched, in hiding, my nostrils stopped with the dust legions of conservative housemaids had reverently neglected to disturb with their brooms, it became apparent that Clark was ahead of me, and had brought his defence with him in a garbled account of my mishap and subsequent disappearance. My name was being shouted. People with voices sharpened by anxiety were calling me everywhere. Along the porches, in the gardens where August muskmelons were ripening; up and down passages, halls, reception rooms as bleak as armouries, I was being sought! And once I heard my mother questioning somebody excitedly.

On another, later, occasion, I concealed myself in the same fashion; but with a companion, in a basement lumber room, where we giggled and joked, and enjoyed the success of our ruse, until our alarmed families telephoned for police assistance in their search. That was different. I did not feel, then, my original despair of a leprous but noble character in a novel by General Lew Wallace!

By peering, my nose sometimes pressed into bed-springs and a mildewy mattress, I secured a circumscribed glimpse of a long window and floor-length shutters ajar on a veranda. For only a second or two, the windowpanes flashed vanishing sun; then turned pearly and opaque. A tree frog began a steady, tiny, bell-like clamour from adjacent creepers on a colonnade. Smells of cold, soaked grass and dampening weeds began to steal into the room. A bat entered, flittering staggeringly, around, around, around, around. In a no-world, dewy, and all vaguely heliotrope, a star began to shimmer lucently, confirming my worst dread. I felt settling upon me a vast melancholy. It was night! And sprawling now upon my belly, I began a monotonous keening, like a chant spoken over my own insignificance, my own oblivion: at once my Requiem and a reproach for those who had forgotten me! I, who was still the captive of my senses that would not cease reminding me of dangers to be lived through before the relief of morning! Until my mother arrived; and I accepted her comfort greedily; but with a reservation—!

As she talked, I gathered an impression that sensible devices for avoiding colds were the end and aim of man. How could I be so silly as to spoil my slippers and a new sash for the sake of a dare from a silly, cocksure little boy? And why my obstinate muteness when I must have guessed how I had frightened her? She didn't seem to realize I had passed through a genuine ordeal. I was ashamed of my prolonged seizure of blind terror, and couldn't tell her. How could she think *anybody* could refuse a dare? Grown people somehow didn't understand.

I might as well have said: Nobody understands anybody! Yet experiences such as are represented in this anecdote ought, I believe, to be an inserted prelude to all general statements. When an historian who has just remarked on the convention of nine southern states which met in Nashville, in 1850, to debate the issues between North and South, undertakes to give what are, for him, plausible reasons for Tennessee's demonstrated resistance, at that time, to the idea of secession; I should like to interrupt him, and ask to know, first, where he was born and brought up, what his childhood was like, what sort of parents he had. Tennessee, when the conflict was precipitated, and there was civil war, competed with Virginia as the bloodiest of all battlegrounds. Before listening while he elucidates this phenomenon, I want information about what happened to him when he was a little boy. Tennessee was singular in escaping the worst of carpetbag government; yet the Ku Klux originated at Pulaski, within its borders. Did he hear tales of the Ku Klux Klan when he was in school, and what did the children with whom he played think of it?

Yes, Knoxville, like Chattanooga, is beautifully located: when you turn from its environs, you may choose as you will a climb toward the blue fumes and purple thunder of the Smokies, or up through other rhododendron thickets, through a rugged pastoralness which only gradually becomes grim, into the Cumberlands. But what was the relationship between this place, and those ancestors of the historian who settled in the neighbourhood when William Blount was governor of this "Territory South of the Ohio River"? And when Blount, who founded Knoxville, was impeached, suspected (like Sevier) of conspiring (though with the British, and against the Spaniards), what was the stand taken by the historian's favourite progenitor, while scandal was mounting, before Blount's acquittal? Two famous impeachments of Tennesseeans—Blount's and Johnson's! Surely somewhere Tennessee fostered an arrogant tradition of independence, even lawlessness? And in the historian's family, how was this interpreted? Did he himself, as a small boy, accept the orthodox southern version of an extralegal, coercive, secret organization like the Ku Klux; or contrarily insist its actions subversive?

I find my own deep fear-hostility to such bodies modified a little whenever I recall the lathelike figure of old Judge Tyler, in his familiar absent-mindedness, as I used to encounter him on the streets of Clarksville when I was a little girl. He was one of the original Ku Kluxers, and wrote a history of the society's origin; and the perpetual intensity of his preoccupation with intangible matters not my concern, always affected me awesomely, as if it were a faint madness. The story of the professor who, in his abstract engrossment, politely took off his hat to the cow, was sometimes, as it went its rounds, attached to Judge Tyler, whose human side appeared at its best in his devotion to his only child, a very charming madcap daughter.

Ross's Landing was settled in 1835; its name changed to Chattanooga in 1851; and from the Civil War onwards it grew, and was important. For me, its significance is not associated with Chickamauga, the Battle of the Clouds, or Missionary Ridge; nor with the industrial expansion which followed the period of these events; but lies further back, and is due to highly personal revelations connected with the journey up Lookout in a cable car, and a discovery which rather shocked me—that the Indians, when they named the wonderful silver bend in the river "Moccasin" were referring to an outline of their ordinary footgear and not to the convolutions of an immense, mercurially shining snake.

As for Memphis, though it is the largest city in the

state, and a fine port, and there is a great trade there, by railways and steamboat, in mules, horses, cotton and its by-products; and though it has parks, racecourses and theatres; and though its history, from the days when it was a French, then a Spanish fort, is intriguingly picturesque, I can never forget that it was known in my childhood (this may be injustice) as the "tough" town of the South. Once, a few years ago, I was on a journey, and stopped off in Memphis; and found it developed into such an up-and-doing centre of successful commerce as puts a seal on the business perspicacity of men like John Overton, James Winchester and Andrew Jackson; yet as I strolled, like any tourist, past whole fresh litters of imitation Woolworth and Empire State buildings, sprung up since my days at school there, I found I was regarding Memphis as, still, the "tough" town of which I had heard boast from country youths vain of their acquaintance with a modern Sodom. I was disappointed that there seemed so few signs to indicate a wickedness which used, in my part of the state, to provide proverbial allusions. Despite streets teeming and noisy enough to stimulate to ugly exhilaration, and the lights at night which achieved, like New York's, the beholder's translation into the twentieth-century version of beatitude, there was a look of obsolescence, a feeling, about it all, of premature, insidious decay. Arriving by the Custom House, I stared from the bluff on the roofs of steamboats; saw the Father of Waters, spreading lethargically below me like some great, overflowing ennui which might have covered all Europe; heard the casual, rhythmic mourning chant of labouring stevedores; and felt nothing suggested by the evident triumph of the go-getter—only an immense, overpowering sense of the primeval, of an un-vanquished antiquity.

Even as my train pulled out of a fine new Union Station, the mood pursued me, while coaches rattled and Pullmans rumbled through a débris of stripped cotton plants in fields around Brownsville. Until it was as if the makeshift homesteads of a prolific and subjugate people; the slovenly villages, impermanently constructed of wood, and gaining nothing in substantiality from new billboards erected, coats of fresh paint bestowed on squat mercantile houses since I had passed through this region, were only holding at bay for a while an accepted threat! Though no proudest claim of a Montmorency could have been validated with proofs that anything before me had existed for longer than a century, all confirmed an effect of discouragement and great age. In the East, in New York, it was possible to feel differently; here in the south you knew the landscape would win, and would conquer the invaders.

> *Gilding fades fast,*
> *But pigskin will last!*

was the refrain of *The Old House* in a story I loved by Hans Andersen: here gilding had disappeared, and pigskin (for all the sows and razorbacks in the kennellike farm enclosures) was of an inferior grade. What I felt before me was a blight like senility on a man who has never matured. In deserted pueblo cities in the West are traces of human tragedies unremembered even in legend by any Indian survivor of today. In Kansas plains, with their salt mines like Siberia; or in the beautiful desolation of Wyoming, you can read the prehuman ancestry of the life around you, and believe Africa young. The

182

South, for all an increasing number of persons own jerry-built bungalows, radios and cars—for all the porticoed mansions in which tradition was never able to keep pace with pretension still stand!—impressed me, after my long absence from it, as both ancient in its every natural aspect, and only half-civilized. With its ripely rooted, lavish trees; its clay fields; and little desolately pastoral rivers; its dwellings were the abode of a youth obscurely senescent without any effect from time. For time was around you; and time, in its every true evidence—in all but the pettiest computations of snobbery!—had been ignored desperately! As desperately as it is ignored (more appropriately) in New York! Only the Negroes, among southerners, have the time sense, really, and apply it philosophically in living.

It was equally absent from the apprehensions of most of the generation to which my grandfather Thomas. belonged. And when he, after his dabbling in materialistic philosophies, passed on, to his children, something from his naïve respect for art (something never more than loosely orientated with his more positive beliefs); the time sense was again missing; as the generation of his descendants translated a cult of art for art's sake into mere intellectual snobbery—into that small change of pseudocritical appreciation which is no more than a cor-roboration of a power to purchase objects out of reach of the necessitous. I think my grandfather was lonely; and I love his memory as we love those who flatter us by exhibiting the symptoms of our own maladies.

As for my mother, she has done her best. If the neigh-bour who asked her for the loan of one of the first copies of the original English translation of *Anna Karenina* to circulate in Tennessee, accompanied the request with an injunction to wrap it carefully, lest someone discover her in the scandal of reading Tolstoy; at least my mother was complaisant only on the surface, and was genuinely vexed by such narrow discretion. My aunt, too, was, in her own way, valiant to a degree. She had, at the start, more talent for painting than for maternity; but was fated to the career of the mother of eight children. Still, and despite this, after she had officially retired from the world of social relationships, and had developed a dislike of emotion which prevented her from enjoying first-rate fiction, she continued to steer her own course according to a galaxy of stars curiously composed, and including John Fiske, John Stuart Mill, Huxley and Mrs. Annie Besant; and amused herself by making amateur astronomical calculations with quite a good telescope, installed alternately on the roof of the house in town, or on a hilltop at my uncle's country place. In those days, when the fountain on the lawn in Clarksville dripped sweet moisture that overflowed, at its pediment, into a Nereid's garden of little, exquisite semiaquatic flowers (instead of standing as it now does like a creature petrified without blood in its veins), it was my aunt who inspired my younger mother's uninformed astronomical enthusiasm, which began every evening with the ritualized comment: "There's the Big Dipper. In summer, it is always *exactly* above the fountain!" And she, knowing next to nothing of the business, would show me, as if both of us were laboriously spelling out, from a great, foreign primer, strange words that could never express any intimacy: "Cassiopeia's Chair," "Job's Coffin," "The Dog Star," "Orion's Belt," or, pointing to a little, milky, bleeding wound in space: "There are the Pleiades!" as if, in some glittering, arrogant crowd, she recognized thank-

184

fully—and even *though* Kepler and Sir Isaac Newton were beyond her!—faces homely and familiar! I think it was the example of my aunt which gave me the courage to meet the glances of downright compassion that greeted me, around my sixteenth year, when I "went high-brow," and was often encountered emerging from a public library with quite an armful of books. I was considered "morbid."

Once those terrible post-Civil War days were over with in the south, people expected young ladies to return to normal behaviour and devote themselves to being charming. Men who were scrupulous, and the fathers of families, dedicated themselves faithfully to providing their daughters with social opportunity. Even Grandfather Thomas, who, while his was the inglorious martyrdom of Gibson's Mr. Pipp, was never, like Mr. Pipp, meek, spent his last years on a struggle to maintain the standard he had set himself as "a lavish provider"; and abandoned forever his dream of a Europe he never visited which had long invited him with a bright beckoning. And my aunt suppressed, for a time, intellectual yearnings sure to handicap a belle; and my mother, though her shyness tortured her, appeared faithfully at select soirées which the *Tobacco-Leaf Chronicle* reported in accounts that respectfully noted the "jewels" worn by attending ladies. Until she was finally married to a Yankee, and her wedding, in the Episcopal Church, with the bells of fuchsia and ropes of smilax, described in next day's paper by the brother of the late President Wilson, then employed to write up such events. He remarked of her eloquently: *The bride looked well in train and veil.* (The Wilson family lived in Clarksville during a period in which Woodrow Wilson's father was a professor at the Southwestern Presbyterian University.)

A focus of gaiety in the eighties and nineties was the Henry home, where the rhetorical wings outflung by "the eagle orator," Gustavus A. Henry, the first senator from Tennessee to the Confederate Congress, were often to be heard fluttering, long after his demise. I remember the house for the looking-glass reflection of the Cumberland seen in a mirror in the double parlours, in which, with an etherealized feeling of shock, you explored fairylike minutiae, at once close to you and very distant; your sensations, I suppose, a good deal those of the inventor of a microscope, whose open sesame has given him the entrée into caves of Ali Baba, pleasure palaces of Kublai Khan, and jungles of roving wild things, none larger than Tom Thumb. I gather from my mother Captain Pat Henry and Miss Mamie Martin, descendants of the famous Gustavus, entertained like true southerners. To southerners, waste is a principle. And at any assemblage at which food is partaken of, absent guests must be provided for with a plethora of rations that can never be eaten—maybe a tribute to the glorious dead! Like the petrifying, broken victuals taken from a Pharaoh's tomb! Mr. Hoover, with his war campaign against extravagance, to southerners, must have seemed sacrilegious.

But to me the sum and substance of that era's culture was a wonderful architectural erection known as "Stewart's (or was it Stuart's? surely preferred!) Castle," embracing, in one flight of fancy, Balmoral, the residence of the Duke of Argyll and the Petit Trianon. In my childhood, I got, from somewhere, the pathetic story of a wealthy, exceedingly noble Scotch émigré who, with the world to choose from, had inscrutably selected

Clarksville as his permanent abiding place. Having set out from some Ben or Loch in the north, undirected by any power save that which guided even Bryant's water fowl along a "pathless coast," he had arrived unexpectedly in the "Queen City" where a design of Providence had been revealed. Feeling there, with Stevenson,

> *the sailor home from the sea,*
> *The hunter home from the hill . . .*

his gratitude to God had caused him to employ an architect immediately—a gentleman compelled to reproduce so often the Virginia dwellings of the Fairfaxes and Byrds that he must find surcease from monotony in an early-Norman orgy. Apostrophizing Romance, Captain Stewart (or Stuart), laid bare his bank account to a lady across the water (Annie Laurie's own sister!) who instantly agreed to take any high or low road to America, provided something could be done to make that country seem as little as possible what it was—as much as possible what it had never been! In a live-wire democracy in which any man may wake up one day and find himself president, were any number of masons, carpenters, stonecutters and finer craftsmen ready, for a compensation, to support the manoeuvres of blind Eros; and produce interior ornament of every sort, from the Coptic to the Romanesque and Gothic. The result of this co-operation, despite combinations of English oak panelling with decorations like those of the Mosque of Saint Sophia, suggested, externally, a motif from René Clair's film tidbit: *The Ghost Goes West.* Then, just as the battlements were reaching a height to make them distinguishable at a distance from new factory warehouses going up in unholy proximity to residential sections, their millionaire

187

owner caused a crisis in unemployment by ordering work on the building stopped; whereupon he departed— and forever!—like an albatross going to its island rock to die alone! And what had happened—whether his lady had proved unfaithful to their common future, or he had gone bankrupt!—was never divulged!

No matter that I have been told in recent years there was not an atom of fact in the story I believed as a child! Stewart's Castle remains for me (as it must for many others) a monument to love's disappointments. In its half-finished state, it was a hardy ruin, withstanding snows and winds and rains long after my mother's first youth, and my own; when it became the place of guilty rendezvous competed for by tramps and those whose devouring and illicit passions put them at the mercy of the living to an extent which made the reputed ghost seem, by comparison, a sympathetic eavesdropper. Until finally the very disreputableness of the "Castle" became a tradition, and almost respectable; and there was scarcely a housewife in Montgomery County who had not gone cleptomaniac through sheer sentiment and secured for herself, as a rest for the breakfast coffee urn, one of the tiles stacked like cold battercakes on the terrace. And Sunday School picnics were conducted idyllically on the sward below trees meant to frame an avenue for entering victorias and broughams.

However, the "Castle" enclosure, which was large, continued forbidden to children not under adult supervision, and unsavoury characters wanted for sneak-thieving were suspected of using the cellars as a cache. And when I, at ten, went there with my friend Ellen Barker, we were being flagrantly disobedient. We climbed a hill green with legend, arrived beneath towers like lighthouses, and, stepping to a sort of portico, peered into a dimness from which was wafted a smell as damply foreign as the scent of the sea when it reaches you across deserts. Within, where all seemed filled with portent (as if the derelict foundations had been a relic from an age of Gothic horror), something was distinguishable which may have been an Elizabethan sideboard draped with a grimed tarpaulin; and, beside it, half in and half out of their crates, several marble figures (Pans and heavy-featured, classically robed ladies) probably intended for the garden, and too bulky for discreet removal by tender-minded sight-seers. A spiral staircase, winding upward into rafters, rose from the débris of ancient sawdust and fungi-sprouting plank which crowded the hall; and there sprawled a choleric-complexioned man of unprepossessing appearance, sound asleep and snoring, with a whiskey bottle at his feet!

Though it was the magnetizing report of a ghost which had drawn us, this spectacle of inebriation, satisfactorily sordid though it might have seemed to an iconoclast foe of Romance, far from discouraging our epic imaginings of the "Stuart" who, by this time, was as mythically awesome as Genghis Khan, added at least another cubit to his diabolic dimensions. Looking back into your mind is like gazing into a long cave, its dead end in darkness, where even sunlight is strange and distorting. Any ruin you inherit, and do not have to erect yourself, may be as old after five years as after five thousand.

We had a spiral staircase on Madison Street, too; and when my cousin Frank and myself used to lean over the banisters encircling the rotunda in the top storey and experiment with a peculiarly indestructible brand of tumbler, that could be thrown from the roof to the cellar and recovered again without chip or scar, we felt securely a part of our surroundings, past and future one in long, unalterable association. People I knew then tended to escape their commonplace literal embodiments, and, like genii released from bottles, take on the guise my fancy felt appropriate. Like Dr. Johnson, for instance, who, in his youth, had served the British Army in Egypt in some medical capacity or other—a fact which caused me to regard him wonderingly, as a man who had lived through a previous incarnation in a remote place. And I should have doubted the account of this former existence but for the physical testimony of a portrait of him in a fez which hung in his home—the picture of a dark-browed gentleman of rather fiery appearance; whereas the person of my own acquaintance (who had brought me into the world, but destroyed my gratitude for my presence there by his asserted faith in drugs of reliably violent action, which was equal to his belief in Genesis!) was stooped, elderly, with thinning grey hair, a wide bald forehead, spectacles, and a grim, laconic, irascible manner. The contradiction excited me—it suggested the transformation caused by a witch in a fairy tale! Either because the ghost of Postmaster General Cave Johnson and some ectoplasmic proxy for a living Justice Lurton were presumed to support the evening vigils of Matthew, Mark, Luke and John at each bed of a member of the family, or for reasons of homelier sentiment, I enjoyed what was, for me, in my childhood, a unique privilege in relation to the Johnsons, and was permitted to stay overnight at their house. Then a penalty was exacted for something otherwise delightful; and I, with the Johnson children, had to consume quantities of a special corn bread, made from the doctor's own recipe, which required it to be baked in thin slabs as resistant as hard-tack. He considered it an indispensable part of diet for young people who wanted good teeth; and thus bore out my mother's assertion that, *though* he was a lone wolf in medicine, refusing to consort with his fellow practitioners or attend scientific conventions, he was in advance of his time—the prophet, as I now see it, of a modern American religion! From things I have heard of him which would not be appropriate in this context, I think he was an obstinate but brave man.

As courageous in his way as his homeopathic rival, Dr. Jessie Atkins, who, when she rose, a convert by experience, from the couch of an invalid, to issue a challenge to allopaths, became Clarksville's first feminist: cropped her hair, put on clothes almost masculine and, touring the countryside in a buggy which became historical, dispensed pills with as much missionary faith in their efficacy, as little heed for a selfish return, as would have been shown by a Jesus or a Pasteur. I never met her, but admired her from afar, while I was starving for examples of the personality associated with great deeds. While intellectual ladies in Clarksville (there were a few) were discussing the serious novels of Marie Corelli and Mrs. Humphry Ward, and uncomfortably confiding their own preferences for *The First Violin*, or some of Mrs. Wister's sweet, wholesome translations from the German, or, perhaps, *Saint Elmo* and other works by Augusta B. Evans! Maybe somebody in a pet about Yankees would bring up the names of Harriet Beecher Stowe and Mrs. Julia Ward Howe, provoking indignations which could be shared unembarrassingly and without reflection. Later, Clarksville developed its own literati, its advance toward metropolitan intellectual sophisticatedness led by Hallie Erminie Reeves (not to be confused with Amélie Rives, worshiped distantly by my father when he attended the Mobile Military Academy, before she became Princess Trobetzkoy and was romanticized all over again!). Miss Reeves (with the double *e*) disconcerted potential admirers of an author whose works actually sold for money by being very pretty, and as much aware of how to make use of that fact as though her writings had been limited to love letters. She escaped—and into Russia, too, where she married an attaché at the Embassy; leaving Clarksville disturbed, unable to reconcile her normally adventurous behaviour with the spinsterish cast of mind it considered suitable for the staid pursuit of literature.

Then the banner she had carried was more appropriately upheld by Miss Betty Garland, who, chaste as Hypatia, never wed; and was rewarded, in the end, by outdistancing her competitor, who, at the peak of her career remained a mere inventor of popular tales; while Miss Betty herself (before slang was adequate for distinguishing these categories) attained the pages of the "slicks." Poetry, however, was no more a lucrative profession then than now, and during God knows how many years in which, in Clarksville, she was the official delegate of the Muses, she taught school. A white-haired, pugnacious, and not unhandsome woman, southern gallantry, while she was the town's laureate and a firm dictator in everything appertaining to its cultural life, accredited her with such numbers of lavender-scented and discarded romances as probably removed from her spirit the blight of soured maidenliness certain to have been laid on a female in a similar position in the North. It was a generosity extended, in the South, to every old maid, so soon as she arrived at years which made discretion superfluous; and was probably the one ingratiating aspect of the attitude which commands woman to a tottery position on a pedestal and denies her competence before the law. There was scarcely a spinster in Clarksville of whom it was not said that she had refused "offers" in her glamorous past which would have stirred the envy of the contemporaneous belle. Like my godmother, Miss Clara Stacker, with her eyebrows met together in a humorous scowl, her rapier addiction to the double-entendre (in my mother's day, her "naughtiness" had been proverbial), and her hands, so slight, so white in their perfection, it was reputed of her that she drained the blood from her alabaster skin by sleeping with wrists tied high above her to the bedposts! She had, according to those tender gossips, received and rejected proposals of marriage from most of the eligible men in the state!

But she was impressive to me, not because of her reputation for wanton and respectable coldness, but because she was aunt to a nephew who was a genuine—a *professional*—painter! His name was Richmond Kimbrough; he lived—fabulously!—in London! And he had designed the dust jacket for a novel by a British writer—Robert Hichens! And when he died young, though I had never laid eyes on him, the loss which grieved Miss Clara terribly, was mine as well, and personal! He shared honours with a talented Kentucky boy, named Clive Wilson, who, when he was eighteen and I five or six, quitted Russellville to attend an art school in New York. And when my mother paid a call on Mrs. Wilson, and took me with her; and the two ladies (their rapport established in the important discussion of the boy's career) inducted me into his vacated bedroom and expatiated before me educationally on the charcoal studies of nudes and still lifes thumbtacked on its walls, I was made to feel myself initiate in secrets of an esoteric, extraordinary vocation! Rumour further enhanced this view of an artist's life when it declared Clive Wilson in love with Hildegarde Hawthorne, who, at that time, must have been a very young lady indeed; and whether this was true or not, he *knew* the Hawthornes—and that was enough! Until he committed suicide, adding another to those recurrent tragedies of youthful discouragement we deny with a smile, while we tickle our risibilities and flatter ourselves with condescension, by reading such amusing books as Tarkington's *Seventeen*!

Just as though each of us hadn't experienced—! Unless I was the sufferer from a unique precocity!

At any rate, I always wanted to know, afterward, why, *why* a particular boy here nameless, whose agitating influence on my emotions, while I was between the ages of fourteen and eighteen, left me stricken—mute from joy as a bird unable to sing!—whenever he entered a room where I was; so that when he was gone, hope departed with him, and I felt the signs of a universal disaster, dreadful, irremediable! Something which affected me for my whole life, fixing the pattern inwardly in a fashion which must have constituted my secret demand for happiness ever since! He was killed, accidentally, after I left Clarksville for my first long absence abroad; so I never met him any more; and he can't be explained. And if he can't be, practically nothing movingly important can be—it is really all a job for the physicists, or else mystical and beyond me.

Even as art seemed to me, in a year when, arriving in front of the first schoolhouse I ever entered, I saw the flag usually flown over the building had been placed at half-mast—the first flag at half-mast I had ever beheld! McKinley was dead! And his spirit had returned unto "the God who gave it." And because my paternal, Yankee grandfather, the railway administrator, had promoted McKinley's election to an extent which included personal entertaining recorded in a series of snapshots of my grandfather and the president jovially communing together on the rear platform of my grandfather's private car, and admired, from the ground, by a throng composed of nobody in particular, I understood clearly it was a real man who had "returned to the earth as it was." And yet, as I put down a new, shiny, school satchel (containing, with other oddments, and an equally new and shiny, adored pencil box, even a book or two!), I was less affected by Mr. McKinley's demise, than by the shock it was to see the flag—the red-white-and-blue I remembered as a dance of unquenchable colour and gaiety in the sky itself!—sagging, as on a broken pinion! And I felt what had been own brother to the radiant swan in Hans Andersen's story no longer able to soar and carry me with it as upon gusts of my own ebullience! And as I stared, stupefied, at the barren flagpole, where a flower, living and fit to bloom over everything, had withered, I was conscious only of a horrible, literal vacancy; which constituted my loss! What stunned me was the abrupt realization that there was a language of *things* fraught with significances far exceeding imaginings compelled by my natural animism. It wasn't death that acquired meaning for me through this experience; for the assassination of Mr. McKinley meant very little to me, even later, when I heard it discussed by grownups. What counted was to see the eagle's wing cleft and despoiled by the skulking marksman! The one proud-flying creature that had allured me in wordless fantasies of motion, exiled forever from its home above peaks!

And from that instant forward, I became more and more aware of the precise qualities in happenings which make them beautiful to people with my type of response and limited understanding—responsiveness to what is transiently lovely, never dependable! Until, fearful—disillusioned, if you like!—we begin to cling to whatever offers hope of that permanence we ourselves continually threaten by the overintensity with which we welcome or abhor the passing hour; and, in aesthetics, seek feverishly for the classical antidote—the simulacrum of what may last!

It is perhaps, by this time, almost beyond the point to add I never found it in Clarksville or in Tennessee. Not, at any rate, among the friends and acquaintances of my parents, to whom Richard Harding Davis was still the literary discovery of a decade; and Rudyard Kipling, a young man of talents, almost a god! People were reading O. Henry with the zealousness of initial discovery; and my mother poring over Lafcadio Hearn with an interest divided between his Japanese lore, his mixed parentage, and the shocking unconventionality of his marriage. The most literarily inclined professional of the people among whom I grew up was Mrs. Elizabeth Merriweather Gilmer, who gave me my first birthday party, and was later known as Dorothy Dix. She was plump, brisk, quizzical, dictatorial and engagingly animated; kind, too, I believe, and eminently practical and sensible. When we saw her in New Orleans, after she had reported the Thaw-Nesbit trial, she was sympathetic to my thwarted, hardly clarified ambitions, advised my mother to take me out of school to travel and learn modern languages, and encouraged me to begin a career in newspaper work. Her sentimental generosity, which referred to my babyhood, brought her an unmerited punishment when I, at fifteen, sent her my first attempted naturalistic writing: a full-length novel which contained a message of sisterly compassion for the prostitute! She eluded embarrassment with a confession of her inability to read my handwriting. . . .

At the time, her return of the manuscript was the least of my tragedies—they were too numerous! Occasionally matters (like capital punishment) which preyed on my mind were symbolically treated in stories; when I barricaded moral indignations behind a pseudonym; which was Hiram Hagan Beck, after a fox terrier my father had named Haganbach, because of the animal show. The first of these tales, which reported the tragedy of a man released from prison, was sold to the *Times-Picayune* for five dollars; and appeared, in a Sunday edition, in a guise of such dignified impersonality as awed me, and left me estranged before such remote talents. And I read about spaghetti suppers given by Myrtle Reed, and wondered why she was so popular, and nobody really cared for Turgenev. And my mother and I, and our friends the Hyams, went regularly to the New Orleans French Opera House, partly for the music, but as much because of the foreign language on lips of singers and audience— exquisitely mellifluous exact French tongue! The lovely language of escape!

In those days, hearing any commonplace in French affected me as when, years earlier, at school, I bought a stick of bright molasses taffy which turned out to have a *boiled bee* in it! Then old Barney, who had sold it, and was a cunning exploiter of childhood's weakness for poisonously adulterated sweets, gained in my esteem, through his fortuitous connection with such captivating unusualness! Then his bulby face, as elaborate with warts as the features of those placid burghers who seem to have given a first impetus to Dutch naturalistic painting, assimilated the character of my furtive thoughts about him, which were on the hunt for anything at all exotic and beyond what Clarksville provided.

Beyond even what I could attain by saving, from my allowance, when we were in the city, enough to make it certain that, at carefully selected intervals, I would have an ecstatic hour of riding on a hack from the park or the nearest livery stable! And once—just once!—while I was visiting Clarksville, I had the loan of my cousin's beautifully gaited saddle pony throughout an entire day! And galloped him into an old circus ring, which had been the site of a Ringling Brothers tent; where I tore around madly, with an exalted drunken-centaur feeling! Such as I was able to revive more temperately in the course of two summers spent in Pass Christian, on the Gulf coast; when I never got up in the morning (and I did at dawn!) without whispering to myself, in a rapt incredulity, about the sea: *O God, O God, it's really there!* And it *would* be, which was still more marvellous, day after day! With virgin pines like long, Egyptian colonnades, black on the rising, blood-red sun; the beach, fresh-smelling, stealthily alive with fiddler crabs and conchs; and perhaps, on the water, where I used to row alone, a snowily gigantic pelican furling huge wings and settling its white breast placidly upon scarcely rippled acres, all a silk moiré.

Escape! As if that craving needed an apology! Especially since, actually, accurately, the discontents requiring outlets that were like forays into other dimensions were less evasions of the concrete than passionate attempts to confront it, consummating realizations which were intuitive, which were tacitly ignored or resolutely evaded by grownups. As if semierotic daydreams engendered in excitingly lovely natural surroundings were not ten times closer to a reality than the poor, anemic culture of false pretences offered by adults, with a schoolteacher's emasculated version of Confederate history! Offered to me in particular by a certain Miss —— in Memphis: a poor, overworked unapplauded heroine, whose "spit curls," refined hatchet face and clothes of antique pattern (worn for economy, probably) made her the butt of her classes; until she forced their unwilling respect by coming to school one snowy morning, seated, her high laced boots dangling and her hat askew, on the back of a dray driven by a Negro teamster. Because I had a good memory and was excellent at guessing, I had her favour for a while, and enjoyed secretly the invariable gratification it was to be liked; until several girls, doubtless inspired by envy of the marks given me, accused me of actually *studying* in order to curry favour; whereupon I confessed by indirection a rather despicable weakness, and, on a very small provocation, carried defiance of Miss ——'s authority so far I was all but expelled from that institution of learning. I wish my overt rebellion had been based on a sensible objection to a certain textbook on the Civil War, from which nothing ever emerged but the tiresome literal look of the print, and a special, irrational aversion for the unpleasant name of General Bragg! Miss ——, whose vacations, taken on funds accumulated after what must have been excruciating parsimony, were all dedicated to improving her mind, shamed me by her magnanimity, when, during the summer following our dreadful clash of wills, she mailed me from Colorado an affectionately inscribed postcard displaying the grave, in the Rockies, of Helen Hunt Jackson.

As I think of her today, she is one of numbers in Tennessee pitifully, even bravely, aspiring toward misapprehended "culture," its aims inextricably confused with those of bourgeois snobbery and pathetic gentility. Miss —— was naïve, narrow, hopelessly prejudiced against most things northern, and, in her way, very gallant. There were others in Clarksville whose escapism adopted more ingenuous mechanisms; among them a local poet whose volumes, published at his own expense, contained memorable stanzas:

> Swing, swing, swing;
> Spring, spring, spring!
> Swingtime is youth;
> Springtime is truth;
> So swing, swing, swing!

being a fair example of the wistful exhibition which often humiliated relatively sophisticated aunts, uncles, and cousins; who could not understand his nature of a sixteenth-rate Thoreau, which made him content to pass his days in idleness, perched on stone walls or apple barrels—sometimes on a curb at some street corner—whittling sticks; his gangly, languid figure a platitude of hot weather.

He had the true nature of a poet, and was touchingly trusting, distributing his works himself, and gratis, to the pretendedly sympathetic; whereas Mrs. Pitt, the hairdresser and masseuse, a mother of children, showed the realism of her sex, and combined the talents of a businesswoman with those of a lyricist; peddling her verses wherever she went to apply curling irons or pommel some beauty into condition for a dance. Though her book, illustrated with photographs of the scene, impressed me, only a phrase or two, requoted below a picture of the Campbellite place of worship, has survived my increasing forgetfulness. I remember only:

> *The dear little Christian Church,*
> *Right on the electric line. . . .*

She wrote with a sentiment curbed by a certain reticence; and it is interesting to contrast such expression with the gaucherie consequent on the more direct feeling of a mountaineer poet commemorating a bereavement in a newspaper published near Knoxville:

> *I seen Pa coming, stepping high,*
> *Which was of his walk the way:*
> *I kissed him twice before he died;*
> *His face was cold as clay.*

For this poet, definition was not so final as to preclude a perpetually extending exploration into areas of excitingly differentiated feelings. He was probably happier, amidst sinister aversions and horrid resignations, than are the moderns who dismiss dying as the mere obvious chemistry of an outworn body. He was certainly nearer the real goal of art (ignored by those misdirected ones who have failed to recognize, in the problem of aesthetics, not escapism at all, but the impulse of an everlasting return to a profound reality) than were consulting ladies gathering in reading circles to issue opinions on Francis Marion Crawford, or read William Dean Howells as an intellectual duty—ladies led astray by theories more cogent in connection with Thorstein Veblen's *Theory of the Leisure Class* and "conspicuous consumption" than in a context of vaunted art appreciations. For he was close to the real earth of Tennessee, and, however awkward his childlike articulation, to the simplicity of a vital experience.

There is a place near Clarksville called Dunbar's Cave. Today, it is a resort, with a plank floor for dancing in the cave's wide mouth, and, below it, huge artificial swimming baths—a transfiguration from the natural which was beginning in my day. But my mother can recall when the country silence there would be rudely shattered whenever a surrey, trap, or buggy from town drew up on the slope over the spring which becomes a little creek in the valley. Then curtains of grapevine streamed from the bluff over the maw of the cavern, almost concealing it. Of course people came to invade the quiet: clans from all vicinities (families and their ramifications, groups from various fraternal and benevolent societies—Odd Fellows and Masons) held barbecues there. I myself have seen whole herds of pigs roasting slowly above charring coals tempered with ashes, in an outdoor trench, the smell of succulently scorching flesh distributed through the adjacent woods. After a feast as barbarously lavish as a banquet for Richard the Lion-hearted, male guests, risking a fatal indigestion, would assemble in a cleared space to play baseball; while the women would either retire into a sylvan privacy in which they might loosen their corsets and gossip, or remain, a segregated audience (affectionately condescending toward vain masculine display), beside the sons, husbands and sweethearts who were panting and puffing and defying the heat as devotedly as if they had been workmen in a French village at a Sunday-afternoon game of bowls. But it was the small children who, at that time, best responded to what Dunbar's Cave represented genuinely, before any effect had been shown from the twentieth-century discovery that nothing is so lovely, or so natural, it cannot be distorted by mechanization in a fashion which will render it attractive—therefore salable! —to the perverted mind of our age. Children, at Dunbar's Cave, when they were in ignored possession of the slopes and heights, used simply to go crazy, and revert; rejoicing at last in the satisfaction of every denied yearning of their primitive souls.

It was on the occasion of the yearly Episcopal Sunday School picnic (which I attended in daring mood, so that I was prompted to smoke a surreptitious cigarette—Bull Durham, too, instead of the vine twigs and segments from rattan baby carriages with which I had previously disported myself in the company of certain little boys!) that I, and some others, straying into the mouth of the cavern and reaching a gate usually padlocked to prevent a further careless intrusion of young persons without official guidance, found the entrance into what was, virtually, Pluto's domain, unbarred. It was cold in there, below ledges of rock, in a shadow which introduced you, eventually, to absolute darkness. People who came to make merry used this foyer of the nether regions as a storehouse for iced drinks and watermelons; someone who had borrowed a key from the caretaker had entered on an errand, and left without fastening the gate. We tiptoed in. There were always bats in the cave's entrance. In the evening, when a locally famous Negro band, ensconced shakily on a platform on the brink of this frigidity, executed primeval ragtime for the benefit of young dancers, the bats, hanging in clusters amidst the stalactites overhead, dropped, one after another, as if fruit had ripened for a loathsome harvest; and, their blind grip on one another released, fluttered and circled, flittered and spanked the cold air with dank, monotonous wings; rotating helplessly about the shoulders of sleek boys, and girls too thinly veiled in muslin or organdy. Until even the explosive trombone could not quite cover with musical noise the gusty beat of perpetual flight! And as we—I believe there were three of us—crept forward that day, out of the glittering languor of high noon into a dense, black-velvet chill, the bats, abruptly aware of the alien, and compelled by habit, slunk, with gradual unanimity, into sombre motion. Though we could not see them, the tiny sound of their pursuit followed us tirelessly.

On we continued, bereft of vision; each of us a secret sacrifice to her own bravado in returning into this dead womb. On—and the little light from the front which, for a while, sent after us an offering of courage that never quite reached us, vanished entirely. And we were descending, along a slippery path, toward we knew not what end. In our summer play clothes—alpaca skirts and duck middy blouses, I think we wore—we would never have credited the story of a fire at the earth's core! Trying to reassure ourselves, our reluctant hands fumbled surfaces like the breasts of lizard amphibians; until suddenly the ground dropped from under us, and we rolled; and lay, all in a heap, in a place less secure and more treacherous than any bottom of a pit. For, in a pit, you can, if you will, discover what encloses you—your confinement has investigable limits! Here, though we searched for substance, what we caught at was sable nothing—the same blackness we breathed sickishly, which escaped about us in whispers and rustlings! The river! Abruptly, we recalled its underground presence! The river which, when you passed this spot and were directed by a guide carrying a miner's lamp, shone beside you in the chasm, through which it flowed, liquidly ambiguous, bearing sparks and reflections! Above it, we recollected, ran a muddy ledge, beaten into a path, outlining a precipice, over which vaulted a roof fanged menacingly with the glittering teeth of the stalactites; while, from boulders loftier than the submerged stream, wanly calcareous stalagmites, almost meeting their brothers above, bit crushingly at space. Here the cave, we remembered, contracted, as with a grimace of anger, old, relentless, and unardent.

We had matches—the reward of sin! (We had used them for our cigarettes.) Though the girl who discovered them in the breast pocket of her gymnasium blouse wasted several before finding one not yet overcome by damp; it did, finally, sputter, flare, then shine, for a second, steadily, on mica-glimmering walls. And was gone; and might as well not have been lit!

But we had recovered our sense of direction; and began crawling, deliberately, carefully, back, up the ascent which had deluded us. And as we moved on, like pilgrims of terror, how conscious we were—even we, mere children!—of the evil receptivity of the abyss beside us! Until, with mud in our hair, and dresses torn and legs scratched, we might have been crying to ourselves fretfully: We don't have to die—never! We, so alive at this instant that we shall soon almost burst our hearts with

the pleasure it is to us to take clean air into our lungs—
surely *we* can never be expected to call this place ours!
If we were inarticulately conscious of anything familiar
in that darkness and silence which wanted of us only
final passivity, we put it away, and tried to forget it and
abhor it. Yet all the while there must have been an attrac-
tion, since we had entered of our free wills.

And, again, once, when I was twelve or thirteen, I
went, early in the morning, to a place called Porter's
Bluff—to another cave near Clarksville. Since it was only
a few miles from town, and used, on holidays, as an
amusement park—chiefly for Negroes—there was no true
solitude there; but at seven of a summer weekday, it
seemed deserted; and I, and a friend with me, following
the mounting sun, as it blazed trees that were fire and
dew, were all at once before a crag-hung orifice which
might have led directly from sky above its roof into
abandoned night. The very burrows of creatures at home
in such hiding stressed dehumanization. Rust-coloured
pools by the door overflowed from a shallow stream,
which bore, in a vacant thread of untranslatable meaning, from a burial ground of everything familiar. What
lived here? Skirting cautiously the little Styx at our feet,
we advanced with palms bracing us as they felt over wet
iridescence; and we were *in* the earth—not yet of it! An
earth we even then recognized vaguely in its authentic
character, as the place of our origin! The place we were
to know best!—never to know!—to which we should
return! Feeling, above us, the weight of the land (below
the illimitable blue into which we should never, never—
really!—be able to escape!) we halted to enjoy our excitement. Until, suddenly, we had already died, and
were alone—alone as we had always been, my God;

though, being children, we were not aware of it! When, abruptly, there was a sound—so ordinary, therefore so unexpected, it dumbfounded us and seemed an illusion! A human voice!

And we peered ahead, through a corridor like a slit, and saw, where the cave expanded to become ample and lofty, candlelight consuming the shadows with a furtive, flickering greed. And on the damp sand deposited by the river, five or six Negro men squatted in a circle, shooting craps. They looked like people in ambush. The dice clicked audibly, to the jubilant encouragement of a "Seb'n come 'leb'n!" then someone swore resonantly in disappointment! Atropos was present, in the ensuing, intent quiet, just as she had been at the beginning of the world. Atropos, Clotho and Lachesis. It was unendurable! Or was the gathering here of these Negroes the only secret the cave held? Only this? Did we belong here after all?

For an instant we delayed, helplessly undecided, in this region which almost claimed us; then, stumbling, half falling, we wheeled; dashing, in an ecstasy of panic, toward an outer Eden of greenness; toward the torrential blue vacanies of the sky in sunshine. As we emerged gratefully into the open, we exclaimed loudly, as if uttering birth cries. We were so breathless, so relieved to have escaped, we were hardly conscious of transition, until we were again at the top of the hill, and walking madly along a road made harmless by a streetcar track. It was not until years later I realized we had been where, whether or no, we must go again.

In those days, though the "germ theory" (as they called it in the nineties) had attained to respectability and acceptance (in proof, however belated, that Lister

207

and such folk had not lived in vain); and though, in my first year at school, I had been vaccinated as a tribute to Pasteur, not even the prophets of that era had been fore-warned of Freud and Jung. People whose instinct was for a culture rooted in emotional needs deeply felt and actual, were not encouraged. How could they have been? Their mentors before them had been similarly handi-capped! Those experiences in the caves are, to me, almost symbolic. They represent my conception of a return into the real earth of that country—a wish for a rebirth into some comprehension of its most genuine aspects! An escape, if you will, but out of the shallow or spurious representation into something more authentic.

Poor Grandfather! I wonder how many he entertained, after the adventures of wartimes, when he was in New Or-leans handling supplies for the Confederate Army, and, whenever he made a visit home, perilously running a Yan-kee blockade, ever so much as glanced at the Delaroches and Delacroixs he had hung on his walls (as a not too se-lective reward to himself for his labours) and thought of more than their worth in cold cash! How many saw in his Psyches-at-the-bath and other Salon nudes more than fine figures of none too reputable women? The poverty of the South is sometimes advanced as proof of its free-dom from the taints of our age; but for a convincing sign of a culture superior to the influence of competitive commerce, more is needed than to be businesslike inef-fectually, with indifferent success. After the Civil War, people in the South, just as in the North, if they suc-ceeded at all (and against terrible odds) did so by a forthright pursuit of materialistic aims. North or south, the money standard was the only one which could be appropriately applied; the one which *was* applied, even by people ashamed to be caught doing so. Often it was the poor white, his wits sharpened by hardship, who became shrewd enough to profit cynically by instruction from the carpetbag era. Triumphant as a Babbitt, his pride, already wounded by what he had endured as a representative of a depressed section of society, was unequal to any cultural defence of his origins. Instead of contributing something relieving to the already general inferiority sense of a people suffering the humiliation of a military defeat, he recapitulated, with a vulgarized vocabulary, the snob's apologia; and explained his rise to fortune in terms which were a genuflection to the passing order which had held him in contempt. He felt he had to protest his descent from feudal rulers before he dared lay claim to his new bank account. Thus he, most of all, has falsified tradition.

The bourgeois, when he acquires the wealth required to purchase cultural opportunity and liberate intelligence, instead of utilizing his privileged position to make intellectual emancipation complete, if he does not, in his cowardice of self-seeking, actually descend to deliberate hypocrisy, supports only those shibboleths which can be academically controlled to redound to his commercial advantage; compromising with such truths as he unavoidably confronts by refusing to give them a name. With his educational advance toward a relative "sophistication," he has renounced the emotional birthright of the untutored, whose truth of necessity is single, independent of flaws in justificatory theory. He substitutes, for a poetry of unequivocal belief, not mental integrity, but impure evasion; his progress toward detachment rarely carries him beyond an unexamined cynicism which, neither modifying nor redirecting the content of his primitive emotions, only frees him to a further indulgence of wishful feeling.

Everything had to go, but everything ought to go— to clear the ground for a fresh start! A reassessment of cultural values! A new beginning somewhere or other!

8

TODAY, so many years after a battle traditionally referred to as "a turning point in the War of Independence," the name of King's Mountain—like a memorial to a courageous man's inevitable humility; like a hero's compliment to an unworthy sovereign!—remains to mark the spot where Ferguson died; and the defeat of his British regulars and Tory militia by a force of backwoodsmen, hastily rallied under the commands of Sevier, Cleveland, Williams, Campbell, Shelby, decided the future of a continent.

Two hundred and fifty British died, out of a small force; one hundred and eighty-five were wounded; sixty Americans received injuries and twenty-eight were killed. For the martyrs, whatever their politics, there were no splints, no bandages. There was one surgeon present to assist all sufferers; and no food was available for victors or prisoners until after a forced march.

Since the patriots of that time advertised the British as murderers and ravishers of women, and torturers of children; and were, one suspects, kinder to the memory of Ferguson than to most, chiefly because tributes to the courage of the defeated flatter the achievements of conquerors, it is difficult to come to any just conclusion on the character and conduct of those loyal to the Crown.

"Tories," we read, were to be "slain on sight, without warning," since they were mere "wild beasts." As a child, I resented this; as family loyalty on my father's side had instructed me to admire, in the ancestral line, the last Tory governor of Massachusetts. Today, when I should like to appraise without prejudice the virtues of the pioneers, and must search through high-flown allusions to "men ready without warning to make a last, sublime sacrifice to preserve the Republican hope," that problem seems as difficult as the other; and I marvel at my contemporaries, who, with data on past records of warring opinion open to them, can be deluded into believing that they themselves, in the midst of strife, will afford an exception to the rule of partisan blinding!

I can, therefore, do no more than make conjectures about the "infuriated patriots." A few things seem certain: that those men fight best who, having burned their bridges (and thus committed themselves to the invaded locality), have the greatest concrete stake in their cause; that men who fight for the future are made strong by their faith in limitless possibilities which cannot be realistically tested, whereas people attached solely to the existent, or to a retrospect, may find their convictions weakening as they are compelled to defend obvious imperfections. I would add to this the fact plain to everybody, that the traders, trappers, hunters and soldiers of fortune who had settled the Watauga and the Nolichuky owed it to their enemies the Indians that they had become, through sheer necessity, the finest shots in the world; and that the mountains themselves—those gorges and cul-de-sacs which are sanctuaries of nature to which none are admitted without becoming nature's own!—had already taught them what could be learned from a liberty in which next to nothing erected by tradition was present to support individual courage! It was literally a matter of doing or dying!

Just the same, these settlers were among the actual founders of a nation; and when you look from the rim of a precipice upon some heap of logs, mud and rubble meant to be a dwelling, and see, below a softened grimness of timbered peaks meeting the sky, all that has been the sentimentalist's reward to the descendants of followers of Shelby and Sevier, you feel a healthy nausea for most concomitants of popular applause. Beautiful Tennessee mountains, with their green, empty betraying faces—they have been responsible for a type which, in a more debased way, shows the traits which make the North African nomad impressive! In the Sahara are tribes that are the polyglot descendants of defeated races: they escape extinction by sophisticated competitors because they have decided to possess only a land into which none not hardened by desperation ever want to enter! Terrible men—yet their features, varyingly indicative of their mixed ancestry, are alike in exhibiting pride in blind, unequivocating self-reliance! Men out of nowhere, they used to come to Bou Saada on a market morning, following after the caravans; and, the next day, vanish, making south again, from the fringes of a civilization still in the French empire, into the *real* desert, where earth is enlarged beyond imagination, and man shrinks proportionately; and is constrained to become modest with his gods, where only a few threads of water silver the sands, a few palms give faltering testimony to a greenness that is for other lands. They are individualists to a degree not less than awesome when one is accustomed only to complex societies, and the repressive dependence which must be accepted for a social advantage in the struggle to survive.

Thinking of them, I am reminded of the southern backwoodsman as he is to this moment—the cracker, the "dirt-eater," the hillbilly, as his designation is, according to the fancy of the region—whose single resting place in the world may be some eerie as inaccessible as the nest of a bird. He is not, like the Arab nomad, a really free man, but is tied to the soil. Bound to his miserable patch of corn, his stalks of inferior tobacco, his field of disease-ridden turnips, as inescapably as though his paltry possessions were the riches of the Gaekwar of Baroda! More so, for an Oriental potentate has absolute power in his own domain; while the poor white, if tyrannically disposed, can only lord it over an undernourished progeny and a wife who, though he beat her without great risk of interference from neighbours as savagely retiring as himself, and though she is not his equal before the law, ceased to flatter him with her subservience when, after she married him, she herself, in order to keep the family going, became half a man.

The poor white, alas, calls himself a Christian; and Mohammedanism, if you view life from the standpoint of male advantage, is a religion far better adapted to human nature. For it frankly admits the constancy of the power lust and provides for its satisfaction in ways which require no apologies, even from the lowly! For the Prophet ordained it that every son of woman treading the earth had a right to four wives and as many concubines as he could purchase or otherwise acquire, and it does make a difference, to a man who is nobody at all, that he may still consider himself superior to any female in creation! That is, where a woman can regard herself lucky with one husband, and as many dates and bli-blis as he will give her from the handful he has for himself.

And recalling white trash, I remember the spectacle of a lane in Clarksville that had been dubbed "Strawberry Alley," where, on court days, when I was a child, horse-fairs used to take place, and alarm me, because of the look of folk from the country: the individual figures of poor farmers and their wives (people from the Cumberland foothills, and occasionally from the mountains) so exaggeratedly unique every man seemed a slightly sinister caricature of himself, as though each represented the apotheosis of an unfamiliar species of which he or she was the last relic! The effect was medieval—like a Dürer drawing, or a group by Breughel the Elder, on the order of his *Cuisine Maigre et Cuisine Grasse*! Hogarth would have been too "modern" to do the scene justice! There seemed a demarcation between these men and women and everything that had gone before, or would come after them! And the plump nags, lean nags, gaited stallions and sleek or starving mules, assembled for the "hawse swappin'," would have made a subject for a Rosa Bonheur less influenced than she by the shallow romanticism into which Delacroix and Géricault were translated by the Salon. Such fairs used to be a regional sport in Tennessee and Kentucky, as important to a local population as the National Lottery to the sertanejos of Brazil. Much of the business going forward was transacted without any passing of currency.

And, if it were a Monday or a Saturday, these beings I regarded as from another planet would begin arriving at the county seat (for them Clarksville was a metropolis) soon after sunup: whole families jouncing along in litters of straw in springless wagons; the females, who had been driven for hours over roads hardly better (for all the optimistic murders committed to supply them with a civilization) than the one by which you journeyed from Mausker's trading station to Nazeboro in 1783, erect and indomitable in wilting finery, nursing babies of all sizes, like primitive madonnas suddenly responsible for whole orphanages. The husbands, as a rule in straw hats almost as wide as those worn in Trinidad, would be in front, seated more comfortably; the older children (their numbers a credit to indomitable instinct, but adding small lustre to society) balanced the most precariously of all on top of scatterings of watermelons and ears of green corn preciously to be sold.

Usually, the entry into the "Queen City" was made royally, the mules larruped until they broke into a tired gallop, enough to have shaken the teeth from the heads of the wagon's occupants. And the little girls whose petticoats were never of a length with their frocks; the little boys whose misfit "store pants" were cut of materials as uncongenial as buckram to the human form; the misses in muslin dresses of the diluted raspberry colour known in the south as "nigger pink," would be shooed to the ground; to be followed by already-weary mothers, wearing hats on which reposed entire flimsy gardens and orchards, or else pathetically alighted, stuffed birds! Though most, with hair that looked as if it had been done up with skewers rather than pins, wore the heartbreaking, cheap finery affected by country women visiting a town; and costumes, as shapeless as ruffled sofa cushions, inclined to be elaborate, and shoes high-heeled (below the thick black stockings which were the only sort available in provincial stores before commerce began to exploit a leg fetish); there were other women hard work had made almost immune to vanity. These clung to the practical slatted sunbonnet of the time of the settlements; and to that last true garment of democracy, the Mother Hubbard; guaranteed to reduce a Venus by Casanova, the formidable perfection of the lady from Milos, and the doubtful charms of undernourished, perpetually pregnant Mrs. Slattern to the same level of utter unattractiveness.

With their progeny bestowed on the ground, mothers and husbands separated; the former herding the children before them, down Franklin Street, for bouts of window-shopping, in which stoical hearts and vacant imaginations were replenished (in the way of the poor!) with the marvel it was to see how prolifically objects were manufactured—how many things existed to be bought by *somebody!* The sexes, it appeared, were never in company unless for the satisfaction of some elemental appetite; and the men were off to the horsefair, or to sell farm produce, or make a trade in tobacco. Reunions of families occurred at mealtime; often on the courthouse lawns, where snacks, unwrapped from riddled newspapers or removed from crushed shoe boxes, were consumed al fresco.

Then the wretched children might be allowed the one incentive to good behaviour: a glass of pink lemonade purchased from old Barney who had sold me the bee. Seurat should have had a go at Clarksville on a court day—or if not a pointillist, one of the older impressionists. With the glare of high noon falling through the maples in a subtle rain of darkness (which was light, also, and brilliant) and squatting groups everywhere in the green; and, in the street, wagons and rickety vehicles, shafts on the ground; the animals, unharnessed, relieving disconsolate patience with surreptitious nibblings at forbidden vegetation, or the rich affectionate pleasure a horse can feel when, by craning his neck, he takes a vicious delicate nip at the back of another horse—it was all a *Déjeuner sur l'Herbes*, in an atmosphere glowing as with reflections from deep, clear water. There was a smell about court days—manure, sweat, watermelons, niggers, horses, mules and tobacco! The aroma of a circus—an odour of life! Court days, somehow, always seemed the hottest of the summer!

They fascinated me, yet, tantalizingly, it was on these very court days that we children were, almost invariably, forbidden the street. In sheer vexity of boredom, I used to try to provoke authority by making darts through the front gate; each experiment leading me just a little further beyond bounds. And once, after my cousin Elizabeth and myself had been offered consolation for our confinement in a permission to go barefoot and wet ourselves thoroughly with the garden hose, a rebellious dash was made which carried us, in the perishing heat, almost to the corner grocery at the top of the hill—a grocery which dispensed a certain niggardly adulterated chocolate drop we then infinitely preferred to anything put out by the popular Mr. Lowney (whose lady, with her rose and her picture hat, is like the symbol of a generation!). But we never attained that Mecca, where soda pop flowed like milk from a generous breast, and a pasty cake with a pseudomarshmallow filling came as freely from the hand of the friendly grocer as manna from God to the hungry Israelites; but stopped on the wooden bridge spanning the railway cut, where the planks, we discovered, had been ignited by an invisible conflagration. And there we stood howling—shrieking for wings! Because we could neither proceed, nor turn back! Until a good Samaritan, a stranger, picked us up, one under each arm, and carried us bodily across a flaming pavement of hell into somebody's cool, shady yard; where we were converted, unawares, to a belief in the most ecstatic joy as negative—a sweet relief from pain!

This torment of high noon, in southern towns and villages, produces general, irresistible somnolence: such places, during the early hours of a summer afternoon, are like Spain—gripped by the mood of the siesta. The stores are not, as in Spain, closed considerately for the refreshment of the shop assistants: but if you enter one and ask for what you have come to buy, your voice will seem as prominently loud as Echo's in a resounding cavern. When you accomplish your errand, and depart, you find the sidewalks, bleached as skeletons in the glare of the desert, as deserted as trails through Death Valley in the season of greatest suffering. Only here and there, on a dusty doorsill, will be a Negro asleep, sprawling abandonedly, flies on his eyelids, like a fresh corpse left by the murderous sun.

There will be no revival until, around four, sound recovers an iron tongue, and the bell in the courthouse tower, tolling as though to awaken the inhabitants of buried Herculaneum, releases a slow clock clamour that spells a recrudescence of vivacity, even to remote black people labouring in fields of sorghum or tobacco in the bottom land across the river. Then the town will lose its air of an antediluvian English village, and there will be a pioneer appearance, up the main street, of a feminine figure—perhaps a pair of them!—sauntering toward the principle drugstore! This will be the advance guard in the concerted action of every woman and girl for miles about who has a muslin frock freshly laundered or a becoming hat. Until, by six in the evening, every female not squint-eyed, harelipped or in some manner repellently ugly, will have converged on the most favoured soda fountain, before which the cars (in my childhood there were other vehicles) will be already three-deep! They have come to participate in a curious Masque of Eros which requires it of the celebrants that they drink unlimited quantities of Coca-Cola!

It was only on court days, when the very grown persons preferred voluntary incarceration to the risk corn whiskey becomes when dispensed in a crowd which has nothing to lose, that the worship of Cupid by Psyche, before an altar with a soap-smeared mirror over it, had to be curtailed. After excesses at noon, lean stomachs to which watermelon was an orgy, demanded compensation in sleep; and many of the "white trash" families slumbered companionably on the grass before public buildings; until such islands of shadow suggested parks surrounding palaces of the Sleeping Beauty, with courtiers and ladies enduring a blight of plebeianism as part of the general spell! Even babies slept, during those hours between two and four, and they are almost as notable insomniacs as guinea pigs! The persistent song of flies became the one voice of a living creation!

But at four, the men in their shirt sleeves and dingy overalls, the wives in their dowdy hats and calicoes (who hoped this—the year's single respite from girding toil in field and shack—was "takin' the country out of 'em"!) aroused to the dooming strokes of the clock as to a renaissance. The rackety horse trade in the byway recommenced. The children became playful. Women, warding away anticipations of tomorrow, tried to drink to satiation this last draught of metropolitan liberty.

In Strawberry Alley, the most conspicuous man of the moment was the professional dealer in livestock: a gentleman distrusted for his relative sophistication, denoted in his clothing—puttees, very likely, rather than boots to the knees; a corduroy jacket, perhaps, and a Stetson hat. He looked like a cross between a gamekeeper on an English estate and a professional faro player of the last century. In consorting with hayseed amateurs, he was on what was tantamount to a slumming expedition; but true sportsmen, though they had nothing to "swap" beyond some spavined, broken-winded grandmother of colts, despised such a fellow—even as gentlemen (entered so for cricket matches at the Oval) regard warily the player who has forfeited his technical right to their status.

I remember very well my early impression of an onus attached to trading in horses for a livelihood. As for dealing in mules—it meant social fatality! The man who did so was, virtually, an untouchable! Even poor whites recognized this; and if a mule trader had ever obtruded himself into the home of one of the first families, I am certain the Negro cook with a care for the reputation of her employers, had she seen the shadow of his uncleanliness fallen upon the stove and her scrupulously tended saucepans, would have flung to the ground the whole material of the best meal on earth. Hindus are not the only respecters of caste! After all, Clarksville was on the fringes of "the blue grass," and at that time, however American racing was destined to degenerate under a commercial influence, the gentleman's view of deriving profit from what is, for him, a pastime, in some measure still prevailed.

221

By evening, however, as the day grew kinder, the sun impotent, even horseflesh failed to give ultimate satisfaction to the farmers, who, urged to demonstrate to themselves and others that a man is more than can ever be represented by the cash in his pocket, his social standing, or even his ordinary acts, began wandering into saloons, emerging, shortly, thoroughly drunk. They had to prove that no man can be made a slave of circumstances except in part; that he can, on occasion, break his bonds in a single gesture of contempt for them, and become what he is—angel, hero or diabolist!

Such heat throughout the afternoon; and now, with oaks and maples darkening after the sunset, shadows in the street were dense as in a forest, and cool! Marvellous, the serenity of dusk, smelling of the earth and damp! Girls in fresh dresses, idling on verandas, looked delicate, archaically remote. Figures strolling up paths over lawns, or walking in gardens, moved with delicious indolence, as if just come, refreshed, from a mystic bath in contentment. Then farmers who had hardened their hearts against their wives and children and left them at home, having spent their last dimes, flung themselves into their saddles, and, reeling, bawling songs as they started off, rode toward the country. . . . Through the Midas-touched gloaming—through the golden semidarkness! Through the hour I used to love most of all; when, after the inebriate preoccupations of play, I, too, having undergone rejuvenation at the hands of my mother or a nurse, acquired, like a sort of astral body, the different personality bestowed with cleanliness and well-brushed curls; and moved with the rest on a new plane, above earth, in a lotus land of rarefied perfections; where even the yellow roses on the supper table, amber tea in the glasses, smells of grass and lawn sprinklers, contributed to classic harmonies strangely refining ordinary living.

I remember a certain court day when, in a twilight which translated everything into beauty, I happened to be swinging restively on the front gate of the little property belonging to another uncle-by-marriage, Dr. Drane (where I visited less frequently), when yells, far-off and growing nearer, shocked me out of my half-soothed mood of a pampered prisoner. Two wagons, bumping, banging, rattling, one pursuing the other, were approaching from the town. In both huddled women, bouncing and jolting in the straw, and clasping to them the youngest of numerous accompanying children. Faces, as these people drew closer, and fled by, bore abstracts of expression—they were blots of terror such as are painted on masks. The horror exhibited was explicable! Presiding over each group was a debauched patriarch, standing on the wagon seat and careless of driving, a pistol in his hand! And, bawling blasphemies, the men began exchanging shots. I can still hear the erratic explosions, the shrill smothered cries, the confusion of women's excited, helplessly protesting voices! Until distance silenced the Greek chorus of doom and obscene expletives; and the rattletrap vehicles vanished into a solitude where night was descending beyond the houses; an echo of crazed hoofbeats and the plopping of shot sounding for a while, audibly tracing progressive disaster. When quiet was perfect again, it was as if I had been a witness while a last roiled current smoothed to placidity over the graves of two stranger ships, just sunk with all on board.

I rushed indoors with my story; but it meant nothing to anybody. You could not prevent drinking and brawling among poor whites—life was too short! Let what I

223

had seen be a warning to me! On court days, even sheriff and marshal and the town's constable (I believe there was but one, though I may be mistaken) retired in discretion!

Curious people, those poor—aliens! A race apart, unknown, incomprehensible! As if within a limitless pale, they yet existed somewhere out of confinement, where freedom was laxity. They were the Jews in Poland, the Armenians under the Turks, but were of no nationality! They were the shambling, blear-eyed man in the ragged clothes who begged at the back door from the darky servant, and cursed what was given him! They were a "drunk" on whom my cousin Elizabeth and myself once stumbled, as he lay in the alley behind the stables—a snoring monster! They were "Sis Daly," the mad slattern who wandered the River Road: you had seen her behave with a watermelon rind like a kicked cur that will snarlingly distrust even the donor of the bone that can save him from starvation! The dread of encountering her—of having to outstare those pale eyes, rabidly intent on defence and vacantly above suffering!—made the water front such a place of fear as spoiled even protected drives taken with superior adults in the family carriage. There was Susan Stoner, too: a Negress—a vanquished but undaunted fury, surprised ringed by urchins outnumbering her ten to one, and unwillingly respectful of her marksmanship, as, her apron crammed with missiles picked from the street, her brawn and tatters defied, with the lofty glitter of blank hatred, childish ribaldries of unfeeling bullying! The poor were the chain gangs we sometimes passed on country outings; and when a sullen glance that would murder our comfort met my own, I clung to my mother for protection from such inscrutable menacing. Charles S. Gilpin, whose performance in *Emperor Jones* was a truly inspired interpretation of a poetry wrung from oppression, brought those faces of my childhood like ghosts from their graves in my own buried terrors. He could not show me how or why or when, I, so literally the product of all white anemias, acquired the black identity that made me save the silver bullet for my very self.

And there were other poor—a white family: a man, woman and innumerable children, who lived in a tiny, hideously utilitarian cottage on my uncle's farm; their status, I suppose, that of share-croppers; though I cannot recall that such a term was applied to them. We idlers, irresponsibly allowed to romp, swim, race through orchards, or spend whole afternoons curled in hammocks and revelling in tales by Marryat or Henty, or in new fairy books, sometimes glimpsed, across a yellow mane of beginning goldenrod in August fields, a boy of thirteen or thereabouts, thin-shanked and ascetic-looking, the hoe he balanced on his shoulder a cumbrous implement for a grown man, making his way into the dry remains of the tobacco crop across the road. He was pursued there by a Lilliputian riffraff of still younger little boys: half-naked mites caricatured by their own neuter clothing: a shift of no gender offering freedom to fat, tanned legs; a girl's dress, cut off at the bottom and stuffed into a revised portion of an adult's trousers, serving as a shirt. And you could see, if you watched, how their pretended assistance impeded every effort of their chaperon; who laboured doggedly, like some convict on Devil's Island for whom work has become the soporific for a self-consuming imagination nothing relieves. And when the babies under his bare feet, rebelling, in sheer infantile lightheartedness, against some order of his to pull weeds from the rows, or nip the suckers from a plant, despised his discipline, and rolled on the ground, tittering in shrill delight and exuberance, he would stand, rigid with futility, hardly able, in his angry helplessness, to hold back his tears; his pale, freckle-blotched face, while he savagely reissued his commands, as wanly fanatic as a young Savonarola's—a half-starved little figure in dim blue overalls, already as stern as Cotton Mather; as otherworldly as Saint Francis! These share-croppers gave their children ambitious, archaic names; and his was probably Milo, or Homer, or Cicero.

I remember very well one of his sisters: a bleached, blond mouse of a twelve-year-old (the flat-voiced, dispirited little replica of her mother) who came to the house one day on an errand, and, twisting her calico frock into a string, scratching at her bramble-scarred stockingless legs, timidly admitted to questioners that she was called Ophelia!

I remember, too, once, when my cousin Elizabeth and myself were driving through a district near that same Helen Furnace that had been the invisible demon of so many years: the neighbourhood around had declined to what is, in the south, the last utter stage of squalid self-contempt, its denizens equally divided between the black and white races. A woman, bolting out of the door of one of the paintless matchboard cottages, shouted to us, asking us to stop. She was so dirty, so lean and ugly and scarred by misery, she seemed twice the inferior of the healthy Negro women who were communally washing clothes in two adjacent yards. Yet she *was* white—the fine straightness original in the sticky hair hanging in spikes about her face showed it; as did her eyes, pale blue, and desperate as a harlot's. And there was the white of her breasts: slack, empty pouches wrung dry, exposed for the hungry, disappointed pleasure of a child over the age for suckling and so emaciated it was like a spider—like a little loathsome, half-reptilian fetus, with vermiculous arms and legs continually writhing and re-volving! When we halted the horse, she approached, her cotton skirt, filthy and coarse as old sailcloth, dragging, with a sinuate trace behind, in the summer dust of the road. Children came after her—more and more children trooping up! Almost as when the eggs of a scorpion have just hatched! They grouped themselves about her, and were so alike in their consanguineous ugliness—in the marks upon them of stupefactions of brutal living!—wretchedness seemed to be of their very blood heritage.

"We all's seen you pretty young ladies passin' here mo'n onct," the woman began; and went on wheedling us; hardly able, as she solicited an appeal to our parents for money, food, shoes, any sort of apparel, to keep the viciousness of her hatred for us suppressed in her voice. And she smiled with the cajolery of a witch casting an evil spell, her gums bared, the few fangs left in her head making a snarl of her gesture of seduction. "Anything yer ma'll send me I'll take and be grateful!" she finished, real tears for herself suddenly softening the hardness of her venom. I felt, as she appraised us, how her glances of calculation assessed our dresses, our hats and slippers—as individuals, we were not existent! We were disassociated, perambulating stomachs, not yet prevented from con-suming her children's food! We were strangling her as surely as ivy strangles the oak! When we were thirsty, we drank from her veins! Panicky but polite, we escaped the sugary voice which plunged a knife into our hearts.

Like Florence Dombeys who eluded further horrid episodes with "Mrs. Brown," we started off; our stupid virginal imaginations resisting outrage by incomprehensible resentments.

> *"O there was a Robber's daughter*
> *And her name was Alice Brown*
> *And her father was the terror*
> *Of a small Italian town . . ."*

begins the inspired Mr. Gilbert's account of an early heroine of gangsterdom. And very well indeed did he convey the sinister quality of a mind rendered immune to everything but the egoistic stimulus of revenge on society. Social justifications had not, at that time, been advanced in our hearing. I felt rather like Gerda, in Hans Andersen's *Snow Queen*, when she discovered another child of brigands delighting in the helpless tremors of a pet reindeer whose throat she was pretending to slit with a hunting knife! Besides, with your one preparation of cruelty a sentimental education, apologias for Public Enemy Number One will mean less to your tender imagination than the impact with a concrete hostility. We were intimidated, though we did not know why. We had promised to be helpful, and kept our promise to the best of our ability; but the result was indignity, self-degradation. Sympathy given under duress is too unnatural to appeal to the honesty of a child.

The Mohammedan, when his sick ego requires a tonic, has but to survey his female dependents, and, though wine is forbidden him, it is enough! And the women of his household, instructed to consider men gods, honour themselves in accepting enslavement to divinities. Alas, the poor white of the south cannot, when he is sober, be

228

certain of his superiority to any living creature—unless, perhaps, he is the owner of a cur dog he can cuff about without inviting interference! If he wants further consolation, he must first make himself drunk enough to forget Christian precepts; then he can enjoy physical brutality, and be assured beings exist who are at a greater disadvantage than himself, since they dare not strike back! Inevitably, victims in a society in which a degree of presumed equality has already stirred questionings, will not get the same kick from ill-treatment from some elected male as rewards the subservient female in Algeria or Morocco; and some, in the absence of priest or psychoanalyst, may even rebel and carry their confidences to a circuit-riding, illiterate expounder of Gospel! However, where the background is Deuteronomy, there is not much help, either; and child marriages continue to flourish. For if a girl is old enough to be seduced she is old enough to be wed, runs the consistent tradition of chivalry! That, legitimately, is the medieval view of what will constitute years of discretion for a female! Besides, many a woman mentally keen, who resents a physiological description of the only virtue allowed her sex, is a house divided against itself; ready, where propinquity invites, to glory (on the side of instincts she has technically discarded) in a relationship prideless enough (or sufficiently above pride) to have pleased poor Nietzsche, whose opportunities for exploiting his insight into women were so pitiably few. But when I was growing up I had not been convinced as yet that life on the Nile and Cumberland held something ineradicably common to both! Though my eyes, at thirteen, were opened by Mr. Kipling to his opinion that "the Colonel's lady and Judy O'Grady" were the same under the skin, I objected to the presumption, and felt it only needed faith to demonstrate a contradiction. In this period, the spectacle of a family of "trash," encountered on a mountain road where progress was in ritualistic formation that never varied—the man with his shotgun striding ahead, the woman with the lantern following meekly behind, tagged by the children—made the material for a nascent "feminist" protest.

"But, my dear madame, the male is the protector of his family: it is for the defence of the women that he precedes them in a public place!" an Arab gentleman explained to me twenty years later, when called on in his turn to justify chivalry. He was squeamish—a poet. His refined, idealistic reverences were painfully affronted when he had to see some woman eat. It was not until I had spent considerable time in the New York of the present, where bad manners, originally due to the absence of traditional correctives, are now virtually a cult, that I confessed to myself nothing had been settled by leaving it to women to fight their own battles under the law and elsewhere. If only the duel, once recognized in the speech of action as the fitting language of antipathy, had not fallen into disfavour; then I might, quite recently, have called out the desk clerk in a certain hotel! But in a fist fight I should never be able to make a conclusive show of equality with a male vis-à-vis! Things are not as I believed they were, when I thought the code of a gentleman a casteless acceptance of noblesse oblige to which every man aspired!

Actually, I began life with a number of misapprehensions: one, I remember, gave me a tendency to attribute intelligence to all really "nice" people. A liquor war raged in Tennessee while I was a child; and I, by no means a hairsplitting student of economics, read despisingly, with complacent self-certainty, the signs screaming at you from billboards, fences, even telegraph poles—GET RIGHT WITH GOD OR GET ON FIRE!—expressing the evangelist's and the poor white's support of prohibition. One exhorter, called Mr. Ham, was reputed to have been crushed by a wit who had retorted, to words prophesying his own damnation: "We'll have Ham fer breakfast when we gits to hell!"

To young people taught contempt for those who, uninvited, try to impose their religious views on others of different persuasions, this was an excruciating rejoinder. I could not, then, see excuses for that majority who, starved of cultural entertainment in their homes, were on the side of a free circus, never more popular in the days of the Caesars, before feats of gladiators had been limited to vocal displays and harmless gymnastics. Nor was I aware, at that time, that strait-laced puritanism of the Roundhead variety had been common, even among Confederate generals—far commoner than Cavalier insouciance, so carefully preserved in southern myth! I had too easily taken it for granted that the liberality of my own somewhat "scamped" Episcopalianism represented generally prevalent ideas. Not having accounted for financial influences, I had accepted my mother's word that Pre-Raphaelitism was a more vital issue than moonshining.

I was especially shocked when certain misses, actually daughters of reputable families, put on the sackcloth and ashes affected by trash, disavowed interest in cards, and suddenly refused to dance. Their behaviour I fancied (as I offered unconscious insult to the memory of Great-uncle Ewing) reflected on their lineage! It surprised me that my relatives—such discerning genealogists!—did not forbid the house to such debased exemplifiers of the Vaughn-Moody tradition! Their public exploitation of deeply private matters genuinely horrified me. Even *I* shrewdly suspected they enjoyed public penitence chiefly as an opportunity for being conspicuously dramatic; exacting a parallel indecent openness of supposed confession from infatuated young men! The whole performance smacked of "commonness"—something as abhorrent to a good Episcopalian as fastidious manners to a Baptist or Campbellite, or voluptuous aesthetic revelling to a Presbyterian! Thus reflected, in sum, an infant Samuel fretted by the inconsistencies of adults, and stricter than they (according to the awful direct logic of childhood) in applying inculcated tenets. Tennessee was, for a while, overrun with parading girls, wearing blue or white ribbons or other insignia of purity, resolutely offering themselves as inspiring virgin examples to the menfolk; and I saw in this phenomenon nothing but objectionable fanaticism incompatible with refined "taste." I did not realize the touching quality of such a simple view as theirs of what was at stake. It was not until I went to school in New Orleans that my Episcopalian assurance suffered shock when I heard from the daughter of a gentleman who had been at the head of Southwestern Presbyterian University (Clarksville's single institution of serious learning) that the Presbyterian contingent, regarding itself as the town's intellectual group, had nonetheless sided with the lower order of prohibition advocates and looked down upon Episcopalians as inferior through frivolity.

Certainly I did not recognize while the struggle was in progress that there was a life-and-death combat between vested liquor interests and an individualist trade opposition, and that no quarter was being given on either side.

We have seen, in the East, and very recently, a similar exploitation of a narrowly conservative citizenry by forces of illegality and disorder; and bootlegging, in Tennessee, has a specific historical background.

There was war profiteering during the French Revolution, even as during our own Great War: the Declaration of the Rights of Man resulted in a situation particularly lucrative for persons dabbling in the grain market. Those who stood to gain most from troubles abroad were farmers in coastal regions who commanded the best facilities for transporting their harvests to metropolitan centres of distribution. Frontiersmen in the mountains preferred to dedicate what was left from their indifferent crops, once their families were fed, to the home manufacture of whiskey, which could be disposed of among neighbours. John Bull himself has never despised spirits, and pioneers so largely Scottish, Irish, and Scotch-Irish were, as a rule (their piety notwithstanding), comfortably hard drinkers. Reliance on this consoling indulgence followed the march of progress and the opening of the Cumberland settlements. A distillery called the Red Heifer existed as early as 1787; and even Clarksville, shortly after it sprang into being, was presented with a road which connected it, not with the world, but with Patton's Still House, which soon became famous; as did the Black Bob Tavern in Nashville, which, on its establishment, was shortly a rendezvous for many of our early heroes. Even if whiskey had to be carried a fair distance, pack horses could convey quantities of the stuff at half the expense which would have been required for the export of the original corn. At a time when a lavish meal could be had for twenty-five cents, whiskey was sold at a dollar the quart; and county courts record the numerous efforts of local communities to extract social benefit from the persistent weaknesses of individuals. Yet the first federal tax on whiskey aroused in the bosom of the mountaineer a sense of injured righteousness that caused him to defy the exciseman, even as, later, he defied the prohibition officer. In these United States, the geographical dimensions of the country diversify the problems of the central government, and residents in localities topographically isolated tend to develop the militant aggrievements of misunderstood souls.

When disputes about the ethics of slave trading precipitated a national crisis, felt in Tennessee as elsewhere, an imposing section of public opinion offered clean-cut support to the federal claim to interfere with the business; but in those very districts once the stronghold of abolition, the prohibition issue remains unclear to this day. Persons whose survival could be assured only by resistance to trade monopoly were, in the era of my childhood, not only afraid to make plain statements as to their position, but were, in a mental sense, insufficiently disciplined for the detachment of self-interested motives of finance from religious discontents and involuntary hypocrisies. The "four-mile law," which made it a breach of legality to sell spirits within the radius defined by that distance from any schoolhouse, represented a compromise between the particular realism which has to do with money and conventions of thought which are an outgrowth of the pioneer's cultural starvation and compensatory crude religiosity—conventions which, as the backwoodsman has been translated into the budding capitalist, are preserved and prescribe the state's culture.

Religion has about played out in the Southern Confederacy, runs a Whig editorial from a paper of the sixties; and continues: *but this is especially so in Knoxville.* It is a pessimistic presumption contradicted both by the fervent indignation of the objector himself, and by this (from the Holston *Journal*, a Rebel Methodist organ): *A few days ago a Methodist Sabbath School concluded to have a picnic. It was had; but what followed? Fiddling and dancing and card playing! Beat that, ye rustics of the country and dwellers in our towns and villages! All this did happen in the blessed old town* (Knoxville). And to this very day, cultural taboos are proclaimed and metaphysical systems erected on the basis of moral discriminations no more subtle than this. There is something to wring the heart in the predicament of persons whose intellectual-emotional performance is on this childlike level, confronted with the necessity for justifying socially some cynical problem of daily bread! In my childhood, such a dilemma drew the moonshiner, the bootlegger, and the sincere (usually female) religionist together under one slogan. Most of the women entering, in this fashion, and for the first time, a public arena, were not concerned with the extending intricate political diplomacy which finally involved railroads, telephone companies and every sort of commercial enterprise in a movement resembling a medieval crusade; and their incapacity to produce the ulterior motive put the climax on general bewilderment. Many males gained illicitly when oaths sworn to in church or at camp-meeting were broken half an hour later with a sale of private stock in some spot beyond pulpit espionage. But mothers, wives and sweethearts of habitual drunkards were not notably enriched by this double-dealing even when the profit from it returned into the family.

My own relatives, when "dry" Carmack ran against "wet" Patterson, in 1908, were faithful to Cavalier precedent, and loyal to the "wets." Actually, after 1896, when McKinley, elected president over Bryan, won in Tennessee only by the narrowest margin of superior votes, there was progressive evidence that those with enough bought tradition behind them to encourage discretion even in matters of faith, were departing from previous "aristocratic" fidelity to the Democratic Party; which had gradually been taken over by advocates of the rights of the "plain man." In the resultant conflict of opposing mores were included many spectacular personal dramas: the meteoric career of Luke Lea; the assassination of Carmack, which was immediately attributed to his political opponents.

We, both as respecters of "trusts," and as good Episcopalians who, on occasion, entertained the visiting bishop, were properly contemptuous of the "sensationalism" of the last accusation. And I mean neither disrespect to Episcopal doctrine, nor to the genial ecclesiastical presence I remember so well, when I say that the bishop's rare descents were equally important in inspiring my first distrust of the "demagoguery" of the commoner and in firing me, contrarily, to an adolescent championing of this very same trash. "Jingoism" had been earlier defined for me by my elders; who supplemented etymological interpretations of the word with illustrations of its applicableness to Bryan's "Cross of Gold" speech. This, I gathered, was wholeheartedly disapproved of by the ladies and gentlemen who were my parents' associates—it was the salient example of the falsity of political emotionalism. I must have been eighteen before I conceded that gross inaccuracies, obvious perversions of fact, may come from the lips of rhetoricians without constituting a denial of their unsullied—perhaps terrible!—sincerity! To discover wisdom in a villainous source, or that the good may be, also, foolish, is a dreadful discouragement to the youthful moralist—it was one I could not face for years! Surely, I used to think, the virtue of a fool was no great matter! Virtue, if it was to count for anything, needed the "truth"!

I was five years old—or was it six?—when my nascent feelings of a patriot were stimulated, in their unexamined intensity, evening after evening, during a month in which my cousins and myself lived for nightfall, and to watch a company of militia which drilled methodically at this hour in the half-dark streets of Clarksville. As we crouched behind an iron picket fence which separated the road and a precipitate grassy terrace, we listened to a marvellously regimented thump of marching feet, and exchanged nudges which emphasized thrills. "Right-*left*! Right-*left*! 'Ten-*shun*! Company, *halt*!" would ring out a voice I shall recognize even on Judgement Day above the brazen blare of trumpets! It belonged to one Gaston O'Brien (called, intimately, "Gasoline") who was the officer in command. And in response to its urgings, heroes not less epic than Xenophon's Ten Thousand (though the numbers visible, as they passed the new electric arc lamp at the corner, were only a few dozen) tramped up and down, stubbornly, wearily, in and out of laggard formations. And, now and again, our excitement reached a peak, as the group broke into double-quick time; the volunteers, who were to defend us against defeat by an Armada, finally disappearing, at a plodding run, into the shadows they cast before them as they dashed along Madison Street. Until they vanished; and you could hear, as if it were a tiny whirlwind, cowbugs and electric-light beetles; sounds tracing the orbits of their flights about the lamppost, to us, in our elation, like some minute "music of the spheres."

And squatting there in the pride of our stealth, hugging the angle of a wire fence which already marked the beginning division of my grandfather's property into city lots, we *knew* (while we prayed silently nobody would come to command us indoors to bed!) that the Spanish yoke was about to be lifted. And by southerners! By *Clarksville* boys!

> *Dewy was the morning*
> *Upon the first of May;*
> *And Dewey was the Admiral*
> *Upon Manila Bay!*
> *And dewy were them regent's eyes,*
> *Them orbs of royal blue!*
> *And dew-we feel discouraged?*
> *I DO NOT THINK WE DO!*

we recited into the darkness, repeating the inspiriting poetry we had learned—those of us who could read!—straight from the newspaper! While the fountain smell, rank and delicate, and always predominant at night, bore upon us with its suggestions of the earth we loved; until, like the rest of humanity whose every breath is self-contradiction, we were enchanted again with the glittering, remote architecture of the multifariously mysterious sky! The Spanish yoke was to be lifted—it scarcely mattered from whom, or for what! We had never heard of economic determinism; we were unaware of something gnawing during decades which had eaten a line through the Union so that it fell into two distinct parts, with no more than a simulated entity—a line already drawn corrosively, even through our own unmindful hearts! And when Gasoline and his cohorts boarded a train made as festal in their honour as a blossom-rigged Mardi gras float, I—among the youngest, the most insignificant— was of the most fervent who cheered! In the Philippines, I have been told, the First Tennessee Regiment was brigaded with a regiment from Iowa; but for a long time I was spared any knowledge of this levelling of necessity.

Several of "the boys"—Clay Stacker, Cave Johnson, James Kendrick, Lewis Drane I think—becoming privileged as veterans to whom the Filipinos were indebted for a first taste of liberty and the joys of civilization, collected payment from Uncle Sam to the extent of a round-the-world tour; visited Melbourne, Sydney, Shanghai, Peking, Ceylon, Bombay, Port Said, Greece, Naples, Paris and London; and, to demonstrate familiarity with Oriental arts and customs, returned home bearing ivory back-scratchers! This was no worse than my mother had expected, after an exhibition by a swain of her girlhood, who, calling on Sunday in a proper regalia of morning coat, striped trousers and lavender gloves, relapsed, in the parlour, into horseplay; snatched up a Crouching Venus from her pedestal, and began waltzing round and round with her! And with the back-scratchers as forewarning, even I, finally, began to see, in the flag-embowered tinted photographs of Admiral Dewey which continued to remind people of the *Maine*, only another of my father's tiresomely reputable acquaintances, unsuitably garbed in gilt-bedizened clothes!

Or maybe I had known all along (and refused to acknowledge it) that a romanticizing moralist of extreme aesthetic susceptibility asks too much of life in a small southern town—too much of life, and too much of herself—and is bound to be disappointed! Undoubtedly a premonition of my ultimate disillusion first stirred in me during the bishop's gala entertainment at my aunt's, when we children, reviewing unusual signs which welcomed a superior being, received such an effect of carnival as remained undiminished though we were poked out of his sight upstairs and had cambric tea in the nursery! Once, to console us, we were permitted to dine at midday at a little side table in the very same room with him! And could feast our juvenile eyes on silver and linen which appeared otherwise only when there was a party or a wedding! It seemed remarkable that the decanters of red Bohemian glass, almost invariably empty on the sideboard, had become perfect jugs of Philemon and Baucis, forever miraculously replenished! And that gentlemen who, as a rule, stuck to their toddies and juleps for between-meal refreshment; ladies for whom a thimbleful of sherry with a biscuit in the afternoon represented indulgence, were undertaking to run through the appropriate wines with a misleading, sober nonchalance that might have deceived you into thinking them accustomed!

Though the bishop was famous (and deservedly!) as a raconteur, and, in his rôle of professional guest, must have developed, willy-nilly, those refinements of gustatory appreciation which distinguish the man of crude appetites from the bon gourmet, I would not, for the world, have this record misinterpreted as a hint that he was anything but a gravely abstemious man! It was the drama of false pretences (to be laid at the door of custom rather than of my relations!) which, even as it elated me, inclined me toward scepticism and criticism. Once having appointed myself censor for the affairs of the church, I looked again upon his benign Irish face, surprised a cold twinkle of humour in his wise, rather sad, blue eyes, noted the eloquent flash of an ecclesiastical ring upon the fair, well-tended hands with which he gesticulated gracefully, and began to make him personally responsible for crimes committed by persons who were utter strangers to him—people his amiable discretion had never so much as taken account of!

Still earlier, I had been troubled by metaphysical problems involved in causation; and, labouring with attempts to apprehend God as He had, did, and would exist, in a sort of anticipatory retrospect which included His creations, found myself in such a spider-web tangle of paradoxes as drove me to save my sanity, and abandon the effort. I took, it appears, an orthodox Marxist view of the total irrelevance of the philosophical abstract to anything "real." With the bishop as my example, I then tried to content myself with a more modest demonstration of Jesus as a true liberal. *Because* Jesus possessed a sense of humour (an essential characteristic in one thoroughly humane) He could not be offended if He happened to hear, from on high, His name taken in vain in the course of mere casual profanity, I remember arguing with my cousin Julien; who was older, bolder than myself, and, for that particular adolescent moment, a militant atheist. He laughed at me, reducing me at once to desperate earnestness which had no refuge but in quoting texts. I recollect I almost satisfied myself I had quashed him with: *The fool hath said in his heart there is no*

God! Unfortunately, my authority for this statement was a caption below a photograph of E. H. Sothern in a play described in the *Theatre Magazine*; so conscience robbed me of the inner benefits of victory.

Undoubtedly, at that very instant, thousands more mature of body but quite as naïve in mental outlook, were discoursing on similar topics with an equal misunderstood wordiness all over the state: fellows with the hungry faces of half-starving prophets laying down the law according to ideas of their own before idling audiences in little stores and post offices everywhere between Arkansas and Bristol (which is on the state line in the mountains). In the mountains especially the theological precocity from which I was suffering must develop continually; where patriarchs to whom Lincoln would have been a weakling hesitate in the doors of single-room cabins for some last fling at Scripture interpretation with which to confound wives and grandchildren, before an escape, with dogs and guns, into the woods—away from family life! Preparing, maybe, to defy the prohibition officer! Just as, in 1791, when Hamilton proposed a tax, the ancestors of these contemporaneous prophets defied excisemen!

In such districts, and to this moment, genuflections to science remain perfunctory—as perfunctory, really, as they are in New York! And to corroborate me, I give a secondhand account of a representative of the government, dispatched not very long ago into a district near Knoxville to discourage the happy raging of an epidemic. At a little mountain railway station, he was met by a representative local practitioner, who, instead of inviting him to a comfortable seat in a waiting car, produced, for his convenient use, a lean, moth-eaten mule, which the visiting physician, inferior as a horseman, accepted with reticent thanks. Then he and the white-bearded figure of Methuselah, who had qualified as his official reception committee, and was identically mounted, rode up trails inviting only to ants; down trails fit to test the expertness of human flies experienced on skyscrapers; descending, as if it were via the chimney, upon one lonely, ramshackle dwelling after another; and calling on the hospitable tolerance of gaunt housewives, gran'pappies sucking corncob pipes, and swollen-bellied children, who were either doomed, or foredoomed to hookworm. The local G. P. freely advised everybody to kill the dogs and cats of the vicinity; but the visiting doctor, feeling he confronted problems in hygiene beyond his merely urban capacities, was at last discouraged out of speech. Until the formal tour of inspection was completed, and the experts, bestriding their mules again in exhaustion, were left free to contemplate the torrential green slopes and gorges which seemed cut through the blue air. They had no heart for the beauties of nature! Suddenly, without any explanatory pronouncement, the medical resident drew rein, and leaping briskly from his stoical nag, commenced the businesslike collection of stray twigs and faggots; assembling what, as he produced matches, was seen to be a bonfire. At least this was the plausible reasoning of the other doctor, who quitted his own mule and watched in amazement his host, crouched by the beginning flame in a posture so devout it suggested a religious rite; while he removed from his pocket a paper containing an enigmatic grey powder which he sprinkled upon the pyre. Next, with a gesture releasing him from tortures obviously unfamiliar, he undid his shirt collar; and, as a fragrance rose from the fusion of heat with mystic substance, bent toward the blaze, seized the white beard which was like the insignia of his authority, and began waving it back and forth, back and forth, above the reek of perfume from the dying ash. "Yawl gotta fumergate when you goes through them cabins!" he remarked across his shoulder, his wizened features relaxing in a grimace of ineffably relieved fastidiousness.

Calamitous trust in nature! Yet there are compensations! Patients of the doctor in the mountains would have no acquaintance with that robot mother of modernity—the hospital! It can be guaranteed to feed you, dress you, wash behind your ears—only if you are mistaken enough to yield to so much as one single spontaneous impulse which may cause you to present, to this paragon of mechanized virtues, the *left* ear at a moment when the implacable sequence demanded for its successful operation calls for the *right*, woe unto you! If you have seen Charlie Chaplin in *Modern Times*, you know what you will get—and that it may be a blow which will knock you out for good! And if anyone is criticized for the result, it will be yourself! It will serve you right! It will have been your weakness that you anticipated concessions from a simulated organism acting according to predetermination.

It was a dark and stormy evening;
Round the campfire brigands sat:
Brigands young, and brigands old;
Brigands slim and brigands fat;
And the Captain said: Roderigo,
Tell us one of those stories for which you are so famous!
And Roderigo said: It was a dark and stormy evening;

Round the campfire the brigands sat;
Brigands young and brigands old;
Brigands slim, and brigands fat;
And Roderigo said: It was a dark and stormy evening;
Round the campfire the brigands sat, etc., etc., etc.,

ad infinitum, ran a perverse recital of my childhood
which always threw me into a condition of utter baffle-
ment in which it seemed impossible to hit upon the conclusive metaphysical rejoinder. It might stand today as
the representation of the deadlock one reaches when,
seeing on the one hand attitudes toward God that carry
a prejudice against any advance in literarcy, the single alternative proffered encourages independence of thought
only to the point which will flatter the theory of perfect
living in the mechanized! And laboratory science, though
it supports with proof its boast of the appropriateness of
an inductive method by which to arrive at a grasp of
universal law, holds out no hope of anything that can
supply a justification for living sufficiently absolute to
meet emotion's demands! At its most successful, it cannot do more than find ways by which men may submit,
with the grace of intelligence, to forces that will otherwise break them! Superstition, like religious poetry, is a
short cut by which we arrive ahead of time at the destination so far vainly proposed as that of all thought!

Probably the crudest of men's attempts to find life
meaningful is history, in which we posit a universality
based on the exclusive interpretation (inescapably subjective in its inception) of our own efforts and acts.
Most of what goes as history, is sheer beguilement for
the fictional imagination; but its exercise is irresistible
self-entertainment; and I almost never think of the South

245

(Tennessee especially!) without feeling how aptly its record parallels that of Ireland: Yankees playing, for the southerner, the part of the British. You will find, in the North of America, even in those quarters most tolerant, an air of condescension toward the southerner which is like that with which the English, on occasion, flatter the Irish into complacence toward exploitation of their own fair land. And in the Yankee (still, to a degree, holding the south in his capitalistic grip) are evidences of those latent prejudices aggressors instinctively cultivate to support a self-advantaging contempt for the aggrieved—prejudices typically exemplified in the English colonizer! The least informed northerner is ready to accept, without preliminary examination of the data, whatever statements tend to illumine southern character cynically—even as the Britisher, who will justify the subjugation of other races with his distrust of the subjugate! For we are, for the time being, a conquered people; which may be why we show, in our agrarian poverty, further resemblances to the Irish; who are hard drinkers, love big talk which compensates for inept action, and tend to seek a refuge from contemporaneous humiliations in political rhetoric and a glamorous mouthing over of their unexceptional descent from kings! In Tennessee, echoes of the plight of Ireland are emphasized naturally; especially among the poor whites, and in the mountains, where the Scotch-Irish strain is dominant, and the topography of the country produces the extreme of primitive, individualistic philosophy, expressive in the blood feud and in highly personal and vindictive methods used to promote public affairs. And everywhere there is an anachronistic hearkening to the framers of the Constitution, who insisted: *No person who denies the being of God, or a*

246

future state of rewards and punishment shall hold any office in the Civil Department of this State. . . . And this identification of piety with politics is also Irish—Irish and Scotch!

Irish Catholics entered the territories with the first Ulstermen and expatriate Presbyterian Highlanders; but in an unzealous minority which failed to draw the missionary priest in its wake—a rare instance of the Church of Rome caught napping! And in the settlements dissenters could be vouched for as patriots almost without any investigation of the individual's claim to the title. The peculiar impression I received in my childhood that the nobility of France was a thoroughgoing Huguenot body was in part the consequence of direct Huguenot-American propagandizing crystallized as tradition; it also represented a tinge given theology during a period when Protestantism had a practical value in preserving, in the Cumberlands, the Blue Ridge and the Great Smokies, the united front against Latin invasion via the Mississippi valley, while French and Spaniards were yet tenaciously, persistently, engaged in empire conspiracies. Curious how we inherit ideas and attitudes engendered during agitations for practical ends now obsolete—how the deeds of our ancestors are commemorated by ourselves in prejudices retained after an embalming in sentiment! The outcome of the pioneer's defence against the encroaching Latin has been an identification of "free Americanism" with an anti-Catholic stand!

Besides, '89 and '76 were at least as much related as the last successful Russian revolution and the present war in Spain. In that period of earlier revolts, after the Encyclopedists had inaugurated an era of free thought, free speech and general rebelliousness against instituted authority, scepticism as a world attitude emerged in various progressive societies in terms of whatever specific outlook best jibed with factors conditioning the survival of the particular group. With a majority, individualism, independence, went unquestioned, but was interpreted according to the exigencies of immediate crises and must fit the capacities of the average citizen's mind. There was more than a little relationship between the nonconformist ardours of settlers on the Holston, and the works of Voltaire himself.

Just as there was a relationship between pleasures I experienced at Buena Vista in the company of a Mr. "Lan" Burn (a sort of maître d'hôtel at that place) and certain social-economic significances indicative of the general state of Tennessee at that time—and this, though my recollections of Lan Burn, who had charge of the food stores, concern only a generous way he had of letting us—kids—into a pantry where there were locked bins, unfastening the one which contained brown sugar, and giving us handfuls of it. We bore the sugar into retirement, ate it with toothpicks and pretended we were dipping snuff. I doubt snuff dipping, as a gesture appealing to the imitative, would have captured the fancies of children in any locality less dominated by the snuff industry. When I was a child, in Tennessee and Kentucky, Negroes and unexemplary trash took snuff almost invariably; but the habit probably impressed my interest because it had reputed apologists even among "first families"; divers correct old ladies being pointed out by gossips, on one occasion and another, as possible, excusable addicts. After all, people said, in George Washington's day, *everybody* used snuff! So, though I did speculate on a difference in aesthetic effect between snuff applied to the gums with the macerated, brushlike tip of a split twig (an operation often illustrated for me by Mammy Alice), and that inhaled daintily, its traces dispatched with the whisk of a Venetian lace handkerchief, still, simulating indulgence by either method had the suspect attractiveness of the forbidden but winked at. And for a long while snuff dipping struck me as the acme of dangerous delight; until I did, actually, try the genuine article, which made me very sick. However, even that I attributed to the fact that my experiment had been with *damp* snuff—the sort associated with a prolific flow of saliva coloured a deep brown and very noticeable when hoi polloi spat; whereas the snuff I consistently imagined to be appropriate for my own caste was fine, powdery and dry. The distinction here obscurely drawn had a bearing on differences my elders had pointed out to me which marked the gulf between (for example) any insignificant retail dispenser of tobacco and the purveyor of the same commodity wholesale—between, I suppose, a Guinness and a country pubkeeper.

Snuff, in that country around Buena Vista, which so excited me with its boundless silences, may have been a true opium for the masses, whether they were black or white: the solace it bestowed was very likely as good for social disgruntlement as ten tickets on the Irish Sweeps. Its use induced, in individuals, mild, soothing lethargies; and may have staved off what is now known as "the tobacco war," which precipitated in 1908, when small farmers, their ruin threatened, began openly to fight monopoly. Sometime around 1904 a Mr. Ferigo, I now gather, exceeded any ambition of my grandfather and practically cornered the patronage of the locality by foreign governments. He peddled his advantage to the

American Snuff Company, which fixed prices for the growers, who were cut off, also, from the speculative market in Bremen and from profiting in Africa. As a defence measure, the Dark Tobacco Planters Protective Association was formed, with Felix Ewing of Robertson County, Tennessee, the presiding president. Then began a series of occurrences which caused voices that were critical to reach even my ears with rumours of the "Dortch Law," originally a Democratic implement for installing the Australian ballot in the state, and thus effecting the complete disenfranchisement of Negroes and poor whites. Then the passionately disparate opinions I heard from members of my own generation combined with an inverse influence from my elders, and destroyed my reverence for names like Duke, Reynolds, American Tobacco Company, which I had once regarded as dedicated, not to a mere conjuring of dollars, but to a subtle alchemy! Warehouses to which my connections had given me privileged entrée—warehouses along the Square, warehouses up and down the River Road, warehouses along odd streets!—where I had been allowed to run wild sometimes in an exquisitely haunted gloom (enormous to a child, and filled with almost aphrodisiac odours) ceased to be places from which I embarked for Cythera! The very lure of the "wharf boat"—a queer, dumpy magnification of a houseboat from which F. P. Gracey Brothers sped tobacco shipments on the steamboats plying the Ohio and the Mississippi—suddenly departed. I was thirteen, fourteen—I was growing up! When, cataclysmically, came revelation—I understood! Caste was illumined! I saw, I thought, what had produced the type impressions which have been assembled in this book informally—the class war!

Earlier, when William B. Bate, an ex-Confederate major general, had been elected governor on a basis of the sheer vehement enthusiasm felt everywhere for a defunct cause, I had been apprized of my difference from the multitude—I was half Yankee! Practically an outcast! And when one Mr. Jere Baxter, daring competition with the Louisville and Nashville Railroad, actually succeeded in building another line on money he was reputed to have got from Adolphus Busch, the Saint Louis brewer, and comments from my relatives indicated to me that *we*—even *we*, who appreciated Sainte-Beuve and had reticently overlooked the downfall of Oscar Wilde out of respect to his talents!—might possibly one day find ourselves in seeming agreement with people who refused to play whist and forbade their daughters to dance, "disillusion" proceeded apace! But it was not fundamental—not in that period! Disillusion had not, then, compelled me to seize on implications from witnessed experience in a way requiring me to restate myself in terms that were a new philosophy. Rather was what I suffered, in my inchoate rebelliousness, a first shock felt by the naïve idealist from any quarter of the globe when made to realize, not defects in his theory, but its indifferent application by its professed exponents.

Now all was altered! And indignation, with the voice of Karl Marx, lucidly expounded every public and private matter. Curious how unhappiness begins to be resolved as soon as it is able to associate itself with a reason! Surely here is something which, though the processes are not identical, significantly parallels the emotional artist's promptings to discover a form!

In the Episcopal Sunday School I attended in Russellville, Miss Q., the daughter of the English emigré parson, played the organ. She was robust, sandy; physically hearty, temperamentally neutral; and would have been in her element in a Sussex village; where her circumspect piety and religious concentration on unremitting cheerfulness would have been best appreciated. Like most Britishers, she was kind publicly, but coldly cruel privately when there was the least threat of exposure of her feelings or other people's. I did not care for her; or, for that matter, for her father, whose reminiscences about Rugby detracted from my interest in *Tom Brown's School Days*. My mother compassionated him for his waste of a genuine erudition on duty visits to ladies who were important contributors to church funds but were, otherwise, obstacles to the scholarly pursuits which absorbed his heart. For my own part, though he seemed authentically benignant when he stopped small girls like me on the street and patted their heads, my instinct accused him of treating me to a condescension equalling that with which he encouraged, in the masses, an appropriately lowly and reverent view of their betters. Indeed the excessive decorousness of the Q.'s was so oppressive to a spoiled child bound to become an individualist, that my feeling about them accumulated until it was actual dislike; expressed whenever, during a service, I sat in a pew directly below the choir stalls and the organ loft, and could see Miss Q.'s athletic shoulders and the unwieldy, dun-coloured hummock of her hair, which was massively coiled on a freckled neck. Then, with this vision to inspire me, I would hiss at her, under my breath, the new word I had acquired, which had come to me in an erroneous context that made me mistake it for profanity. It was, oddly: "Sarsaparilla!" And I would repeat it over and over, timidly, in a whisper, but in a tone of most vicious deriding: "Sarsaparilla! Sarsaparilla!" the experiment providing the first relief for emotion I ever had from the use of what was, as I esteemed it, downright obscenity.

Until, while the tobacco war was in full swing, and the precise methods of old Ku Kluxers were being employed by "common" persons my relatives condemned as terrorists (which they were), I discovered Karl Marx; and was prepared with a language in which I could tell things that were at least half the truth; and so put my long-accruing inferiority complex to a really dignified use! For, as others have remarked before me, without that shove from the unconscious which an inferiority complex can provide, no society would ever have progressed. But for malaria and boils, and the collapse of my vanity in a creek, I might have been unable to resist agreement with people who were generous to me, and had paid me that highest compliment of assuming me one of themselves! Yes, undoubtedly, had my father not been Yankee-born, and the bishop, during his visitations, a trifle overpowering, I should have been incapable of essaying, as I did, an uneary guerilla warfare on behalf of those logically, "normally," and by every traditional right, my enemies!

All during a summer in which Clarksville's most prosperous citizens were in virtual ambush, while my male cousins and other young men with conservative affiliations were serving conspicuously as volunteers in a home guard, and embarrassed at their duties in tobacco warehouses converted into barracks, because the culinary tributes to their bravery were so many that they were threatened with a death from indigestion and their own gallantry, I secretly fermented righteousness; and, without any accurate data for controversy, came, verbally, to the defence of the Night Riders again and again. At night, in the Square on the bluff above the river, young and valorous recipients of hams, layer cakes, beaten biscuit and fried chickens donated to chivalry by a grateful womankind, made bonfires before the old Tobacco Exchange and bivouacked in the street; under a harvest moon rising red, and soaring, until a veil like luminous frost was laid across the open sky; and the Cumberland, stripped of shadows and nakedly silver, was exposed like the frank face of some utter stranger, never previously seen.

Then "the boys," with rifles stacked, crouched in reflections from the flames which distorted the scene heroically; so that they might have been mistaken—as they sang *Nellie Gray*, or *My Old Kentucky Home*, or *Skip-ta-ma-Lou, Mah Darlin'*—for their own grandfathers, cheering themselves in a wide darkness somewhere while waiting for news of the advance of General Grant and praying silently for General Lee. True, time had reversed the tactics of the two parties of opposition; but without altering the fundamental character of the traditional allegiances represented in struggle. They were, like their grandfathers, on the side of an aristocracy— such as it was! And if they seemed, contradictorily, to support a union, it was no more than a union of forces to insure further profiting for those who had already profited disproportionately.

Meanwhile, on some road between Clarksville and Hopkinsville, masked men (incited, it was said, by a Dr. Amos and a Dr. Champion, both of Kentucky) might be calling in at the lonely farmhouse of John Doe, who had refused to join the Association, and, after scraping

254

his plant beds and destroying his seedlings, commanding him into his front yard for a horsewhipping. Worse things happened—when Farmer Smith (or Farmer Jones), riding peaceably along a turnpike, reeled suddenly and toppled from the saddle, the bullet of a hidden assassin in the small of his back. And if you drove out of Clarksville, you had to pass sentinels. In the covered bridge beyond the tollgate over Red River, when vehicles rolled into an artificial cave filled with rumbling echoes and smells of water, people who were in transit there met men with rifles, tramping back and forth methodically, suspiciously, in a dour glare from lanterns.

The two physicians reputed to have betrayed Saint Luke so deliberately were rumoured to have planned an organization operating under a severe military discipline; each tobacco-growing section in Tennessee and Kentucky being allotted to selected leadership. There was a colonel for every county; and a captain, supervising two lieutenants, engineered the strategy in separate districts; he accepted, for enlistment, only young men noted for expert horsemanship. Old men rendered service chiefly by providing alibis for those directly guilty. There were secret rituals; rebels' oaths were sworn. So young Tom Sawyers lived again what had been legends they inherited from carpetbagging days. I remember a dance given for young people which was almost disrupted by the spectacular announcement of a late arrival—a young man about eighteen—who appeared breathlessly to declare that, this time, for a certainty, the Night Riders were *coming*! Then Clarksville became Brussels on the evening before Waterloo! Then children between fourteen and twenty "carried on" with a cool hilarity, terrified, but poised and elated, too; their fearful fatalism like a strong, steadying potion.

And over the countryside hung, repeatedly, odours of burning; as barn after barn, ignited by the mysterious incendiary who stalked the byways, burst into flames which reduced the stored crop, collected after a year of labour, to reeking cinders, scattered by the wind. In Kentucky, Augustus E. Wilson, a Republican governor, moved troops from Louisville and from the mountains into the tobacco regions. In retaliation, those in revolt descended openly upon Hopkinsville, dynamited and burned all non-Association warehouses, wrecked the town's light, power and telephone systems, and even imprisoned some of the police. Clarksville was very near—it is only thirteen miles from the state line—and when Night Riders and a National Cavalry Guard clashed outside Princeton, and news came through of a pitched battle, in which, it was said, Dr. Amos, charging with the insurgents, had been wounded, my own juvenile principles were eclipsed by my blank, dreading feeling of revulsion and objection to the general violence of everybody.

Not long ago, in New York, I was aroused, after I had gone to bed, by hostile noises from the street. When I peered from the window toward the watery satin of the asphalt road in its broad, postmidnight desertedness, I saw a tangle of human bodies, like a multiplied Laocoön; and could hear the impact of fists, mindless and merciless, belabouring quiescent flesh. Worse were the clamouring voices, stupidly delirious with aggression, repeating and repeating the single, indecent expletive phrase which was the whole vocabulary of hatred, and its adequate expression! And gradually (because I did not act quickly and interference was too late!) I distinguished the five victors from the single vanquished—the prone man now too torpid to respond to torment, from those who attacked; the ten hands with clenched knuckles, the ten cloddish feet from the *thing* they kicked, with which they denied their identity! Until, at a cry, "Cops!" the object they attacked (become for them all the world save themselves) was seized and slung, with life's contempt for inanimates, into an areaway. And a policeman arrived, and began, with cautious inefficiency, a concentration of the law's force on an examination of garbage tins he illumined with his electric torch. Until the victim, who had passed out, suddenly reviving, rose, punch-drunk, and began, in a scream of frustration, to curse after his vanished assailants, using their identical words, with an intonation so like theirs his profanity seemed allegory.

Which it was—an allegory with which I had begun to struggle even in that time when my confused yearnings for abstract justice were inspiring me to espouse, in my complete unimportance, a cause little girls knew nothing about. And I began to wonder. For to conclude that life—even "righteous" life!—was best served by militancy was obvious logic! Then was my concern for humanity only a Liebestod sung by a sublimating masochist? Yet this love-death, it still seems to me, is below the superstitious surfaces of all popular religions. And in the real leaders—like Jesus, like Buddha—it was nearly pure. And year after year I went on looking for a "right" decision on behaviour which should take account of such a mystical paradox, which was at the very basis of all being.

9

TWO years ago, I was in Sheringham, in Norfolk, and stopped, one day, in the high street, before the window of a photographer's place; and found myself confronting a portrait of a mature, but not old, and certainly still handsome woman, "taken" at her desk, where she was surrounded by the paraphernalia of professional authorship. Written in a boldly distinguished hand, across the corner of the picture were her compliments, and the signature: "Cynthia Stockley." So she was an actual woman! And I was moved by this discovery—really apologetic! Though I shouldn't have been so surprised, for I have learned since that a successful movie, founded on her story *Poppy*, was at that time either being filmed, or had already been produced. So, to her own public, she had been, all along, very much alive.

To think that I had bracketed a writer—a human being—according to the predisposing dictates of people known to me in childhood—people against whose literary and ethical shibboleths I myself was in rebellion!—shamed me. I really should, I decided, buy one of her books and reread it. I might, afterward, find I had entirely revised my opinion of her works. My previous acquaintance with them had been confined to a surreptitious perusal of paper-back copies, presented to the Johnson girls and

258

myself by the Johnson's coloured cook, who produced a series of them, in a flatteringly tattered condition, from a drawer in a kitchen table. All these years, Mrs. Stockley had been somewhere writing (like myself), sad or happy according to the occasion (like myself), and, like myself (though it seemed more fortunately) growing older! And all the while she had stayed in my imagination where she had been placed at the beginning—the half-forgotten, disappointingly boring symbol of what fathers and mothers, in Tennessee, in the early nineteen hundreds, were displeased to consider pornography!

Poppy—if I had not found it almost as dry reading as the diary of President Polk—might have stood, as Olive Schreiner's *Story of an African Farm* did later, for a great moral and literary influence in my life! Alas, Mrs. Stockley, like Mrs. Glyn, was anticlimactic in the impression she made. Though I opened her novel with thrills which prepared for an initiation via her pen, the effect on me was so ordinary, I turned from her in secret relief and resumed Crockett's *Sir Toady Lion* with such an ardent preference for it as embarrassed me. As for *Three Weeks*—when I was fourteen, it was loaned to me by a fatherly young man a few years my senior, who wrapped it in a mackintosh before he delivered it to me with as much caution as my mother had been required to employ when trying to circulate *Anna Karenina*. I was at Red Brook, my uncle's place in the country, and to make sure I would be able to investigate a grand passion uninterruptedly, I used to steal from the house with the book, and sit with it under a copper beech tree. But it never made me indifferent to foraging ants, or to unpleasant "devil's riding horses" and "devil's darning needles" that, all too frequently, dropped from the branches over me.

That was a compliment spontaneously reserved for the Brontës and Jane Austen! And I could not help feeling, though I dared not say so, that I had got more information on falling in love from *The Mill on the Floss*. For one thing, beside the bad style, Mrs. Glyn supplied me with no draughts of nobility. She was much too genuinely pagan for my moral appetites. Defiance to society, I might support wholeheartedly; mere sordid "sin," though she suggested it might be enjoyable, struck me as flat and only dull.

However, by that time, I was in love myself, and, though imperfectly analytical, tended to test literature by a character recognized in my own emotions—for example, by an obscure, stifling joy continually engendered in me during a week end in which I was permitted to be under one roof with my beloved. It was at Idaho Springs; and in the years that have followed, I have never forgotten a single hour in the three days I spent there; or the lovely nonsense of affection with which he filled his notebook, making it a surreptitious gift to me. . . .

And the excruciating, precocious suffering he caused me by neglecting me, altered my conventional light-minded view of the relations of the sexes as something divinely provided for female exploitation, to a degree which makes my debt to him very definite and permanent. It was he who discouraged permanently a desire I had had previously to shine, like all my little maidenly compatriots, as the professional southern belle. For it is as sensible to demand of a man whose hand trembles whenever he grasps a knife that he make fame as a surgeon, as to insist that a girl who falls in love too easily develop expertly as a coquette. He drove me at last, for two years, into virtual retirement—into the self-absorption which follows heartbreak—and when I emerged, graduated, after this premature experience of major grief, it was into a new way of living. One career had ended, another begun. Though I was wretched at college and did not study, I was metamorphosed and a "highbrow." My usual acquaintances looked at me pityingly and rather fearfully, as if I had contracted a disease. Until, as though it were to demonstrate to them I still had a clean bill of mental and emotional health, I found myself "engaged" to a young bank cashier of highly uncongenial views.

However, I did, at any rate, emancipate myself from further obligations to that relic custom of feudal pioneering which ordains it that marriageable girls in the South pass their time, year in and year out, in rounds of exchange visiting! No more for me either the penalties or the benefits of a species of co-operative matchmaking, exemplified in such hospitality as will test the endurance of both hosts and guests! In the rural, and semirural South, a visitor invited to your house for a fortnight may linger for months! There can be no complaint! Reciprocity may be valuable, and has been taken for granted! The father and mother of the girl from Texas who has decided to make Tennessee her hunting ground for a winter will do as much for your own daughter when the time arrives!

At my aunt's (for we, as city people, were never typical), where the normal composition of the family included eleven souls, there was rarely a meal for which housegirl and houseboy were not required to provide seats for from fifteen to eighteen persons—the extras being, for the most part, impromptu additions to the company; though there would be among them, also, the young lady from Georgia, Alabama, or "The Lone Star State," who had arrived for Christmas eggnog and holiday junketing and might remain until the dog days of August, should it be her whim to do so.

I recollect but a single outburst protesting this presumed right of any female after a husband to seize on board and lodging in whatever quarter she considered convenient, and stay on where she willed for as long as her optimism endured. Then it was my uncle who exploded one day in disgust, admitting himself, in a rare moment of privacy, sick to death of a particular perky face and inane giggle, that had come together in the spring when swallows were being welcomed, and had been present for ten months! He never, he said, hoped to be able to enjoy a meal exclusively with his family, but he *did* ask for variety!

I don't remember when the visitor left, or how she was finally got rid of; but I suspect nothing could really be done about it until she had run through her wardrobe—the clothes she had bought and brought, and an equal number of borrowed dresses. With a risk before her of having to wear the same party frock three times in succession, she may have become suddenly amenable; or may even have resolved, of her own accord, to transfer her activities to another place. In the matter of costume, it was regarded as hardly less than disgraceful for a girl to reproduce her own effects too frequently and obviously. So travel became a double economy, a change of venue sometimes equivalent to an entirely new wardrobe. It was all made easier, too, by the freemasonry existing among girls, who agreed liberally to appropriate one another's belongings, often for weeks at a time.

Probably it was the constant stressing of the dramatic importance of physical appearances, which caused me to supplement preparations following a first permission to attend an evening party for children, with a trip to the florist's, from whom I ordered red carnations, sent to myself with seemly greetings from myself, signed "John." (I was twelve.) I wore my flowers, not too certainly, with a new scarlet point d'esprit.

Not (I must add hastily) that I commanded only invented tributes! One of the privileges of old age I have noticed (and they are few enough!) is a shameless dilation on the flattering aspects of the personal past—a habit of retrospective boasting that the more self-respecting modesty of youth would abhor. However, after my own fortieth birthday, I decided every woman able to survive such an ordeal was completely justified in claiming for herself, as an inalienable right, a share in contributing to complimentary legends (in memoriam) of "the glorious dead." I was not a beautiful child, but neither was I stupid, except as I reacted with blind impressionableness to demands made by southern custom upon the vanity of womanhood. It seems improbable that a child in the North would have been aware, as I was before I was seven, that Santa Claus, for example, though his supernatural powers elevated him to the status of the angels, was, also, a man. Yet I remember clearly a Christmas Eve after the sacrifice of my chief adornment to malaria, when my mother, in despair over my appearance and anxious to have me shine at the next day's festivities, sent me to bed with my hair done in curlers improvised from strips of soft rag. Something warned me not to object openly against the libellous effect she was willing to let me make on Saint Nicholas; but I had in mind the jacket design on *The Night Before Christmas*, and, while I hung up my stocking, rebelled privately against an invidious comparison the expected nocturnal visitor was bound to make between a little girl whose head was encircled by disgusting humps and knobs, and that chubby-cheeked, golden-orioled sum of infant perfections depicted by an artist. And as soon as my mother, ingenuously oblivious to the havoc she had wrought, had kissed me and left me to what she imagined would be innocently selfish dreams of gifts, I snatched off the curlers, and, settling myself upon the pillow carefully, arranged my locks in such a fashion as to make the utmost of their temporary paucity. In my realistic conception of things, I was rewarded for my cautious foresight—it was the Christmas I received a dollhouse which, to this very moment, seems to me like the apotheosis of all dollhouses, and even far superior to the Queen's.

Such premature concern for male opinion may strike the Yankee as only idiosyncratic and perverse; and it may well be that I was abnormally sensible of what was expected of a little girl. But the background for my behaviour was general suggestion, which affected other children, too. For me, pervasive innuendoes were embodied in a jovial, portly bachelor called Mr. Blakeman, who had claimed me as his sweetheart from the age of three. He owned a dry goods store; and when my mother took me with her on a shopping tour, would pounce upon me from the door of his emporium, decoy me in with gifts of chocolates and peppermints, swing me to a vacant counter, and entice me into giving recitations from the works of Eugene Field, before an audience of males who always laughed uproariously. The pact between us was sealed finally when I received from him a little silver "friendship bracelet" with a jewelled, heart-shaped lock engraved: "with Blakeman's love." And once, on Sunday, he invited me to drive with him behind a tandem pair which he manipulated dashingly. I wore a new blue cashmere frock from New Orleans, and carried, for the first time, a small blue silk parasol with pale pink frills; and proudly, almost suffocated by the steaming bulk which towered beside me in the narrow seat of his smart vehicle, endured an ordeal of discomfort compensated for by the display.

Though I may have represented an extreme, all little southern girls, as I remember them, were almost frighteningly precocious in developing sex-consciousness. For one thing, constant contact with the coloured race both stimulated and informed them about matters veiled by late-Victorian, white taboos. And in the case of boys, strictly conventional white parents were incredibly obtuse, often employing, as a paid companion for a lonely child, some small Negro, who was called "a play boy." At ten, we priggishly reared daughters of "first families" were familiar with a language we half comprehended which would have been proper for a bawdyhouse. It seeped in from untrammelled sources with a curious, poisoning incongruity that made our natural guardians into egregious hypocrites. While we tripped forth politely, with our miniature cardcases, and, under adult supervision, called on one another formally, like polite "little ladies," we adventured, simultaneously, into forbidden territories we found terrible and strange. Odd indeed it is to think that such tender maidens as we were, occasionally escaped in a nursery pony cart into a province perilously near the sort exposed by Brand Whitlock in one of the earliest of "muckraking" novels: *The Thirteenth District!*

We were attracted there by a large, drably unimposing frame house, which was a conspicuous salient for our expeditions because, extraordinarily, though it was on the fringes of a Negro settlement, it was inhabited by white women. On this account, and by reason of numberless semi-intelligible explanations of its significant repute, it fascinated us as if it had been a Castle of Otranto, or the villa into which Count Dracula descended from his mountain stronghold for variety in summer months. And every now and then, quaking, but gleeful over our own daring, we would turn the pony from the main road, and make a detour by this awesomely mysterious place. Y., the mistress of the diminutive vehicle in which we crowded, cowering, would then try to put a brave front on her own timidity and defiantly curb the pony's trot until it became a walk. Then we could covertly and deliberately survey a seedy yard containing poor grass and a few shrivelling cannas; or scrutinize the dirty curtains before upper windows where the blinds, even at midday, always seemed to be drawn. I remember, once, a sharp glance given us by a thin-featured girl in a wrapper, who, as we passed, stared at us from a lawn swing in which she was idly enjoying the sun; and that the casual look she bestowed upon us turned back on me like a weapon the dangerous feeling of my own guilt. As Y. lashed the pony into a gallop, it produced in the lot of us an explosion of hysteria; and as we rattled on along the regained public thoroughfare, we might have been fleeing for our lives.

What had most amazed me in this exploration of a demimonde had been the evidence of poverty. From a

House of Usher, bound to fall in the end, I had anticipated sinister grandeur. Instead—shockingly!—we had
discovered only a shabby dwelling, in need of paint and
repairs! Why, *anybody* might have lived in it! And the
girl in the swing—not pretty, with a slovenly air of discouragement and languor, her clothes without a single
touch of luxury! By her mere appearance, she annihilated
forever the "romance of vice."

The stories whispered surreptitiously by little coloured
children had primed all of us, voluptuously, for horror;
but, actually, quite simply, I remembered Mary; and my
heart was sick. Before this, in *Eva Gay*, I have tried to
write of Mary—she was one of three or four literal in-
gredients among the many fictional elements in that
novel—one people not initiate have questioned on the
score of plausibility. Though I have frequently, indignantly, protested against such an interrogation of cor-
roboratable plain fact, I incline, now, to accept the
aesthetic basis for these objections. After all, though I
am telling the precise truth when I say I, at seven, loved
Mary, who was fourteen, more than I have ever loved
anyone else; I know, also, that, when she fell into disgrace and was carried off into concealment, so that I
never heard of her again—ever!—certain feelings she engendered, which belonged to her, and to no other being,
were forced so deep underground they cannot be
brought to the surface again. As well insist a dumb animal eloquently articulate devotion to a lost master, as ask
me to express, today, what Mary used to mean to me.
Yet she belongs here, in a chapter which might be fit-
tingly concluded with a discourse on chivalry, which,
it is reputed, flowered in the South of the early nineteen
hundreds as never elsewhere since the disbanding of the

Round Table! It is particularly appropriate to mention her, not only because she was physically beautiful (with a profile like that of Henny Porten, a German cinema actress, now retired I believe, and the loveliest human object I ever saw in this world), but, more notably, considering her tragedy, because she was such a *good* little girl—docile, dutiful, as instinctively housewifely as Meg in *Little Women*! As naturally domestic and "normally" kindly as little Daisy in *Jo's Boys*! Indeed Mary was as lacking in those impulses which make for sexual precocity—as really stupid, in one way of looking at such things!—as Louisa M. Alcott herself!

And why didn't they take *that* into account? I used to wonder; after I was commanded to forget her; after I was told—incredible!—she had become a *bad* girl! Because, if you please, she had had a baby—and it took three years to ferret *that* out! And three years more to make literally certain the baby had come into the world with a father, who went about uncastigated (appearances deceived me then) by what, for her, had been calamity no one could mend! And whether or not those militant feminists who, for a while, during my adolescence, commanded my admiration and respect, in the end, made it impossible for any little girl to share Mary's fate, I don't know even yet. Mary was a Kentuckian—as a victim, she was universal. As universal, and as much a victim as so many of her male contemporaries—poor romance-starved and semiliterate little adolescent, would-be profligates in southern towns and villages!

The Portuguese tell an apocryphal tale of Dom Pedro Segundo, whose beloved mistress, Inez de Castro, was hounded to her death by the jealousies of a political opposition which had refused to recognize her as his Queen.

In the city, my father, affected by the general American contempt for leisure as immoral, compromised with antecedent custom, and seldom reached his office before ten o'clock; but my uncle, after his morning toddy and a breakfast scarcely distinguishable in its dimensions from the dinner itself, often did not leave the house until eleven. As for "the girls," they were allowed a lenience which exceeded even his! Small children, whose nurses had more to do in a day than sit about pampering the whims of the dilatory, might be fed, clothed, or deservedly spanked, before the sun was well up and the dew dried on the grass; whereas "the girls," in as many years as had to be lived through between puberty and the attainment of their goal in marriage, received consecrated treatment—even as western American Indian maidens, or native female Central Africans.

And so did I. . . . Until, as though on purpose to demonstrate for those psychiatrists and psychoanalysts who attribute to a disappointment of the glands every imaginative work of man, from the stone paintings in caves in Europe to the poetry of Shakespeare and the novels of Mrs. Wolf, I left off attending parties in a professional spirit, drew the works of Schopenhauer, Nietzsche and Karl Marx from the library, and settled down to write. And if the gaze so devoutly fixed on the typewriter sometimes swerved, as it were inadvertently, toward the mirror, who reared in Tennessee will dare to condemn in me a certain inevitable fidelity to type? Renegades strayed from the early worship of Aphrodite ought, at least, to make better Christians (if not invariably better Marxists) than persons from regions which love mankind in glorified abstract, but incline toward persecution when man manifests his character in the flesh—better Christians, that is, once maturity has made them tolerant!

Though I acknowledge it true that not all the budding little Saphos, Manons, Adrienne Lecouvriers, Toscas and Becky Sharps I once admired for their ability to produce from the ether, and with the lift of an eyelash, limitless numbers of five-pound boxes of crystallized fruits, while, with equal effortlessness, they caused American Beauty roses at a dollar the blossom, orchids at five dollars the boutonière, to spring like daisies in a country field, quite bear out my thesis. Some, unhappily, having forsaken the pagan gods of love to be consoled appropriately by Mrs. Emily Post. And, in justice to them, there are as many who, after adversities, have accomplished, without any weak nourishment from theories, conservative, biologically approvable heroisms. For however one may rail against the standards responsible for the cultivated, naïve, yet eminently practical, cynicism of the southern coquette, women are the backbone of the South; and it is they who have kept the South alive, and even lively, through dark days threatening it with cultural extinction. Having myself given over, to a degree, an earlier perfectionism which interfered with realistic evaluations of the attained existent, I now recognize, in dozens of families, in which the males had become inept through discouragement, women whose practical courage, veiled by self-obliterating tact, was the one rock to be relied upon, where everything else tottered.

And whether it was Mrs. P., who rallied from a tubercular "decline" (it was genuine) to reform (yes, successfully!) a husband whose drunkenness had annihilated his professional career, while his inebriate gallantries made him the town joke; or Mrs. J., whose pallid gentility concealed the iron will which gave her strength to accumulate, with a slow, sub rosa disposal of jams, jellies and beaten biscuit she made herself, enough small change to pay for the social entertainment of her five pretty, poverty-stricken daughters, who went to all the dances in wonderful dresses cut and sewed by their mother by night, and thus finally effected the matches she had hoped they would make. Or Mrs. Z., a widow with two boys and two girls on her hands, who, subsisting with them on next to nothing in an antebellum ruin forever offering to collapse on their heads, so cleverly exploited local snobbery in its relation to her own brood, that she not only warded off the starvation logically to be expected for them, but married the girls to rich men who felt honoured by her condescension, and wisely sent the boys north to become wealthy, too. Whether it was Mrs. P., or Mrs. J., or Mrs. Z., or scores of other self-effacing, softly-spoken females, these—the women!—were the South's dependence, and its resource in calamity.

And as I look back, it seems to me that, in Clarksville, at any rate, in my generation, even the most frivolous and parasitically inclined members of my sex, supplied, after the Negroes, whatever there was in "atmosphere" which might have been considered colourful. This may not have been true previously—my uncle-in-law, Dr. Drane, was rumoured to have fallen ill of a grave bronchitis, contracted through standing with his head uncovered, in the street, in an icy wind, while he was greeting a talkative lady! But, in my day, male youth had already succumbed to the spreading effects of growing Babbittry: it was, for all its boasts of profligateness, somewhat neuter, and, in the main, not very attractive (though there were, of course, exceptions). And among married men I used to observe, in contrast to my father (and to my uncle Julien, so impeccable in his winter riding togs or in his white duck in summer), there had begun that yielding to slovenly personal habits—that tendency to go collarless in hot weather, and to attend only segregate gatherings!—which is now characteristic of all America; and is such a terrible implied commentary on the Anglo-Saxon conception of romantic monogamy! Such a powerful inferential argument for the realistic code of France!

However, whatever the shortcomings of the men, whose minds were entirely preoccupied with that poor thing business is at best, while they sottishly resigned themselves to the interminable pretext of matrimonial fidelity in the same spirit prisoners under life sentence will, on occasion, outrage their warders with a show of indifference to both censoring and punishment; the women, though you may disparage their ideals, never gave up. Wed, or unwed, successful or confronted with defeat, they seldom lowered the banner they had agreed to carry, on which was inscribed, together with some genuinely noble sentiments: FIRST AND FORE-MOST, SEX APPEAL! And there was the beautiful Mrs. Jones, with her smart equipages and her plumed picture hats à la Lillian Russell, who, when she appeared in Franklin Street, produced a manoeuvring by the male population in which the actions of individuals synchronized with a perfection not surpassed in the German Army! Mrs. Jones, who, though her "social standing" was unexcelled in the community, and her husband a respected, solidly prosperous citizen, so fired the fancies of the masculine gossipmongers peering at her avidly

276

from bars and banks that the least imaginative man among them outdid Paul de Kock in scandalous inventiveness. On the one hand, Mrs. Jones and a younger following of pert misses parading a forlorn pseudo sophistication, which, though it was not much, still embraced nuances in seduction which were wasted on the audience; and, on the other hand, Miss Mae Murray and Miss Arthur Bishop, who were "not received," and may hence appear with their real names in print.

And there were other names, known to every adult in the town, and to us children by the time we were ten when we used to con them from the telephone directory. Unhallowed names, which were luridly attracting—names of strange heroines who, while they suffered social obloquy, figured periodically as provocation for recurrent bruitish brawling consequent upon sex rivalries; all furtive, and all carefully suppressed. I don't know which of the million tales I heard at the time might have been verified, and maybe their common extravagant improbability cancelled them all. To have credited one would have been to establish a dangerous precedent since neither the humblest nor the leading citizens escaped. For that matter, if you apply a psychoanalytic theory of inverse compensation for omitted acts, tellers and listeners, in their interchangeable roles, were equally exemplary. As exemplary, according to this reasoning, as the billion other purveyors of destructive gossip residing in the small towns of the world. Where scandalmongering takes the place of novel writing and expresses sex frustrations and divertible desires! And people who, in this way, seem to work off such fancies as come to them from a realistic source, develop, curiously, an acutal aversion for books that display the earmarks of a similarly literal origin; and want to read only the grown-up fairy tales of Eleanor Porter and Harold Bell Wright! To an amateur psychologist, it is bewildering!

I was bewildered indeed when, around 1908 and 1909, I used to join the evening procession to the soda fountain, and would realize, as I passed a line of drummers ensconced comfortably in chairs tilted against the front of the Arlington Hotel, that I was running the identical gamut of furtive appraisals turned on the girls from the establishment I was not supposed to mention, who were driving by, before me, in a usual conspicuous ignoring. And once, as I have set down in *Eva Gay*, rebellion prompted me to attempt conversation with one of these inoffensive-looking, reticent pariahs, who was much embarrassed by my well-meant tactlessness.

I suspect she was not only perturbed lest my minor outrage of convention be paid for by herself, but was faintly shocked, too, as by something aesthetically unfitting. Even as I was shocked, and my sentimental defence of those pursuing a calling I had decided to consider only unfortunate, was strained, when, a little later, in the Pullman, on a train to New Orleans, I had the car to myself until I was joined by two brazen-faced damsels who, as soon as they had settled themselves for the journey, commenced a patently indecent flirtation with a passing conductor. They demanded from me a yet greater adjustment of my preconceived ideas when, the next morning, I discovered them in the dressing room in bright scarlet sateen camisoles and chemises, and noticed they had very dirty necks, and preferred cosmetics to soap and water! (In that day, intimate garments for *ladies* were *never*, under any circumstances, anything but *white*.)

278

Probably my persistence in championing unpopular causes defied dampening experience chiefly because of the undying moral weakness previously indicated here, which continued to make it next to impossible to take a dare. The dares, oddly, always seemed to come from boys; as from my cousin Frank, disporting himself in a skiff on Red River one afternoon, while I, from the shore, admired his skill. "I dare you to climb up to the fork and hang on to the rope," he challenged, pointing to the large sycamore tree which swept tall boughs above a thirty-foot swimming hole. "Go on—I'll row below you when you can't hold on, since you can't swim!" And almost before I knew it, I found myself obediently scrambling up the trunk, forced on by that will of the timid which solicits desperately approval from the brave. And I remember how, quaking inwardly, I grasped the rope affixed to an upper branch, and leapt; and the sky flew toward me, and the river, tolerable while it had seemed remote, became, instantly, a lapping, leaden, too-actual substance. "I'll count to a hundred—see if you can stick it out. One, two, three—!" Frank began, with that bored air of a sultan for which I adored him; as, drifting an indifferent distance from me, he watched me dangling like a corpse from a gibbet, and half-suspended by entangled hair, like Absalom. "Seven, eight, nine, ten—five hundred, can't you? That'd be five minutes," he encouraged, taunting me with his deliberateness.

Five minutes! . . . Already my wrists trembled. Already the weight of my body wrenched at my armpits and drew the last strength from my shoulders! My fingers, tortured with rope burn, had suddenly begun to numb. . . . "Ninety-six, ninety-seven, ninety-eight, ninety-nine, one hundred! Pretty good," he conceded, his voice lacking the enthusiasm that might have been assuagement for my pangs of hell. "Sixty-one, sixty-two, sixty-three, sixty-four, sixty-five—! That's O.K., kid! Don't be a quitter! Almost to two hundred now!" And I don't yet know just when I gave up! But I recall the river, as it brimmed, swollen, and seemed to rise closer; and that its surface, all at once, looked turbid; and that it seemed to be magnetizing me slowly into its cryptic, inscrutable depths. And that the sun, a moment before, merely brilliant, grew dazzling, blinding with abrupt ferocity. Until my ears, as though catching from afar the song of the Lorelei, rang with invocations to abandon—and I was slipping. . . . Gently, gently slipping, not even caring to resist. . . . And it was as though the stream, with its unremitting wandering, while it moved on, sucking and hissing at the mud bluff, had almost covered me, while I sank ineffably into a liquid, fear-obliterating, terrible embrace!

Yet in this decline of resistance, some contrary instinct, protecting me from myself, must have survived, causing me to cry out, though it might have been in joy; for Frank brought the skiff about, rowed a few yards rapidly, and I dropped; startled when I received an unfriendly wooden impact from the bottom of the boat. And I was surprised, as, exclaiming and pushing myself to an elbow, I stared about at a world strangely unaltered by the passing of a crisis. "So so," Frank condescended. "Guess it was pretty good for a girl. Pretty good when you can't swim, and had your clothes on. But it wasn't any five minutes!" As usual, he was taking pains to safeguard me from demoralization by conceit. "Say, guess that took it out of you—you're white as paper. We might as well get on back to the house—it's dinnertime anyway." And he regarded me with the compassion naturally engendered by my sex (with the very glance so often cast by male—particularly young—reviewers upon the works of women novelists!).

"I wasn't scared—only I reckon my wrists aren't as strong as yours," I defended humbly. Secretly, I felt a burst of exhilaration—some sixth sense told me Frank was unadmittedly impressed! And exhausted, but in the peaceful satisfaction following an ordeal, I became, again, happily aware of the day's hot stillness; and of the green song of silence and motion from the river and the trees. Far off, on a hill, a woodpecker bored; drilling minutely through vast spaces; as though it escaped determinedly, out of the glittering perfection of high noon, into somewhere else. And on a rock ashore, a squirrel, its tail fine-flaring like the handle of an urn, arrested rigidly, set up a chuckle of exasperation; the small voice of impotent rebellion loud like that of a conspirator in a huge, hushed theatre. Ahead, logs, inert like alligators, nosed at a sand bar; and on the skimming currents, water spiders traced a jerky course in a handwriting of stiffly darting legs; where twigs and shed leaves half-eaten by caterpillars were webbed together with scum and soaked dust. While away, over us, in a blue like blue ice, above this heat which consumed clothing until we were as nakedly warmed as children in the womb, flapped, as usual, an indomitable buzzard—a majestically sailing dot, too remote to menace; sinking, rising, circling, and accentuating peace with its own poise. Until the freedom it displayed as an infinite possession might almost have belonged to ourselves; and seemed but to wait for us to claim it. A freedom to be attained without more effort than went with acceptance in the flesh of this plenitude of summer, in which one lingered, desireless, and as though forever, without any want save for what one had. And I could feel—almost!—though inarticulately, imagination replaced by a stasis in thought, in which every bit of me saw, without need or excuse for commentary, the green, aqueous details of a whole world wrapped in lovely lethargy, in which time—even that important five minutes of clinging with my whole self to a rope like a symbol of destiny!—counted not at all!

But there was Frank, whose thirteen-year-old proclivity for doing and daring had still to be considered, his excellent opinion of me bought and rebought! For who was I—a girl, and only eleven!—to despise his requirements! And at this precise moment, the old farm bell on the rear porch of the house, tolled remindfully when children were late to meals, began sounding alarm. "Come on—guess you're strong enough! Gimme a hand!" he ordered, grounding the skiff with a jolt; and I scrambled out, and meekly assisted him to drag the boat onto the mud and rock; where it lay like a harboured crocodile, with that look of ignominy peculiar to things made for locomotion when they are in disuse.

"Don't know what the dickens to do with these oars," Frank remarked absently. "They're too heavy for you, and I've got all this fishing tackle and a lot of other junk."

"They are *not* too heavy!" I disputed recklessly, "and I can carry them!" And I accepted with assumed carelessness what he casually discarded. And we began climbing, through a quiet desecrated by the tiniest insect activity, where the windless sloth of the forest regretted lost ecstasy. But if the oars, long before we reached the summit of our nearly upright path, were like a burden of

282

Saint Christopher, increasingly weighted with each yard gained, there was the passive delight of Frank's commendation to blend with weariness and relieve my awkwardness as a mountaineer. Until rewards were added to when we emerged from the silence of the wood, into the less candid fields, where bouncing Bets, black-eyed Susans, and Queen Anne's lace, under a miasmic veil cast by the sun, spread, tossed and fretted by a sudden hot breeze.

Yet, as we passed Uncle Charlie and another, more presentable coloured man (not an habitual retainer), who were spading flower beds, the glare beating upon them like rain on the just; and skirted the back veranda, where Mammy Alice and a gangly, volatile housegirl named Lizzie were quarrelling in the mellifluous, ungrammatical tongue which is Negro-English; and stepped from a blenching oven into a refrigerator coolness, where honeysuckle, balsam creeper and white clematis screened a line of deck chairs and hammocks, my contentment with myself wavered. And as we went indoors to store our impedimenta in a nook beside a stone fireplace, where they were companioned by shotguns and rifles, the house, though I was familiar with every corner of every room, seemed suddenly alien—inhabited by strangers! I did *almost* hang five minutes! I thought; as if conjuring a necessary sign of something demanded to save me. But what had stimulated like a physical intoxicant was all at once gone; the sharp, impure exuberance of gratified vanity was not enough. And even if Frank should recount my exploit, it would only leave me excited and miserably self-conscious, with my dearest wish a desire to run off and escape notice. It was as though I had, continually, to accumulate evidence which would prove me "not guilty." Though I never really knew of what I felt myself to be accused. Only that when *they* praised me—even to tell me I wore a becoming dress—I somehow always thought they were lying. And decided, underneath, belligerently, that *I*, at any rate, would tell the truth.

10

O N ITS northern border, Tennessee is four hundred and thirty-six miles across, and its southern boundary line contracts this measure to some hundred miles less. The state's most singular topographical feature is the Sequatchie valley; and the highest point of land in its acreage of forty-two thousand and fifty miles is Mount Guyot, which is six thousand, six hundred and thirty-six feet above sea level. So says the *Encyclopaedia Britannica*, which is a genuinely informing book. All I can contribute to such valuable assembling of data by scholars and educators is some early personal impressions, which were intimate and prolonged only in the restricted neighbourhood of Clarksville. Though I did, now and then in my childhood, venture as far north as Gutherie, Kentucky, as far south as Memphis and Chattanooga, as far west as Nashville, as far east as Knoxville; still, what I am able to remember is too overcast by subjective emanations to rise above what is, informationally speaking, a very low level. It may be little more than self-portraiture; and that is trivial subject matter for the reader with an eye on universalities from which to compute a future for the whole human race.

Though I have tried to select, from a plethora of memories, some which may bear on a conditioning peculiar to a particular locale, I cannot pretend to certainty even in this choice; after all, Tennessee and Mississippi, though quite distinguishable, are also very alike—like all the South, and like all America, despite its many differences of place. And there has been a further complication due to the gradual erasure of geographical demarcations after a child begins to read; when Mark Twain or Herman Melville will as probably figure equally in the development of a life passed in Georgia and one in Maine. While I was at school in New Orleans, the works of Stephen Crane, Frank Norris and Theodore Dreiser influenced me far more significantly than did my half-creole milieu, discussed idyllically in the stories of George Cable. And as I matured I owed more to conversations with Cyril Kay-Scott than to the accident of a residence in France or South America or North Africa.

In effect, the personal derivation of these somewhat anecdotal reminiscences puts the detachment of the compilers of the *Britannica* beyond me for the time being. And as I conclude, I feel an almost overwhelming yearning to abandon both my wavering attempt to capture a regional-mindedness never my talent, and the feint occasionally here made at contributing a little to visions of statisticians, who have a patience I lack and are able to wade through contexts of small, specific physical happenings when there is a sufficiently important abstraction in view. Instead, I want to remember and remember, without searching for explanations in self-justificatory theories, qualities of adventure and excitement in my own beginnings—maybe they are everybody's beginnings after all!

And the failure, so far, to mention a large, rock-sugar Easter egg with a peep show inside it seems a terrible omission, for which compensation is urgently required. When you squinted an eye and peered with the other through a tiny magic casement, you looked on fairy lands forlorn, where, amidst pink pasteboard houses and acid-green, two-dimensional trees, shepherds and shepherdesses wandered tenderly in pursuit of lambs that might have been an innocent inspiration to Blake. No object in this scene as sensitively elegant as a picture by Watteau was more than half an inch high! And surely it deserves *some* notice in a cultural reference to Tennessee!

And all those Christmas mornings, Biblically holy, with a scent through the house like the smell of a forest at dawn, and the tree, like a pillar of fire, lighting the Assumption of a doll-angel in a spun-glass dress made by the glass blowers—those wonderful people who came to Clarksville with a show, and drank pure flame, and miraculously trapped diminutive, naked china babies inside amber and transparent imitations of a real cigar!—aren't they significant?

Far more impressive to us children than the recognized contemporaneous heroines of Tennessee, was Millie-Christine; and we felt privileged when we paid to be received by her where she—or is it they?—sat on a platform in a dingy, ill-lit little tent, benignly bowing and dispensing smiling condescension with the kindly dignity of a dumpy twin Victoria. Her duplex armchair made every whit as impressive to her reverent audience as a throne in Buckingham Palace. She wore her fascinating strange misfortune far more gracefully than many martyrs wear their crowns.

And as a figure stirring to young imaginations, how much more an influence was Bosco, who "ate 'em alive," than bronze gentlemen like Lee or Forrest, superiorly inactive on their stony plinths in public parks! Bosco, whose rabidly anonymous presence, menaced from the bottom of a canvas pit, where snakes, striking at air with fangless jaws, continually seething, re-embraced themselves in rage! It was his example which induced us to erect a barrier across the nursery floor, surround ourselves with every necktie in the household not in use, and attempt swallowing them. He converted a succession of Elks' Carnivals into freshly rewritten chapters from *The Jungle Book.*

And despite the lessons in caste we children, perforce, attended, memory still stores accents which ignored them! For instance, Mrs. B., who "sewed," lived in a cottage crowded with plush furniture, lace cushions and preposterous embroidery, and owned a grey-jowled pug! It sat, as if forever, on a hearthrug woven with pink roses and a couchant and bombastic-looking Saint Bernard; the live dog an asthmatic symbol of those passive virtues of persistence with which petty realists reduce romantics who delude themselves with posturings! Symbol, in fact, in all but antlike industry, of the whole pious, eminently practical class to which Mrs. B. herself belonged. Is it for implications of a culture I remember her, or for twelve pairs of durable, detested, lace-edged drawers my mother ordered made for me? These seamstresses impressed me—elderly Miss S. remains a far more fascinating recollection than the socially imposing D.'s. I see her as a gentle, obstinate, self-deprecating ghost with pin-filled mouth, in limbo—in a twilight, like her spiritual effluvium, which filled her huge, deserted drawing room perpetually. Great gaunt pier glasses—someone's aspiration for magnificence—reflect a tired, dyspeptic, genteel wraith, who, as she stitched the web of other

288

people's clothes, spied fearfully on Main Street, filing by a Lady of Shalott!

Such immortality as my brief life can undesignedly bestow is shared by her with the two Misses M.: one lean as leather and the other like a wilted barrel lacking hoops. These moustached virgins, driving in a rheumatic buggy, drawn by an unwilling, weedy horse, belaboured with monotonous insistence by the pepperishly kind, elder Miss M., were tailpiece ornaments for every funeral wending through the town. Their very comments on the weather rang with their delight in wholesale banqueting on corpses. Even the younger, who, when she greeted you, warmed with a glow of spurious maternity, betrayed consistently her possession of a suppressed harpy's soul. I used to go to them for fittings, among lares and penates, where ranged crayon portraits of deceased and still contemporaneous M.'s, alike in bold, hermaphroditic features bearing testimony to the family's sexless moral uprightness, glared from the walls, on horsehair sofas and accumulated rigid bric-a-brac, as on the shambles of a battlefield.

Quite recently, my son and I, motoring from Kansas to New York, made a detour from the Lincoln Highway into a familiar-unfamiliar region where the country teemed with black people; a road sign, which invited us to be conducted by the victim's brother through the cave which was the scene of Floyd Collins's tragedy, brought back that pair of gruesome spinster poets of my earlier days. As we sped through fluent ruts traced by some car which had preceded us, and dust, as fine as antheap powderings, bizarrely covered us as if in preparation for a masquerade, I recalled accounts of men and women, gathering, with unembarrassed heartlessness, to guzzle soda pop, consume hot dogs and scatter peanut shells, before a tomb from which the buried gasped the record of his own advancing anguish. Were crowds like those the true inheritors here? I wondered suddenly. Were they legitimate descendants of pioneers whose star was greed? Was the America I had envisaged as a child completely dead—like Buffalo Bill; whose slim, unaged audacity, and profile, purely perfect and as abstract as the graceful and incredible mathematics of his never-failing marksmanship, had inspired laudatory contests between me and Frank, who always claimed, in cowboy games, the male prerogative to be called Bill? It was hot, with the torrid heat of the South one forgets to compare with the stringent blaze of New England in summer; and yet I shivered to some dank, pursuing and too-mortal breath.

We were nearing Gutherie, in my childhood, quite as much a focal point for travellers as Rome had ever been. Surely in Gutherie—! . . . In my callowest youth, these roads had swarmed with juvenile Orlandos and demurely perky Rosalinds, rebellious against cold authority, and eloping in hordes to Bowling Green, where marriages were possible without parental consent; until this landscape along the state line became a Forest of Arden. Alas, though I had done my best, and not too badly, to be seen for weeks together with a different stripling every evening and competing braces of them at each dance, not even in my valedictory sixteenth year had I eloped! And still, when we had passed new stores and the fine movie theatre which had not been here previously, oh, *surely*, there would be the park! Unless in Portugal, where, in the gardens surrounding the Palace of Penna, at Cintra, are artificial Moorish "ruins" built

290

by a dead, Byronic king, nothing resembling that park has ever existed!

And I recalled its band kiosk, which had been derelict already around 1904, its mildewed wooden railings so mould-padded they were like green rubber. Trees grew densely about it, and the slightest shower instantly accumulated scores of pools reflecting moss-grown trunks and untrimmed grass, below the level of adjacent fields. I had never seen a human being enter the confines of this little acreage, along two sides of which excavations for railway embankments had produced the equivalent of an impassable, medieval moat.

When I visited Gutherie in my childhood, it must have rained very often; for my memorized sense of the park was never complete without a plain song of frogs; an eerie, sonorous bedlam, permanently linked with hasty snatches made at underwear and shoes and stockings in a foreignly exciting hotel room; from which my mother and I, followed by a couple of Negroes who had recognized us as "from Clarksville," would emerge, through corridors plaintively filled with another mystical music from invisible snorers, into an inscrutably expectant darkness which anticipated morning. Then, as our private entourage, bundling us, with our valises, along a platform and over indistinguishable crossties, prepared to deliver us into the hands of a Pullman porter, whose natty duck jacket put to shame their own sleazy misfit mohair livery, and we were thrust abruptly up steps into the sophisticated atmosphere of real journeying; a *knee-deep, knee-deep*, from the little shattered park, always came to us as a last word from everything we were leaving. Until the express we had boarded was off, like a rocket lit from within, across a world of stars and farms and towns.

Surely *now*—! I thought, noticing, ahead of our car, the station hotel; and how shrunken, worn and tired it looked, after its long haphazard service to the railway company. . . . And I remembered a steel engraving of Charlotte Cushman as Lady Macbeth—it had somehow seemed to belong with the park. And with it a certain family of buxom little girls whose loveliness had been so lachrymosely advertised in Russellville by their hard-working mother who was owner of a boardinghouse, that my parents had dubbed the daughters "the Ken-wigses." Once, for a fortnight, when we were without a cook, "Mrs. Kenwigs" had supplied our breakfasts, sending them in little covered dishes which made simple things like ham and eggs alluring as a fairy feast; until it had seemed as if you had only to clap your hands and command softly: *Little goat, bleat! Little table, appear!* to be fed as regally and almost supernaturally as Sara Crewe, when she was rescued by the "Indian gentleman." The whole experience had become marvellously extraordinary when my mother had accused "Mrs. Kenwigs," seriously, of putting perfume in the sausages! So surely in Gutherie—! I decided, as we turned into another street as dry as baked confectioner's sugar.

There was not even a relic! Not even a skeleton portion of the bandstand! Not even a section of fence! The trees had been felled; and the plot, filled in and levelled, and as bare as your hand, was a stubbled scrap which glittered cinders tossed there from the railway line. Even I could have thrown into it empty tins, and bottles cleared from the medicine cabinet, and not cared a whit! It was the same as anywhere. . . .

I knew, of course, this happened to everybody—but it was surprising just the same. Just as death, whenever and however it comes, however much you have prepared for it, will certainly come as a surprise. There was a strange place in my mind, and I began to be frightened. Had I only *dreamed* the Pullman porter wielding our bags with his insolent ease of long practice and ushering us into dim sanctities of green-enveloped berths? Had there never been any frogs?

When I was a child, the people among whom I lived were very superstitious. I have never forgotten the horrified face of Mrs. R., when she called on my mother and happened to catch me in the very act of opening an umbrella in the house—it was a death warrant! If you saw the new moon over the wrong shoulder, or spilled salt, and failed to ward off evil consequences with appropriate rituals, you were sleepless for nights. If you were so feckless as to walk heedlessly under a ladder, there was really nothing to be done! And *nobody*—at least nobody *sane!*—ignored the sacred attributes of hay wagons and rabbits' feet! Besides, in Clarksville, there had always been a local bogey to propitiate—old Kate, the Bell witch, who had settled demoniacally in the Bell homestead on Red River, shortly after 1804, and reigned there ever since; extending her malicious operations periodically across two counties. After the murder of John Bell, in 1846, even Andrew Jackson had believed in her! My problem, when I was a little girl, was to destroy her —to extinguish her by the sheer force of cultivated scepticism! Because I thought my own involuntary faith in her revived her powers, it seemed to me the gravest matter to draw on a *left* shoe before you had shod a *right* foot properly. (*Three Negroes!*) Kate detested numbers which were multiples of three! In a top-floor bathroom was a clothes chute which descended to a basement laundry; for years, I never passed it without opening the door and spitting down the vast, black shaft three times—or again three times three! I recognized the externality of these devices as no more than palliative. How kill conviction? Lying wakeful, thinking how best to preclude my grey, presistent thoughts of Kate, I felt her loathly being fattening. Combating her, affirmed her! How invoke the blankness of true disregard?

How almost good those *positive* terrors, compared to my dread upon discovering the park was nothing but a space it had once occupied! So mean! Now, where there should have been conviction, warm and solid as a beating heart, there was this hole which looked on nowhere—only a tiny rent, but it destroyed a complete fabric of imaginings. At Soria Moria Castle, the Knight, stumbling on the ogre's secret, had found bones, at least—not empty cerements!

At *least*, in 1900, there had been a game called "Brownies," played by Frank, Elizabeth and me! *They* would uphold me—at least *that* occurrence had been actual! It really *had* required us to remove our footgear to safeguard ourselves against surveillance, while we committed depredations on a store of sweetmeats in a secretary in the bedroom of the Gracey grandmother! Then we, who despised common thievery, entering on tiptoe, would wriggle, with a slight gymnastic effort, underneath her bed; from which we could reach forth and turn the key of the old secretary where her stock was kept, her deafness aiding us conveniently. We pilfered shamelessly, retiring later to the attic where we had a cache—not vulgar criminals! Rather heroes, with the unscathed con-

sciences of New York gangsters, or bold members of
the K.K.K., who complimented Palmer Cox! A *fact!*
. . . Perhaps I could begin upon a certain night when
Mammy Alice, cleverly pretending she detected rats,
fetched a long broom and mercilessly tried to prod us
from our hiding place! Suffering for our delusion that
a mouselike quiet was a satisfactory contradiction of the
sense of touch, we bore her pommellings stoically; until,
later, she betrayed us openly. And weren't we girls, escaping adult condemnations for which Frank had to bear
full brunt, reaping our first reward from the despising
double standard which immediately put us down as dupes
of a superior masculine initiative? So *that*, at any rate,
was verifiable, and *might* mean something which related
me specifically to Tennessee. Even to shadowy female
figures upon pillions, and to soundless men in moccasins,
who trod the Indian traces through the Blue Ridge and
Great Smoky gorges around 1784, when women in the
wilderness had extra value as a rarity.

Oh, let it be that, after all, that park—that strip of
earth which might have been a potter's field!—was not
anonymous! Let there be resurrection for those drowned
in puddles under withering oaks and maples around 1904!
Instead of this cold, bare compartment of the brain, let
there be yet a furnished mind!

Otherwise, all loved and lovely long ago would be a
knife turned in the heart—turned first perhaps in 1895.
In—was it Sioux Falls, South Dakota, or Dubuque, Iowa?
In the bright summer afternoon we left a siding where
the railway company had considerately disposed Grandfather's private car, and took a carriage for an hour of
sight-seeing. The town, though large and thriving,
proved to be without incentives for the tourist. Unless

we cared to drive into the country to a newly built and modernly equipped state penitentiary, our expedition threatened to be on our hands. A small, informal village lockup, shown to me in Russellville, had not prepared me for the majestic proportions of the grimly spotless edifice before which our coachman halted us. The warder's dwelling, brick, with pleasantly irregular bows flanked by neat, gaudy flower beds, and situated just outside the prison yard, put extra emphasis upon the law's impersonal, inhuman character. When he himself emerged with offers to become our genial host, and led us, with appropriate pride, through kitchens large as factories for food, and dining rooms like warehouses; an incongruity between the setting for his hospitality and the general adult attitude appeared conspicuous to a child.

We traversed corridors like mammoth vaults, and lined amazingly with open grilles. Astounded, I stared through the rows of bars, not at anticipated lions and tigers (in Chicago we had visited a zoo), but at ordinary human faces, neither more nor less revolting than the faces of the warder, turnkeys, and my family. Confronted suddenly with a phenomenon so inexplicable, my heart beat thickly in quick fear.

My father, probably, had realized the spectacle a shock, and I remember how he bent to whisper to me: "These are all wicked men—that's why we have to lock them up. They're dangerous."

I trembled. "Would they hurt us if they were let out?"

"They might. They've lied and stolen—some are very likely murderers; and every one's a lawbreaker."

"What's a lawbreaker?"

"I can't explain it to you here. Abstractly speaking, that just means they're bad. You're bad sometimes, but what these men have done is worse than anything a little girl can do."

And yet the warder urged us amiably to linger, and indulged in conversation with these menaces. He even called them "Jim" or "Tom" or "Dick" or "Jack." "Here, Jerry," and he pushed me into prominence, "this little lady's come to visit us. . . . It's all right, sister—don't be scared! Shake hands with him."

The convicts, grinning surlily, as though they forced re-entry into a lost land, addressed to me pathetic, witless jokes. Spiritlessly jovial, they named me "Susie," "Sally," or used sheepish, half-facetiously endearing terms, inveigling me into approaching them. "Howdy, young sunshine!" "Gona leave me one o' them thar curls?" "I got two little gals like you back home, but I ain't found no sweetheart here; you gona be my sweetheart, ain't you?" As onlooker, we had a trusty, whom the warder self-commendingly presented to us as a man who had spent forty years in jail and deserved every confidence reposed in him. He had a mild, scarred, stupid, vacant, unembittered face. Grandfather, tenderhearted, passed him money surreptitiously; he received it more submissively than gratefully. Obscurely I was conscious of an ageless, eunuchlike, and utterly indifferent personality.

Our tour terminated below concrete stairs which mounted, with bewildering uniformity, past tiers of balconies, toward a rotunda, overhung by something like a quarter-deck. My father lifted me; we climbed; the cells beneath us, joining one another, now like an exposed honeycomb. The sound of milling feet; a glimpse of joyless ranks, shuffling together after sustenance provided for those no one wants to see alive, is an uncertain memory. But a precise recollection of rich, muted quiet shed through hideous cathedral windows on a mechanism which obtruded from the stony floor upon that topmost variant of a captain's bridge, remains as clearly vivid as the happiest day of a first love affair!

With levers *so*, the warder was elucidating, every inside door was wide; and every prisoner had pure air. They could be neighbourly, and exchange greetings and profanity. Whereas, with levers *thus*, reversed—! "Say, sister, catch a-hold o' this, and see if you can't shut the cells all by yourself," he urged paternally. "A three-year-old could manage this! We don't need turnkeys any more." He seized my clammy and reluctant hand, and, keeping it inside his own, pressed with me upon chilling metal. "That's right—keep pullin'! While we're pullin', peek downstairs."

My family beamed benignly on the novelty of this experiment; and suddenly there rose from under us a gentle rumbling, like beginning thunder, re-echoing oddly through the institutional placidity. I had a tail's glance over railings—apertures were closing slowly, like deliberate wounds that healed themselves! Abruptly, came a sharp, reverberating, heavy clangour, and a final steely snap and bang! And miseries were shut away! Applause for me! But still, as we descended toward the open freedom of midwestern fields, the adults talking casually, I carried with me horror for trapped victims who were lingering after me behind that masking iron!

My mother sighed relief. "It was all very educational, but it seems nice to be outdoors."

As we strolled on, beyond the prison yard, I looked

298

up furtively into a window in which a smiling, rugged, stubbly face had suddenly appeared. It was Jerry! He grinned broadly, threw a kiss and waved. "Wave back! He said you were his sweetheart," my grandfather ordered me. "He likes you—they're just men like everybody else. Don't be so timid. Throw a kiss." I hesitated; and Grandfather, so affectionately proud, was like the warder and directed me. Settling me upon his shoulder exhibitionistically, he made my fingers flutter an appropriate response. And I found myself waving; no longer only in obedience, but frantically, desperately, despairingly; my tears, of which I did not understand the meaning, dampening my cheeks. And now other windows filled with those people who might have been penned, haggard denizens of the jungle; and they crowded together, spying obliquely down upon us; until *everyone* was waving, and the burst of kind jocularity, initiated by Jerry, had carried almost the length of the terrible wall! It was, for all the world, like the suddenly spontaneous proclamation of good will on earth! Like the enactment of a beatitude!

My grandfather himself was moved; though, as I burst into sobs and he consoled me, he did not understand what I was feeling—had no idea what paradox disturbed me! Hitherto, I had accounted for but two sorts of persons: the "good" people, who petted me, admired me, and were generous to me in ways congenial to my self-esteem; and "bad" people, who were unfriendly to me, hence the natural enemies of my parents and myself. Yet here, obviously, were men who approved me—they had shown themselves my friends!—who were considered "dangerous"; and had been shut away! I felt guiltily confused—as though I owed them something I could never pay. That old debt, so nearly metaphysical, still haunts me. . . . And the emotion then aroused, recurring, foolishly, blindly, violently (even wisely, as in the demonstrated case of Sacco and Vanzetti) never alters its essential character.

We seated ourselves in our hired surrey, the wheels turned with a scrape, and the prison was behind us; as our horses jogged, in the declining, heat-hazed sun, across a landscape ample as a Claude Lorraine. Dakota (or was it Iowa?) lay broad and strange before us, half-enveloped in an amber mist. Until we were descending a hill, and, having passed another plain-faced structure with a gilt cross flashing white fire from an insignificant tower, were able to stare over a wall into a terraced garden, enclosed on three sides; the fourth wide to raw farms lying, with their barns and silos, beyond. Where there should have been vineyards! For the whole character of the garden, as I now recognize it, was Italian, in a certain sculpturing of nature of which the horticulturist had taken advantage. Within the garden, and sweetly secret among ilexes and cypresses, were little whitewashed dollhouses—my mother called them "shrines"—in which stood little sentinel, bedizened statuettes. Among them, gliding footless along chalky paths, moved pale-robed figures—like the Bible! Like the Lac des Cygnes in the ballet! A few sat stilly upon marble benches, in the classic spell of wrapt devotion to small black-bound books. Before a well, beside a rustic belvedere, silent elder women and young novices—Ruths and Naomis, all their sheaves cast down!—watched, with fond, submissive contemplation, the approach of the long-gathering night. Or floated on; their sumptuous garments of simplicity ethereally lost beneath the cloudy